GREENE & GREENE

GREENE & GREENE

The Passion and the Legacy

RANDELL L. MAKINSON

*Ceiling panels for dining-room
bay windows, James A. Culbertson
house, 1906.*

 Salt Lake City

DEDICATION

To the volunteers of the Docent Council

of The Gamble House,

who, for over three decades, have given of themselves

by sharing the spirit, the principles,

and the educational lessons of The Gamble House

with all who enter its doors.

Half-timber and clinker-brick infill detail, Adelaide Tichenor house, Long Beach, 1904.

First Edition

02 01 00 99 98   5 4 3 2 1

Published by
Gibbs Smith, Publisher
Post Office Box 667
Layton, Utah 84041
Orders: 1 800 748 5439
Visit our Web site at
www.gibbs-smith.com

**Library of Congress Cataloging-
in-Publication Data**

Makinson, Randell L., 1932-
Greene & Greene :
the passion and the legacy /
Randell L. Makinson.
1st ed.
p.   cm.
Includes bibliographical
references and index.
ISBN 0-87905-847-1
1. Greene & Greene.
2. Architecture—California.
3. Architecture, Modern—
20th century—California.
I. Title.
NA737.G73M335   1998
720'.92'2—dc21
97-43568
CIP

CONTENTS

PREFACE

Carved-redwood, watercolor and gold-leaf detail in the entry hall, James A. Culbertson house, 1906.

Over the past twenty years a considerable amount of information about Charles and Henry Greene has surfaced. More structures have been identified; the independent roles of the two artist-architects have become clearer; and time and experience has brought about a better understanding of their work and their passionate belief in the role it would play in our national architectural heritage and in the Arts and Crafts movement as a whole. During this same period a number of houses have suffered outrageous indignities either through ignorance or greed, thus denying an appreciation of the Greenes' entire body of work. Fortunately some of their work remains, and by bringing together new information about Greene and Greene that is now available, this book complements my earlier books, *Greene & Greene: Architecture as a Fine Art* (© Gibbs Smith, 1977) and *Greene & Greene: Furniture and Related Designs* (© Gibbs Smith, 1979). Also, in order to contribute to a greater understanding of their building vocabulary, the role of color has been developed as a significant element in the Greene and Greene style.

■ The extraordinary unity of their work is so important that I have chosen to combine architecture, landscape, interiors, furnishings and the decorative arts in a single volume. The sheer amount of the Greenes' work has necessitated a selection of commissions to be included. This has been difficult. For the most part these selections have been made according to the significance of their design in the evolution of the Greenes' work, by the existence or condition of a structure, the accuracy of its present state as a correct example of the architects' vision, and the extent to which the imagery conveys the genius of its creators over a period of years. Only on rare occasions has additional work been separated from the discussion of the initial construction.

■ The Greenes' heritage, youthful experiences and training are handled in the introduction. Chapter 1 addresses the first designs of a beginning practice, the struggle to break free from the eclecticism of their MIT training and the popular demands of that era, and their own search for a logical criteria for architectural designs appropriate to that time and place. This is followed in chapter 2 by a discussion of Park Place, a small neighborhood in Pasadena with the highest concentration of Greene and Greene

designs, and in chapter 3 by a description of the evolution of their style and the events leading up to the masterworks, which are dealt with in chapter 4. The final two chapters identify the changes that brought about a new direction in the work of the firm and, finally, the independent work of the two brothers after the era of the masterworks. An epilogue describes my first visit with Charles Greene two years before his death.

■ The date and the name for each client follows the format used in the Greene and Greene office and appearing on the working drawings. This system allows for the dating of a particular design to be placed at the time of its final resolution by the architects and their clients, and compensates for the wide variation in the time a project entered the office, the number of preliminary studies required, and the work load in the office affecting the completion of the final design and working drawings.

■ After pointing out the difference between changing fashion and the logical determinants leading to the origin of new designs that "possess style," I have chosen for the first time to discuss the brothers' creative works as having a distinct and unmistakable "Greene and Greene style."

■ During the years when my attention was focused on the Gamble House, the development of the Greene and Greene Library, and the permanent Greene and Greene exhibition, the growing international recognition of the Greenes' work has prompted many enlightened owners of Greene and Greene houses to appreciate and protect their investments and to insist on the accuracy of any restoration or alteration. This has not only enhanced the value of the property but has contributed to the integrity of the surrounding neighborhood. Such visionary owners have also provided scholars with an opportunity to study designs that represent some of the highest aspirations of the Arts and Crafts movement in America.

ACKNOWLEDGEMENTS

From the central courtyard, the roof forms of the Cordelia Culbertson house express the light wells, which allows the morning light passing over the inner corridor to shine into the raised ceiling areas of the north and western bedroom wings. Iridescent Pewabic tiles in the fountain compliment the colorful variation of glazes Charles chose for the Ludovici roof.

This book was made possible by the assistance and goodwill of the scholars and administrators of the three research libraries that house 99 percent of the Greene and Greene archives. My sincere thanks to Angela Giral, director, Janet Parks, archivist, and especially Dan Kany, assistant to the curator, Avery Architectural and Fine Arts Library, Columbia University; to Professor Steven Tobriner, Documents Collection, College of Environmental Design, University of California, Berkeley; and to my colleagues Edward R. Bosley, director, Louise Mills, library chairperson, and the volunteer members of the Greene and Greene Research Library Committee, all representatives of the Gamble House, School of Architecture, University of Southern California. I am also indebted to the administrators and volunteers of the Pasadena Historical Museum and staff members of the Long Beach and Pasadena Public Libraries.

■ Margaret Meriwether's many years of research and her intensive study of the microfilms of newspaper files dating back to the early days, when there were few city records, has enabled her to identify many of the early works of Greene and Greene. With each new discovery added to the body of existing knowledge, she has produced one of the most valuable chronological listings of the complete works of Greene and Greene to date. She has now placed this important resource in the archives of the Greene and Greene Library, a gift which will be of genuine value to future scholars. Researchers will also benefit from the information on the Greenes' work that John G. Ripley has entered into his computer, providing a valuable cross-referenced data bank.

■ Stephanie DeWolfe, assistant planner, Urban Conservation, and Mary Jo Winder, Brian Goeken, Leon White and Bill Welden of the Permit Center, City of Pasadena, helped with access to and interpretation of the city archives and records, which were essential to the documentation of much of my work.

■ I am most grateful to those owners whose appreciation of the integrity of their houses has encouraged my research over many years, to new owners whose eyes sparkle with enthusiasm as they take possession of their houses, and especially to those owners who in recent years have had the foresight and will to carry out thoughtful restoration of their homes. In particular, I thank Ellen and Harvey Knell, Denise and Zachary Snyder, Edna and Alex Whittle, and Dr. Robert and Ruth Peck for reasons only they can truly appreciate.

■ Through four generations, members of the Greene family have become valued friends and provided information essential to the piecing together of facts, have brought life to my images of Charles and Henry Greene, and continue to enrich the Greene archives with their own extensive research into the genealogical heritage of the family. I am especially indebted to the Greenes' children: Bettie Greene, Gordon and Betty Greene, Nathaniel Patrickson Greene, Harriet and William Sumner Greene, Ruth and Henry Dart Greene, Isabelle and Alan R. McElwain, as well as the grandchildren: Nancy Glass, Isabelle Greene, Alan G. McElwain, Virginia Hales, and Alice Cory. The families of woodworkers Peter and John Hall and glass artisan Emil Lange have also continued to provide us with information and documents necessary to a full understanding of the important roles of these master craftsmen.

■ My thanks also to James N. Gamble, who has chaired the Gamble House Board of Overseers for three decades, and whose wise counsel has been continually appreciated, and to the deans of the School of Architecture who have been willing partners in the great Gamble House adventure: Sam Hurst, Ralph Knowles, A. Quincy Jones, Panos Koulermos, Emmet L. Wemple, Robert S. Harris, Victor Regnier and Robert Timme.

■ I am indeed grateful to the heirs of Cecil and Louise Gamble, James N. Gamble, Margaret (Gamble) Swift, Elizabeth (Gamble) Messler, Edwin Cecil Gamble, David Gibbs Gamble, and Margaret Corinne (Gamble) Ritchie (Scherr), who, with remarkable vision and generosity, placed the Gamble House in the protective custody of the City of Pasadena in a joint agreement with the University of Southern California, and to the university for its enlightened leadership, its pioneering of the preservation program and its operation of the Gamble House through the progressive curriculum and administration of its School of Architecture.

■ I also express very special thanks to the many individuals who have supported my belief in the cultural values of the Gamble House by donating their time to the volunteer Docent Council or participating in the support activities of the Friends of the Gamble House. I also thank the administrators and staff of the Henry E. Huntington Library, Art Galleries and Botanical Gardens for their joint effort with the Gamble House and the University of Southern California in establishing the permanent exhibition *Greene and Greene and the Arts and Crafts Movement in America*—located in the Virginia Steel Scott Gallery at the Huntington.

Many individuals have been important to this book in a wide variety of ways, and for their particular roles during the course of its preparation, I want to express my thanks to:

Brian Aamoth
Lillian Adams
Eleanor (Bush) Allen
Marilyn Anderson
Randy Ayers
Juan Barraha
Narda Bateman
Helen and Delmer Beckhart
Judith Benda
Mrs. John (Louise) Bentz
Beatrice (Bush) Bissell
Virginia and Robert R. Blacker
Paul Boehm
John Boothby (Blacker family)
Mary Borgerding
Edward R. Bosley III
Charles Bowyer
D. Eric Bowyer
Janet Becker Brown
Kathryn Jill Brown
Daniel Nelson Bube
Mary and Scott Randell Charles
Austen Randell Charles
Trevor Scott Charles
Carolyn Chenoweth
Dennis Chesney
Michael Citron
Robert Judson Clark
Leonard W. Collins
Pat Copley
Joseph Cotter
Jeffrey Cronin
Harley and Jennie Culbert
Phillip Culbert
Stephanie Culbert
Lynette, Barry, and Michelle Culbert

Morgan Lee Cunningham
Shannon and Paul Cunningham
Dave Davenport
Cliff Douglas
Paul Duffy
Jacqueline Dugas
Desiree, Rodney, Anna, and Robert Dye
Flavia Louise (Flavin) Edgren
Daniel Estrada
Manny Estrada
Margaret Fackler
Sean Flavin
Martin Flavin
Janet and Mortimer Fleishhacker Jr.
Mortimer Fleishhacker and family
Barbara Ann Francis
Robert Fu
Arthur B. Gallion
Alan Gallion

Gamble Family
Sidney and Elizabeth Gamble
Catherine (Gamble) Curran
Louise (Gamble) Harper (Shouchat)
Anne (Gamble) Symchych
Clarence J. and Sarah Gamble
Sally (Gamble) Epstein

Rudolph H. Garfield
David Gebhard
Doris and Constantine Gertmenian
William Gillan
Merlin Glass
Brian Goeken
Elizabeth Gordon
Thomas Gould Jr.
Virginia and Richard Gould
Herb and Nanine (Irwin) Greene
Michael Greve and Associates

Greene Family
Anne Greene
Thomas Casey Greene
Charles Sumner and Alice Greene
Nathaniel Patrickson Greene
Bettie Storey Greene
Betty and Thomas Gordon Greene
Jane Stacey Roberts McElroy
Alice Cory
Henry Mather and Emeline Greene
Alan R. and Isabelle (Greene) McElwain
Isabelle Clara Greene
Alan G. McElwain
Ruth and Henry Dart Greene
Nancy Greene Glass
Virginia Dart Greene Hales
Harriott and William Sumner Greene
Elbert Mather Greene
Soozi and Patrick Greene
Christopher Greene
Nathaniel Greene
Serena Adair (Greene) Goen

Marianne Hadden (Prentiss family)
David Hadden (Prentiss family)

Hall family
Juanita and R. Donald Hall
Robert J. and Nadine Hall
Mark Hilton Hall
Gregson Brice Hall
Chad Tyson Hall
Gary and Betsy Hall
Alice Hall Hodgkins
Walter and Marilyn (Hodgkins) Zaiss
Doris Hall Campbell

Richard Harder
Steve Harold
Harwell Hamilton Harris
Jean Harris
Robert S. Harris
Cynthia Richardson Hart
Douglas E. Hart

Edna (Breiner) Heartt
Patty Heather
Thomas A. Heinz
Donald C. Hensman
Glenice Hershberger
Edna Hicks (Culbertson family)
Margery and Max Hill
Sam Hurst
Patricia and Hart Isaacs
Mrs. Laura (Ware) Isham
James Ipekjian
Ron Ives and Associates
Daniel and Lilith James
Lili James
Margaret (Cole) Jarecki
Mrs. John N. Jeffers (Bentz family)
Russ Johnson
Joan Kaas (Lange family)
Dan Kany
Virginia Ernst Kazor
Roger Kennedy
Donald Klein
Carol Soucek King
Diane L. Kuki
Kathy La Shure
Clay Lancaster
William H. Lavey & Associates
Robert Leary
Lawrence Lee and Associates
Cindy Maines
Alfreda and Sam Maloof
Phyllis Manley
Robina Mapstone
Erika Marrin
Janeen Marrin
James Marrin
Delaney and Robert Marron
Virginia and Howard Martins
Margaret McCord
Dennis McGuire
Kelly Sutherlin McLeod
Dorothy McMillan

Mrs. Stephen Mengos
Margaret Meriwether
Brian Miller and Associates
Charles Miller
Denver Miller
Irene and Kinsey Miller
Louise Mills
Elliott Morgan
Amy Meyers
Kirk Myers
Mrs. Richard P. Nash (Prentiss family)
Maggie Nelson
Ann Nourse and Ken Ammissow
Kathryn Novak
Ed Nygren
Susan Ogle
Virginia Olkowski
Thomas Cram O'Sullivan
Vernon and Madelyn Parrett
Nancy Parsons
Mary Jane Penzo
Leif Petersen and Associates
Brad Pitt
Mr. and Mrs. Howard W. Porter
and family
Helen Rempel
John, Beverly and Julia Richardson
Tania Rizzo
B. J. Robinson
Nels Roselund
David Salazar
Edward Lee Sanders
Louise Saurenman
Helen Schevill
Joyce Schiller
Edward Schwartz
Margaret (Halsted) Seamans
William Searle and Julia Wyman
Abram Singer
Boyd Smith
Bruce Smith and Yoshiko Yamamoto
Sosha Smith
Janice and Craig Randell Stewart
Harold and Paula Makinson Stewart

Calvin C. Straub

David C. Streatfield

Cynthia Swanson

David Swanson

Kathryn Swanson

Hope and Crombie Taylor

Rea Taylor

Rose Terrones

Jeanette and Frank Thomas

Eleanor and Michael Thompson

Elsa and J. Eric Thorsen

Stephen Tobriner

Rick Travers

Mary Tumilty

Nancy (Bush) Bissell Turpin

Betty Ullner

Robert and Nancy Ullrich

Jane Unruh

Richard Valdivia

Walter Johannes (Jack) van Rossem

Sarah Venn

Bill Wang

Dr. Robert Wark

Robert Warren and Associates

Beverly Wayte

Luther Paul Weber

Martin Eli Weil

Meguila and Emmet L. Wemple

Cole Weston

Leon White

Claus Willenberg

Mary Jo Winder

Robert W. Winter

George D. Wittman

Lloyd Yost

Winogene and L. Morgan Yost

Sally Zaiss

And to those privileged owners of Greene and Greene properties I extend my deep appreciation for continued assistance and friendship:

Sofia and George Adamson

Catherine and David Alexander

Leslie and Harry Anderson

Barbara Babcock

Mr. and Mrs. John Bowman

Judy and David Brown

Douglas Brown

Marilyn and George Brumder

Stephanie Buffington

Ann and Andre Chaves

City of Carmel-by-the-Sea

City of Pasadena, California

Mrs. Lorton L. Clough

Mr. and Mrs. Thomas Cotter

Marie Duffy

Mortimer Fleishhacker family

Fuller Theological Seminary

Myrtle Giles

Betty and Gordon Greene

Gould Trust

Jacque and Robert Heebner

Jan and Wallace Hurff

Keith Jamison

Maria and Robert Kelly

Mr. and Mrs. Robert Kincaid

Ellen and Harvey Knell

Ann and Mark LaSalle

George and Dr. Judith Lowe

Patricia and Dr. C. Burke Maino

Leon Max

Louise K. Mills

Mrs. Robert Morris

Jennifer and William Moses

Mrs. George K. Mullins

Neighborhood Church

Ruth and Dr. Robert Peck

Kathleen Pulliam

Mr. and Mrs. Thomas Reitze

Margene and Edvin Remund

John, Beverly and Julia Richardson

Marjorie and William B. Richardson

Mr. and Mrs. Joseph Ritchie

Doug and Mary Robinson

Sigma Phi Fraternity, Alpha Chapter

Winifred Staniford

Susanna Gregg Smith

Denise and Zachary Snyder

Mr. and Mrs. Alfred Ulan

University of Southern California

Martin Eli Weil

Westridge School

Gwen and Robert Whitson

Edna and Alexander Whittle

Mr. and Mrs. Orland Wilcox

Special acknowledgement goes to members of my family and those I choose as family, for their support and encouragement; to Brian Aamoth and Daniel Nelson Bube for always being there; to Margaret McCord, whose editing has greatly enriched the manuscript and gives me the courage to write; to James Marrin for the magic he brings to the graphic design with the invaluable assistance of Erika Marrin; to Gibbs and Catherine Smith and Madge Baird of Gibbs Smith, Publisher, for believing in this book and for keeping in print over two decades my companion books on Greene and Greene; to Marvin Rand for the photographic talents he brought to my prior books; and especially to Thomas A. Heinz, Erika Marrin, and Toshi Yoshimi for stepping in and enduring the travails of the winter storms to photographically capture the spirit in the work of Greene and Greene for this book; to D. Eric Bowyer, Daniel Nelson Bube, Dennis McGuire and Luther Paul Weber for the new illustration drawings; to Robert M. Perkins III for his invaluable assistance with the research.

Finally, I express my deep gratitude for the loyalty, friendship, and encouragement of Thomas A. Heinz, Donald Hensman, Brad Pitt, and Robert Ullrich, who each has been steadfast in his support throughout the most challenging periods in the final development of this book.

*The Greene family farm, The Forge, was
established in the Potowomut section,
East Greenwich, Rhode Island, in the late
1600s and remains in the family today.*

INTRODUCTION

The Greenes' family history goes back to England before the first Greene came to America. The path followed was not unlike that of the Arts and Crafts movement itself, which had its origins in England and culminated in America with the architecture and decorative arts designs of Charles Sumner Greene (1868-1957) and Henry Mather Greene (1870-1954).

■ Charles was born on October 12, 1868, and his brother Henry on January 23, 1870, in the town of Brighton, just outside the corporate boundaries of Cincinnati, Ohio. Their father, Thomas Sumner Greene, a bookkeeper for the Greenwood Pipe and Supply Company, and their mother were both descended from distinguished New England families instrumental in the origins of this country.[1]

■ The Greene lineage can be traced back eleven generations to A.D. 871.

■ Early ancestors included Katherine Parr, the sixth and last queen of King Henry VIII, and the beheaded Lord Chief Justice Sir Henry Greene and his Lady Katherine, all residents of Greenes Norton in Northamptonshire. The direct line to Charles and Henry goes back to Robert Greene of Bowridge Hill, near Gillingham, Dorsetshire, in 1543; and it was his son, John, a surgeon, who came to America in April of 1635, who settled first in Massachusetts and later in Rhode Island, where the Greene farm, The Forge, still remains. Among the Greene forebears were Catherine Ray, wife of Governor William Greene of Rhode Island, and Elizabeth Sumner, who married John Franklin, postmaster of Boston and brother of Benjamin Franklin. Upon her husband's death in 1756, she became postmistress of Boston, allegedly the first woman to hold public office in America.

■ Charles and Henry's father was the direct descendent of colonists John Greene and Sir George Sumner. In the family were Generals Nathaniel Greene and his brother Christopher Greene of the Continental Army, Governor Increase Sumner and Reconstructionist Senator Charles Sumner of Massachusetts, and Lieutenant Governor George Sumner of Connecticut.

■ Mrs. Greene was the former Lelia Ariana Mather of Virginia, descended from John Cotton and Reverend Richard Mather. The Mather family roots have been traced back to John Mather and his son, Thomas, of Lowton, Winwich Parish, Lancashire, England. It was Thomas's son, Reverend Richard Mather, born in Lowton in 1596, who came to America with his sons, Timothy and Increase, and settled in Dorchester, Massachusetts.

Greene family home on the farm in Rhode Island.

1. Ainsworth R. Spofford, LL.D., advisory editor, *The National Cyclopædia of American Biography* (New York: James T. White & Company, 1897).

Henry E. Turner, M.D., *Greenes of Warwick— in Colonial History* (Newport, Rhode Island: Davis & Pitman, Steam Printers, 1877).

The Greene Family in England and America with Pedigrees (Boston: T. R. Marvin & Son, privately printed, 1901).

Livermore, *History of Block Island, Rhode Island* (1877; reprint, Block Island: Block Island Committee of Republication, 1961).

Greene family members, interviews by Randell L. Makinson, 1955-1997.

1

Charles Sumner Greene, above, and Henry Mather Greene, below, circa 1874.

2. Calvin Milton Woodward, *Rational and Applied Mechanics*, rev. ed. (Saint Louis, Missouri: Nixon-Jones Printing Company, 1915).

■ Increase Mather became president of Harvard, established the first public library in the United States, was representative to the king of England and was appointed governor of Massachusetts. His son, Cotton Mather, gained notoriety for his involvement with the Salem witch trials.

■ By the time Charles and Henry were of school age, their mother had moved with them to the Mather family farm in Guyandotte, West Virginia, when their father enrolled in the medical school of the University of Cincinnati, Ohio. Those were the years during which the boys developed a genuine respect for the integrity of the natural environment, a respect that would become a part of their lives and would imbue all aspects of their professional activities. Of the two, Henry was the more active and outgoing. Charles shared Henry's youthful curiosity about the rural landscape, but he was quieter, less robust and somewhat introspective.

■ When their father completed his medical training in 1880, he set up his first practice in Saint Louis, Missouri, where his wife and sons joined him. His office was on the lower floor of a rented three-story brick row house that offered little light or cross ventilation, an unhealthy arrangement that Dr. Greene, with his sons' future in view, continually pointed out to the boys. He had already decided that they should become architects like their great-great-grandfather, Thomas Waldron Sumner of Brookline, Massachusetts, an architect who had been distinguished for his work on Harvard's Divinity Hall in 1825.

■ Charles was twelve and Henry ten when they started in the public schools in Saint Louis, the year Calvin Milton Woodward, professor of civil engineering, founded the Manual Training High School of Washington University, the first of its kind in America.[2] Woodward, widely acclaimed as the father of manual training in America, had been strongly influenced by the philosophies of John Ruskin and William Morris in England. He believed in the dignity of craftsmanship and was responsible for the introduction of handcrafts into American secondary education.

■ Dr. Greene was enthusiastic about Woodward's educational theories, believing that training in actual workshops each afternoon would provide an important foundation for his sons' architectural careers. Charles was enrolled in the fledgling program in 1883 and Henry in the following year. Throughout their lives the Greenes acknowledged the influence of Woodward and his program on their own work and adhered to the school motto, "The Cultured

Shop scene in the Manual Training School of Washington University, Saint Louis, Missouri.

Mind—The Skillful Hand." They responded eagerly to the shop classes, absorbed the theories of Ruskin and Morris, and learned that design determinants stemmed from function and from the appropriate analysis of materials handled in a direct manner. This was a logical approach: forms resulted from the nature of materials and the tools and skills employed. Because of the hands-on approach in their high school training, both boys developed an appreciation for craftsmanship that was to be reflected in their design process and in the details of their own original work.

■ Charles graduated from the Manual Training School a year before Henry did and spent that period pursuing his interests in painting, photography and poetry. He was not interested in a university education nor an architectural career, although, in time, his father prevailed and he reluctantly agreed to the abbreviated program in architecture at MIT, which offered a two-year course, at the end of which a Certificate of Partial Course was awarded. With this certificate, graduating students could either continue on for a bachelor's degree or accept apprenticeships under architects in the Boston area in preparation for professional registration.

■ The Greenes entered the MIT program in 1888. Here the courses in design, the Orders of Architecture and the History of Ornament, were steeped in classic traditions that seemed to Charles and Henry to be completely at odds with the

*Charles Sumner Greene, left, and
Henry Mather Greene, right, in 1888.*

fundamentals of the Arts and Crafts philosophy as taught in the
Manual Training School. Both of them, however, were interested
in the history of architecture and in the derivation of historical
styles, ideas that were more important to them than the surface
imagery of the styles themselves. To them, understanding the
sources could be an important lesson in the development of designs
or styles in the future. But at MIT they must have felt that the
architect was regarded more as an "artisan" than as an artist, an
attitude that stifled creative thinking. That these rebellious feelings
remained with the Greenes is clear from the quality of their work.
Charles's continued opposition to the MIT curriculum was borne
out in 1913 by portions of his unpublished novel, in which he poses
the question:

*Why is it that we are taught that it is impossible to invent anything
worth while in architectural art? . . . Isn't invention the life of science?
Don't men of science do it every day? And science has not had the last
word yet. Why not art? . . .*

*The great trouble is that the schools ignore principles and teach
too much detail. One gets a mass of disjointed facts. No inspiration,
no insight. . . .*

*Our students go over to Paris and learn a jumble intended for educated
Frenchmen. When they come home they think upon everything
American as hopelessly illiterate. . . . So they put Louis Quinze's
interpretation of a Greek temple into the first story of an office building.
A thing that the Greeks used as a sacred thing, a place of divine
worship . . . it's true that we worship there too! ...worship the dollar.
Oh, it's damnable!* [3]

■ In spite of their frustrations with the MIT studies, the Greenes
found their years in Boston culturally invigorating. They attended
the opera, joined the Shakespeare Club, continued their music

lessons, visited relatives scattered about New England, spent many
of their leisure hours in libraries and museums, and expanded their
classroom work with reading on a variety of subjects.[4] Charles in
particular delved into Greek history, studying basic principles that
influenced his own beliefs throughout his life.

■ Although it has been commonly believed that the Greenes were
first introduced to the arts of the Orient at the Chicago Exposition
in 1893, this was not so. Their frequent visits to the Boston
Museum of Fine Arts during their student years provided them
with access to the finest exhibition of Chinese and Japanese arts to
be found in America. Okakura Kakudzo, a leading critic on
literature and arts, pronounced the Boston Museum[5] preeminent
among the Oriental collections of the world at that time, and
Professor Edward S. Morse,[6] renowned for his own books on the
subject, attested to the similar quality of the Japanese pottery
exhibits. In this extensive collection were fine examples of Chinese
and Japanese sculpture, metalwork (where Charles may have
developed his interest in the *tsuba*, or sword guard, for his later
collection), Japanese prints, pottery and porcelain, much of which
was exhibited in gardens and structural surroundings of Chinese
and Japanese origin.

*Oriental exhibition of the Boston
Museum of Fine Arts frequented by
Charles and Henry Greene while
attending MIT and apprenticing in
Boston, 1890-94. This was their first
introduction to the arts of the Orient.*

3. Charles Sumner
   Greene, *This Thayer*
   manuscript, 1913.
   (Pasadena: Greene &
   Greene Library, The
   Gamble House, USC.)

4. Archive letters,
   Documents
   Collection,
   Greene & Greene
   Library, The Gamble
   House, USC.

5. Julia de Wolf Addison,
   *The Boston Museum
   of Fine Arts*, rev. ed.
   (Boston: L. C. Page &
   Company, August
   1924).

6. Edward S. Morse,
   *Japanese Homes and
   Their Surroundings*
   (Franklin Square, New
   York: Harper &
   Brothers, 1885).
   Charles Greene's
   personal library
   contained a well-used
   copy of Morse's book.

Henry Greene photograph of row housing along Saint James Avenue, where the brothers lived during their four years in Boston, shows the looming presence of H. H. Richardson's Trinity Church in their daily lives.

7. Documents Collection, Greene & Greene Library, The Gamble House, USC.

8. The sequence of apprenticeships of the brothers is from their own hand on their Western History Forms, Los Angeles Public Library, executed in 1906. For an extensive study of the Greenes' years in Boston, see Barbara Ann Francis, "The Boston Roots of Greene & Greene" (MFA thesis, Tufts University, 1987).

■ The Greenes spent the summer months with relatives in Nantucket, where the contrast to the densely populated row housing of Saint Louis and of their own housing along Saint James Avenue in Boston undoubtedly reminded them of the open spaces in West Virginia. Various of their sketches and watercolor drawings found in sketchbooks show that the Greenes seem to have developed their keen interest in the landscape early. Throughout their careers they paid much attention to the context of their designs as they related and contributed to the neighborhood environment.[7]

■ Charles and Henry attended classes in the Walker Building of MIT, which was situated directly across the street from Henry Hobson Richardson's Trinity Church (1872-1877) in the midst of Copley Square, Boston. During the five years they lived in Boston, all four of their residences on Saint James Avenue, on the opposite side of Trinity Church from the school, placed Richardson's masterwork in the center of their daily activities. The dominance of Trinity on Copley Square and on the surrounding neighborhoods was captured in a photograph by Henry that shows the diminutive scale of the three-story row housing along Saint James Avenue. However, it was not just the scale that captured the interest of the Greenes but also the imagery and the color. Their own original work indicates that they drew inspiration from the stained-glass windows of the church, the form of the escutcheon plates of the entry doors, the brazen use of expressed iron hardware, the bold expression of the nature of materials, and the powerful use of color found on the interiors of Trinity. Whether intentional or not, and whether through his architecture or from those who worked with him in his "atelier," Richardson exerted a powerful influence on both Charles and Henry Greene.

■ The certificate from MIT opened the door to various apprenticeships in the Boston area. Charles's first apprenticeship was with the firm of Andrews, Jacques and Rantoul, the result of an introduction arranged through family friends in New Bedford.

■ Andrews and Jacques had formerly been in the office of H. H. Richardson, the first real Arts and Crafts architect in America. While Richardson had attended the Ecole des Beaux-Arts in Paris and was exposed to the rampant historicism that the Greenes opposed, his experiences there served him more as a basis for his understanding the opportunities to be found in the inherent nature of materials and in the crafts that were the driving force behind his logical designs. It is the strength of these principles in Richardson's work and in that of his followers that prompted the Greenes to become intimately familiar with the characteristics of the Shingle style so ably carried out in the large residences of New England, characteristics easily recognized in the Greenes' later works.[8]

9. Personal letters, Documents Collection, Greene & Greene Library, The Gamble House, USC.

10. Okakura Kakudzo, *The Ho-o-den: An Illustrated Description* (Chicago, n.p., 1893), 21.

■ Charles was working briefly with the firm of Sturgis and Cabot when, on March 10, 1891, he received a letter from H. Langford Warren offering him a position. Warren had joined the office of H. H. Richardson at the age of twenty-four and, following Andrews' departure, had served as Richardson's head draftsman for several years. Charles, unhappy with Sturgis and Cabot after leaving Andrews, accepted Warren's invitation immediately and again fell under the shadow of Richardson.

■ His last apprenticeship was with Winslow and Wetherall, whose larger office may well have provided him with his most intense involvement with commercial architecture.

■ Henry Greene's apprenticeships were more satisfying than those Charles experienced. However, he too worked in several different offices between 1891 and 1893, for a time in the Stickney and Austin offices, both in Lowell and Boston. Although he later spent less time with Edward R. Benton, it was a very rewarding period because of Benton's former association with the office of McKim, Mead and White. Henry's most valuable experience, however, was in the offices of Shepley, Rutan and Coolidge, successors to H. H. Richardson's practice, following Richardson's death in 1886.[9] Thus, Henry too was influenced by Richardson's ideals, and throughout his life expressed great pride not only in having worked for this firm but also in his involvement with the drawings for the construction of the Quad, the dramatic Richardsonian arched courtyard and related structures at Stanford University in Palo Alto, California.

■ During the years of apprenticeship, Charles grew more and more independent in his thinking. He developed a strong interest in Impressionist painting, continued his studies of poetry, philosophy and history, and found himself more and more in conflict with the prospect of an architectural career. Letters flew back and forth between the two boys and their parents, dealing with the question of funds, prospects for better-paying apprenticeships (Charles and Henry were receiving between ten and twelve dollars a week), and Charles's expenditures on books, considering the costs of shipping them if he should move from Boston. There was also mention of Dr. Greene's dwindling medical practice and the failing health of both parents, which was attributed to the smoke-filled air of St. Louis.

■ During their sons' apprenticeships, Dr. and Mrs. Greene moved to the "little country town" of Pasadena, California, at the urging of their relatives the Howard Longleys, who had already settled in South Pasadena. Although Dr. Greene again established his medical practice and began to associate with the movers and shakers of the community, he and his wife continued to suffer ill health, financial problems and loneliness. Before long they were urging the boys to come to California, if only for a visit.

■ In spite of the family assumption that the best prospects for young architects would be in Boston, New York or Chicago, Charles and Henry reluctantly decided to travel to California. This was not an easy decision and the boys changed their minds several times, but in mid-August of 1893, when Charles again lost his position, they both left by train for Pasadena.

■ According to stories recounted by family members over the years, Charles and Henry stopped in Chicago to attend the World's Columbian Exposition, where they were both impressed by the design and the simple but dramatic construction of the Ho-o-den, the official exhibit of the Japanese government. This was a half-scale replica of the Ho-o-do of Byodo-in at Uji, near Kyoto. Its parts had been shipped from Japan in pieces and assembled in Chicago by Japanese workmen. It was an excellent example of Buddhist temples of the Fujiwara period (895-1185).[10] The structures, built primarily of unpainted wood, straw, plaster and paper, intrigued the Greenes by their system and order of composition, their use of heavy timbers, their exposed joinery, and the subtle way in which they were sited on the landscape. Here were the fundamental principles they had learned at the Manual Training School. Nowhere in the grouping of structures was there the rampant eclecticism that had confronted them at MIT and now completely dominated most of the exhibits of the exposition. Had it not been for the progressive vision of Louis Sullivan's Transportation Building, the surprising design of the Turkish Pavilion, and the Ho-o-den, the Greenes would probably have looked upon the fair as a great wedding cake, devoid of principle and excessively gaudy.

■ So impressed were Charles and Henry by the Ho-o-den that the following year they made a special effort to attend the Mid-Winter Exposition in San Francisco in order to visit the Japanese hill and water gardens. Here again they found an architectural expression that to them was a marriage of the craftsman's respect for natural materials and the care with which he fitted his work into the environment.

■ The popular historical styles of the day were so prevailing, however, that in spite of the Greenes' enthusiasm for these beautiful Japanese structures, it would be over a decade before they would be able to infuse their own work with similar integrity, style and confidence.

Previous page, archive overview
photograph of early Pasadena and the
foothills of the San Gabriel Mountains.

Pasadena downtown crossroads of
Raymond Avenue and Colorado
Boulevard, circa 1900. The first Greene
and Greene architectural offices were
located in the Stowell Block on the far
left, across the intersection, from 1894
until their move across the street into the
newly completed Greene and Greene
Kinney-Kendall Business Block in 1896.

I

When Charles and Henry Greene came to Pasadena to visit their parents in 1893, they had no intention of settling down in Southern California. But upon their arrival they found the scenery spectacular and Pasadena a far more active and vital community than their parents had indicated in their letters.[1] To the north the San Gabriel Mountains overlooked a valley of citrus groves, which the architect Harwell Hamilton Harris later compared to a great chenille bedspread. Two miles to the west of the Victorian house that Dr. and Mrs. Greene had rented on Colorado Boulevard (now renowned for its annual New Year's Rose Parade) lay the great Arroyo Seco canyon with newly developed neighborhoods on its perimeter bluffs, trails leading down to its natural streams, varieties of sycamore and oak trees, and a seemingly unending supply of cobblestones—a popular source of building material. In addition, the Pasadena Board of Trade publications described a wide variety of wildflowers, rugged trees linking the present to the past, and a perfect climate attracting visitors during the winter months.[2] Perhaps even more surprising to Charles and Henry were the announcements of business opportunities and the listings of various social and cultural events for a populous interested in music, art, literature and religion.

■ Between 1886 and 1888 Pasadena had undergone a reckless growth. Real estate was booming and a fever of speculation had led to rapid development and a mixture of architectural styles ranging from Queen Anne, Spanish Mission, Moorish, Gothic, Grecian and a great many combinations of unnamed origin. In 1891 the Throop Polytechnic Institute (now California Institute of Technology) had been founded with an emphasis on manual training, a program developed by Dr. Calvin Milton Woodward at his Manual Training School in Saint Louis, which both Charles and Henry had attended.

The Decision to Stay

Within three months of their arrival, the two brothers apparently abandoned their plans for returning east. In January of 1894 a local newspaper mentioned Charles Greene at a meeting that founded the Arcade Sketching Club and in mid-January announced the opening of the Greenes' first architectural office in the Eldridge Building (renamed the Stowell Block the following year), on the main thoroughfare in the center of town. As their family background and social experiences had taught them, they placed themselves in the center of business activity and social influence.

■ Their first job, though not their first structure, was a design for "those concrete boxes for old Mr. Hutchins, the candy man," who, with his brother, operated a confectionery and ice cream parlor a few doors from their office.[3] Family members recall the two brothers describing another early work on the design of a tombstone.

■ For the Greenes, the next decade was a period of experimentation. They were searching for the forms, materials and expressions appropriate to life in Southern California and finding their way through the confusion of client demands, the eclecticism propounded by their professors at MIT, the fundamentals taught at the Manual Training School, and the popular styles of the time. It is therefore not surprising that their work during these years reflected a variety of expressions that can be divided into three distinct eras. At first, modest budgets allowed for a straightforward simplicity but within an eclectic theme. Then, as their reputation grew, clients of position and means began demanding large homes reflecting the most lavish combinations of popular imagery. Finally the Greenes broke away from this historicism and turned to stripped-down designs with a strong reliance on bold geometric forms carried out in simple, honest materials and straightforward detail. This, then, would lead them into the new century with its prospects for new ideals and new thinking.

1. Greene & Greene Library, The Gamble House, USC.

2. E. Norman Baker, *Environments* (Pasadena: Pasadena Board of Trade, 1893-1894).

3. Letter from Henry Greene to Charles Greene in late life, Greene & Greene Library, The Gamble House, USC.

4. Though located only a block off Pasadena's main thoroughfare, Colorado Boulevard, and near the center of town, the Flynn house resisted demolition until 1947, though still some years prior to local preservation ordinances designed to protect the works of Greene and Greene.

5. The Breiner house exists today in spite of the original construction directly along Colorado Boulevard. In 1915 it was moved north onto Stevenson Street (now Mar Vista), north of Orange Grove Avenue. Subsequently, unfortunate modifications to the exterior deny the integrity of its original clean design.

First Designs

The first documented work to be built by Greene and Greene was the house for Mrs. Martha Flynn, apparently designed about the same time as the house for Dr. Greene's neighbor John Breiner. A legend in both the Greene and Breiner families claimed that the Breiner design was the first commission and was responsible for Charles and Henry Greene making the final decision to remain in Pasadena. This may well have been the case, but according to local newspaper accounts at the time, the Flynn house was under construction a few weeks earlier than the Breiner house.

Mrs. Martha Flynn House, 1894

Martha Flynn was the widow of Thomas F. Flynn, a successful businessman who played a major role in Pasadena's short-lived building boom in the late 1880s. In 1886 he and three partners organized the Pasadena Park tract Land and Water Company, and the Park Place tract on the bluffs overlooking the Arroyo Seco. This neighborhood now boasts the greatest concentration of Greene and Greene designs.

■ The Flynn house, the larger of the first two houses built by the Greenes, was a full two-story design with a large gable roof and dormered attic. The plan, a basic square, contained elements of Victorian imagery in the ground-floor arrangement of the entry porch and the related hexagonal bay windows of the adjacent rooms. A strong roofline and the dominant gable of the facade strengthened the horizontality of the front elevation by the use of clapboard siding and trim detail, which gave distinction to the first and second floors. A stronger horizontal trim was introduced to organize the second-floor windows. As such, there is a fundamental

simplicity about the design. As if to cater to the popular imagery of the day, the facade is adorned on its central axis with a modified Palladian window in the attic and, directly below, a hexagonal bay window on the second floor.[4]

The John Breiner House, 1894

John Breiner was the owner of the prestigious City Meat Market that catered to the so-called "carriage trade," the virtual "Who's Who" of Pasadena. Although considered successful, he was not in the same league as his clientele, many of whose large homes on the west side were located along or at least near Pasadena's Millionaires' Row, with South Orange Grove addresses. The Breiner house, the second and smaller of the Greenes' first designs, was not a pretentious house by any means, but it was considered well built, differing from similar houses of the time because its utilities were all inside the structure. It was basically a single story with a few rooms in the multi-dormered attic, with a full covered porch across the front, with central entry steps, and built upon the popular cobblestone foundation.[5] Its lines were cleaner even than the Flynn house, which was also a basic square plan of bilateral symmetry.

■ Work during 1894 and well into 1895 all came about through the Greenes' association with local bankers and investment houses near their downtown office. Most of these early buildings were for a downtown clientele and therefore located along or just off Colorado Boulevard. This led to their early demolition or relocation, making way for downtown commercial growth. As a result, very few examples of the Greenes' experimental work during this first decade remain for observation. But several houses built a few blocks away from the business center (i.e., those for Robert and Willis Eason and Conrad A. Covelle) exist today and offer an opportunity for academic scrutiny.

Left, Robert and Willis Eason houses, 1895.
Right, Conrad A. Covelle house, 1895.

First Presbyterian Church Sunday School

In March of 1895 a notice in the local newspaper cited plans in preparation by Greene and Greene for a major addition of Sunday school rooms to the large and impressive Presbyterian Church on Colorado Boulevard. When the entire church was torn down in 1907, the Greenes' addition was dismantled and some parts given to the Calvary Presbyterian Church in South Pasadena. Although assembled differently and much altered over the years, the interior design still reveals the Greenes' unique concept as described in the original newspaper story:

The architects have very successfully arranged the interior so that from a central point, the superintendent of the Sunday School may command a view of every part of 12 class rooms, which are to be located in circular form on the north side and to be divided by sliding partitions which may be removed during general exercises. This arrangement for overlooking the rooms is accomplished by the two systems of radiation which overlap, so as to give the appearance of entire symmetry.[6]

By now the brothers were each becoming involved in a variety of town activities. Charles had lectured "On Architecture" before the Fortnightly Club, both had joined with a Miss Sutton to perform a piano/violin trio before the Tuesday Evening Club, and by the end of 1895, along with their father, both had become charter members of the Twilight Club, whose membership did and still continues to represent the leaders of the community. This was

6. *Pasadena Star,*
   August 3, 1895.

7. Dr. Walter A. Edwards,
   *The Twilight Club, Its
   History and
   Regulations* (Pasadena:
   Published privately,
   1935).

a social club with a specific number of elected members who met, as the name implies, at the twilight hour— "when twilight falls the garish day departs and we enter the circle of softened light shed by theevening lamp."[7] The club was not a political body and refused to take on any causes; yet, at the same time, it took great pride in the openness of the subject matter presented and was always eager for speakers, whether or not they were members, to provide "intellectual feasts." The list of guest lecturers and subjects covered was extremely broad, including Dr. T. S. Greene, "The Duties and Responsibility of American Citizenship," followed by a violin and flute duet by Charles and Henry Greene; George S. Hull, "A Talk on Venice"; E. W. Claypole, "Mental Epidemics"; Edgar W. Camp, "Some Anarchistic Reflections"; and Charles S. Greene, "Color in Art and Architecture," to name but a few. Each of these speakers would become a Greene and Greene client. The Twilight Club, composed, as it was, of the virtual shapers of the community, had benefits for the young architectural firm as no less than sixteen significant clients came from its membership. It was here, too, that Charles and Henry met such guest speakers as Charles F. Lummis, A. C. Vroman, General Harrison Gray Otis, Ernest Batchelder, Myron Hunt, George Ellery Hale, and Upton Sinclair, among others.

■ Charles and Henry had learned their lessons well. The days of family gatherings in New England had prepared them to move easily in social surroundings, yet they were never comfortable using their social contacts to promote business. Later in his life Charles joined the Annandale Golf Club at the urging of Myron Hunt but let his membership expire at the end of the year without having attended a single event.

Kinney-Kendall Business Block, 1896

Just two years after opening their office, the Greenes received the commission for the Kinney-Kendall Business Block, one of the largest office buildings yet to be built in Pasadena and an extraordinary opportunity for the young architects. The site was located directly across from the Greenes' office on Colorado Boulevard at Raymond Avenue. Mr. Kendall, whose office was also located in the Stowell Block, originally requested a two-story structure, but prior to breaking ground a third level was added to the design.

■ According to the newspapers this was the first building in Southern California with a steel frame.[8] The design took full advantage of the iron and glass construction materials to enhance the qualities of light and air circulation throughout the working spaces, in accordance with the admonitions of Dr. Greene.

■ The design had a forthright simplicity in its composition and this set it distinctly apart from surrounding buildings. Between the large horizontal bands of windows allowing the sunlight deep into the heart of the interiors were great horizontal spandrels and cornices with a rich textural relief that responded to the shadows of the passing sun, contrasting dramatically with the columns and windows. Unfortunately, little of the progressive concept of the design remains because of the substantial alterations over the years. Upon its completion the Greenes moved their office into the Kinney-Kendall Block, where it remained until the firms move to Los Angeles in 1903.

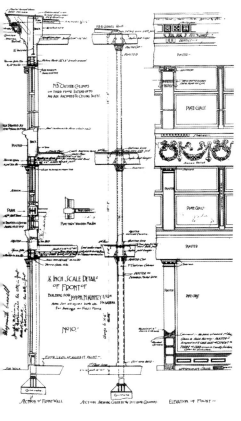

Top, Kinney-Kendall Business Block, 1896.

Bottom, Greene and Greene drawings for the steel-frame construction and detail for the Kinney-Kendall Building.

8. *Pasadena Daily Evening Star,* June 11, 1896.

9. Greene & Greene Library, The Gamble House, USC.

■ Although the recipient of much favorable comment in its day, the Kinney-Kendall Block would be one of only two business blocks the Greenes would build throughout their long career. The second, built half a block south on Raymond Avenue in 1901, housed the sales rooms of oriental imports for John Bentz. In the latter part of the Greenes' career, they turned down a million-dollar opportunity offered them by client Mortimer Fleishhacker of San Francisco for a large structure providing loft space. By choice, both Charles and Henry Greene preferred the personal quality inherent in residential work.

■ By 1901 the building boom in Southern California had slowed down. Although the general building industry was bleak, Greene and Greene continued to attract new clients. But this was not altogether satisfying, particularly to Charles. He and Henry had both become architects to please their father, and there were times when its demands were not to their liking. Their extensive correspondence with their friends from MIT days and their relatives in Massachusetts and Rhode Island reveals much about their activities and feelings at this period in their lives. Their letters comment on theater, music, polo, literature and poetry.[9] They admit to missing the libraries and museums of Boston, and Charles, in particular, complained about the demands of the practice when he would rather have been painting or writing poetry. He was excited by the landscape of Southern California and captured it in word, drawing, painting, and photograph, sending examples to his friends with detailed instructions on how a painting or photograph was to be framed. He also wrote of moonlight sailing at Long Beach and of reading the Bible, which prompted one lady friend to ask whether he always took the opposite side in a discussion for the fun of the argument. Of a painting of the Santa Barbara Mission, she wrote, "It is an odd bit—and interesting, exceedingly I think. You sure made a happy choice in your subject." Many of these friends from the East would winter in California, and in his correspondence Charles would write of trips to Santa Barbara and the California missions. There is little doubt that initially Charles Greene was less enthusiastic about his architectural career than his later work demonstrates. He wrote to another friend:

Things crowd in so in the day time: there is more responsibility in building a barn well when one has to carry it through one's self, than in building a state house when others fight the outside battles. I can't always leave my cares at the office as I used to, and so you see the

Right, Dr. and Mrs. Adelbert Fenyes house, 1897, designed by architects Dennis and Farrell following the Greenes' withdrawal from the project, refusing to carry out an ersatz Algerian design.

action things push aside the passion ones. But I seldom lie down at night without thinking of the things that give me most pleasure (I try to put the others away) and then I often think of dear old Braintree. I half close my eyes and imagine I can hear the gentle rustling of the little river, the frogs croaking by the water in the meadow. I imagine I'm in the little room and the wind is swaying the apple boughs under the window. I begin to wonder vaguely what we shall do next day and pleasant thoughts of pine woods picnics come and long beautiful drives (the Braintree drives will always be beautiful to me) and then I open my eyes and look out, but I see only the lights of Mt. Lowe faintly shining five miles away, with the dark mountains rising far above them and the cold north star glistening over them.[10]

10. Charles Greene's letter to a cousin in Boston, written in late 1895, Greene & Greene Library, The Gamble House, USC.

11. Ibid.

These carefree days of the late 1890s would come to an end. In later years he became so devoted to his work that he would stay at his drawing board until late into the night, often forgetting family activities and even meals. After his visit to England and the Continent in 1901, Charles became totally absorbed in architecture. As Alice Greene told me in 1955, "Charles was pantheistic: that is, his religion was his work. . . . He was devoted to his family but his work always came first."

■ But back in the mid-1890s Charles was just beginning to find himself and was still searching for the real meaning of life. He stated in another letter:

No, no, I haven't grown callous yet. I know you think that I'm not very affectionate and I think so myself sometimes, but I always come back to the feeling that I am only different from others. I'm sorry I'm different but it's pretty much the same case as poor Jacob Faith feels,—What's done can't be helped.[11]

Henry Greene's letters are more upbeat. He discusses work for new clients and expresses happiness that the firm is doing well. But he also realizes that the demands of the office are difficult for Charles, who seems to need more time for his music, painting and photography. Henry, however, appeared to thrive on the day-to-day business of the firm. At the same time he became more and more

involved in various community activities, including the Americus Marching Club and a society of young actors and singers who put on musical shows in the popular Lowe's Opera House, and the Amphion Quartet, of which he became a member.

Standing on Principles

Although the brothers had not yet embraced a personal expression in their architecture, they certainly had strong feelings about what it was not. Early in 1897 they accepted a commission for a residence on South Orange Grove Avenue (Millionaires' Row) for Dr. and Mrs. Adelbert Fenyes, only to reject it a short time later when informed that the design must be of Algerian derivation. Within a month the Fenyeses commissioned Los Angeles architects Dennis and Farrell, who carried out their wishes, as described in a March 31, 1897, story:

The plans show a front entrance into an Algerian hall. The reception hall will be finished in Italian Renaissance style and the parlor after the popular Louis XV style. The patio is the distinctive characteristic of Algerian buildings and in the Fenyes home it will indeed be a beautiful feature. The apartments on the upper floor will open onto it and it will be crowned by a dome of art glass.

Winthrop B. Fay house, 1898.

Howard Longley final design, 1897.

The Winthrop B. Fay House, 1898

Typical of these larger commissions was the 1898 design for Winthrop B. Fay, a complex combination of disparate styles from Queen Anne to Colonial Revival. Wrapped in a simple horizontal clapboard siding, the exterior materials belied the variety of semicircular windows balanced by an octagonal tower at each end of a central entry portico. Above, in the third-level gable, was a Palladian window with French doors opening onto a narrow balcony with a heavy balustrade in deep relief. All that held the variety of stylistic elements together was the strength of its bold roof form.

■ Throughout the mid years of the Greenes' first decade of work, it was the strength of their powerful roof forms that brought order to their complex historical design expressions. This was true of both the earlier Longley house and the later Swan house, where a mixture of historical styles resulted from a combination of client demands and the brothers' classical training at MIT. While they were uncomfortable with the criteria of the times, such commissions kept the office going until they were able to develop more clearly their own feelings and the direction of their own architectural work. As students at MIT they had considered the teaching of classical styles illogical and distasteful. The Manual Training School, with its emphasis on the relationships of design, form and character to materials, tools and craft had had far more influence on their thinking. Even so, it was difficult for the young architects to buck the prevailing tastes of the day.

It was just this kind of eclecticism that reflected the tastes of many a client at the turn of the century and was frequently rejected by the few young architects who, like the Greenes, possessed genuine courage and convictions.

■ The rejection of the Fenyes commission did not free the Greenes from the pressures of other clients who were caught up in the popular styles of the day. Although their own work showed a progressive interest in the Shingle style and the work of H. H. Richardson, which they had encountered during their respective apprenticeships in Boston, their fourth year of practice brought in wealthier clients, and the stylistic pressures on them continued.

The Howard Longley House, 1897

The Longleys were relatives of the Greenes and had had much to do with Dr. and Mrs. Greene's decision to move from Saint Louis to Pasadena. The Longleys and the Greenes spent much time together, so it was not surprising that they should choose Charles and Henry as their architects. The closeness of the two families probably accounts for the fact that the Longleys abandoned a complete set of detailed ink-and-linen construction drawings for a more simplified design proposed by Charles and Henry. Their first design represented an eclectic mixture of historical styles, including a Mission-style parapet over an attic dormer. Altogether the design was almost humorous and undoubtedly disturbing to Charles and Henry.

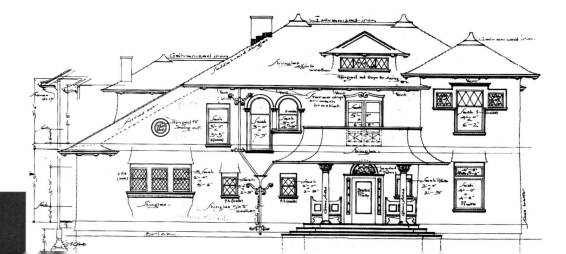

Stairway detail, Howard Longley house, 1897.

■ Pencil-on-tissue sketches of revised elevations for the Longley design, saved and placed in their scrapbook, demonstrates the brothers' effort to clean up the design desired by their relatives. From these sketches there evolved a new design that affected the interior configuration as well as the external character. Each of these sketches progressively rejected more and more historical precedent and allowed for function and the expression of structure and space to impact the final form. The resulting design, somewhat in the Shingle style, finally met the combined interests of the Greenes and the Longleys. The imagination of this original interior octagonal configuration of the plan, with its free flow of space and the long line of the roof organizing and giving strength to the front elevation, was lost in a Greene alteration for later owners in 1912. While nowhere near the expression of their later beliefs, the Longley house illustrates the Greenes' struggle to extricate themselves from the prevailing classical and traditional work of this era, a struggle reflected by the unique combination of balcony railing and entry roof for the Longley house.

The James Swan House, 1898
The largest and most prestigious of the residences of this period was Torrington Place, an elaborate and costly mansion for James Swan, Esq., and his wife, socialite Francis B. Swan. Located directly on Colorado Boulevard just a short distance from the

Top to bottom
James Swan house, 1898.

Entry hall and elevator of the Swan house.

A carved-wood panel of the second-floor elevator door of the Swan house.

This wood-cut detail of the elevator fan light of the Swan house originally occupied the two side arches as well.

Left, stair landing and stained-glass window of the Swan house, 1897.

Lower right, Charles W. Hollister house #1, 1898.

center of business activity, the Swan house became a focus of many a social event. Like several other clients, the Swans wanted their house designed along traditional lines. As with the Longley and the Fay houses, the Greenes softened the classicism of the facade with the bold form of the predominant gable roof, giving it strength by carrying it across the side porte cochere and producing a long, clean line similar in feeling to the beauty and simplicity of the 1887 Low house by architects McKim, Mead and White.

■ An earlier and more formal plan of the Swan house incorporated a large central receiving hall with dual stairs leading up to a central landing. While the change in the balance of the house was affected very little, a study of the sketches for the interiors suggests that the original plan called for an elaborate vaulted ceiling supported by columns and capitals, richly carved wood paneling and a high degree of formality, which would have been much more costly than the Greenes' altered version.

■ Even in the Greenes' final and more simplified form, the house was highly ornate, with sculptured plaster ceilings of flowing sinuous lines. In these interiors was the first appearance of the fluid forms of Art Nouveau to be found in the work of the Greenes.

The Charles W. Hollister House, 1898

Though smaller in scale than the Fay, Longley and Swan houses, The Charles W. Hollister house also demonstrates the continued struggle in the Greenes' minds regarding design determinates. This, the first of two houses for the Hollisters, is still more Shingle style, though simpler and cleaner, than the Longley house. While incorporating the Greenes' much-used broad-roofed dormer, here it adds to the horizontal line emphasized throughout this design in its careful composition. Although the historical stylistic traits, which were being gradually eliminated from their designs, are felt more on the interiors than on the exterior, their detail is dramatically restrained here in stark contrast to that of the Swan house.

Competitions

Along with their work for their more affluent clientele, the firm began to enter competitions for various projects in town but, with the exception of that for the Presbyterian Church, were unsuccessful. Their 1897 proposal to provide for a major annex addition to the popular Green Hotel was lost to architect Frederick L. Roehrig, to whom they had lost a residential commission the year before. In 1898 they lost the design for a major addition to the Wilson Public School, and a year later the addition to the Pasadena Public Library, with both commissions going to architect C. W. Buchanan. On other occasions initial proposals for clients were rejected in favor of local architects who had no trouble producing Moorish and other exotic or eclectic designs.

Personal Lives

Toward the end of the 1890s, the Greenes were spending more and more time with their growing architectural practice. They were also spending considerable time with two young ladies in the community—Henry with Miss Emeline Augusta Dart and Charles with Alice Gordon White. There were bicycle outings to the nearby poppy fields in the foothills or picnicking and painting in the adjacent arroyo, Rubio Canyon or Devilsgate Dam, and, as time would allow, individual trips to the Southern California beaches for Henry's photography or to the California missions for Charles's painting. Letters indicate that Charles was wrestling with a painting of *The Flying Dutchman,* which he rejected, retrieved and finally completed before having it framed. This painting was kept in his home throughout his life.

Charles dated July 28, 1899, he expressed his continuing concerns for the day-to-day business of the firm and his worry about the firm's reputation if any chimneys had fallen during the earthquake or "if any plaster fell from the Fay house." The rest of his letter is full of questions about the completion of the Swan house and the status of various other commissions, and ended with just a quick comment on his health and wedding preparations. The wedding was held at the home of the bride's aunt on August 22, 1899, with his close friend from Boston "Tech," Willie Gamble (no known relation to the later Gamble house commission), as his best man. After a honeymoon in Kansas City, he returned to Pasadena and quickly became immersed in the work of the firm.

■ By this time Charles was focusing his attentions on Alice White, for whom he had designed and built his first piece of furniture. Taking scraps from the various job sites, he crafted a simple square, pedestal dining table with a geometric-pattern top made up of flooring strips. Far from being representative of the furniture designs now identified so closely with the work of Greene and Greene, this first table spoke clearly of Charles's disdain for the prevailing furniture styles and for his desire to work with his hands. Certainly the years in the Manual Training School shops had instilled in him a love of materials and craft.

Small portions of the natural arroyo exist today, offering scenes similar to those enjoyed by the Greenes and their friends a century earlier.

■ Around the turn of the century a series of events took place, each of which, in one way or another, affected the dramatic new directions in both the brothers' lives and in their professional work.
■ In the spring of 1899 Henry took ill and was out of the office for some time, requiring that Charles pay attention to the business as well as to the design activities of the practice. While still regaining his strength, Henry traveled to Rock Island, Illinois, to prepare for his wedding to Emeline Augusta Dart. In a letter to

12. For a detailed discussion of the trip, see Edward R. Bosley, "Greene & Greene: The British Connection," *The Tabby* (Berkeley), vol. 1, no. 3 (July - August 1997).

13. Charles Greene's contact prints and negatives of the 1901 trip are part of the Documents Collection of the Greene & Greene Library, The Gamble House, USC.

Emeline Augusta Dart.

Alice Gordon White.

This table, designed and made by Charles Greene for his fiancée, represents the first furniture design by either of the brothers.

Oil painting by Charles Greene entitled
The Flying Dutchman.

14. Documents Collection, College of Environmental Design, University of California, Berkeley.

■ In February of 1901 Charles married Alice Gordon White, one of four sisters who had emigrated from England with their father several years earlier. The following month they left on a trip to southern Europe and England.[12] Charles's photographs document their travels throughout the six months of their stay, capturing the countryside and waterfront scenes, fountains, plazas and gardens that seemed to catch his interest.[13] Careful study of these photographs indicates that he paid careful attention to the composition of his images and waited a considerable length of time for the light to change so as to achieve the effect he wanted. Part of their time in England was spent in and around Lancaster with members of Alice's family and in the Lake District, where their exploration of the English countryside deepened their appreciation of nature and the out-of-doors. Just how much

Charles focused his attention on the Arts and Crafts activities while in England and who he may have met and talked with is not yet certain. However, after Charles returned to Pasadena, the work of the firm suggested his deep interests in the English half-timber structures and the materials and architectural forms of C.F.A. Voysey, which he could well have experienced in London, where he had rented a flat for part of their visit. However, it would be over a decade before the impressions from their travels throughout southern Europe would appear in the form of house or garden designs for larger commissions.

■ Meanwhile Henry carried on with the business of the office, the several smaller houses on the drawing board or under construction, the designs for the first of many commissions for the Pasadena Ice Company, the large building block adjacent to their offices for John Bentz, and the donation of his architectural services for

Page from the brothers' scrapbook containing clippings of the Will Bradley articles appearing in the Ladies Home Journal *between September 1901 and August 1902.*

alterations for All Saints Episcopal Church. Additionally, with the birth of his first child in October of 1900, there was much thought given to future plans, the growing architectural practice, and how those considerations would affect Henry's growing-family situation.

■ Records of Charles and Alice's return to the United States include a train trip from New York to Buffalo, giving rise to speculation about a possible visit by Charles to East Aurora and the Roycroft Arts and Crafts shops of Elbert Hubbard, which had begun operating in 1895.[14]

■ By August 1901 Charles was back in Pasadena, where his life changed dramatically. There was new work in the office and construction progressing on others. At the same time, Henry, Emeline, and Emeline's mother, Charlotte Whitridge, moved from Pasadena into a two-story rented house near the University of Southern California campus and within trolley distance from downtown Los Angeles. In October Greene and Greene expanded their offices to the Henne Building in Los Angeles within walking distance of public transportation connecting Henry's rental house in Los Angeles and Charles's travel from the Pasadena office. In November new regulations required architects to apply for State of California certificates to practice architecture. With Charles now spending more time in the Pasadena Kinney-Kendall Block office and Henry in the Los Angeles office, there was less opportunity for the close collaboration heretofore experienced by the brothers. As a result, it would be but a short time before they would begin to take personal responsibilities for the various aspects of the work in the offices.

■ In the midst of all these changes taking place in the firm was the arrival of exciting new publications espousing the ideals of the Arts and Crafts movement. In October 1901 came the first issue of *The Craftsman* magazine, which had a profound impact on the work of the Greenes. It featured the philosophy of William Morris, expressing the ideas and ideals of design and craft, which had been the core of their training at the Manual Training School in Saint Louis and had led them to reject the eclectic training of their MIT years. Its stories, principles and illustrations of the furniture designs of Gustav Stickley lit a spark under the Greenes that was quickly transposed not only into their architecture but also into their integration of the design of interiors and furnishings. Now, through Gustav Stickley, these ideals were being implemented in America.

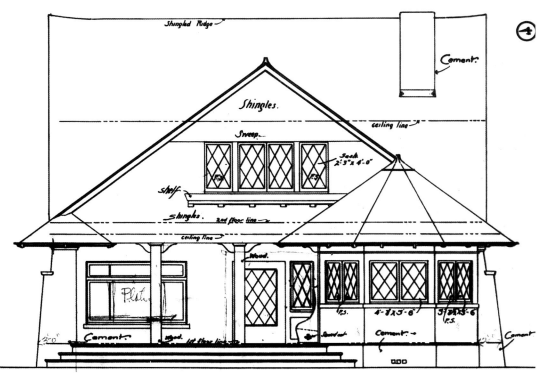

The Mrs. Matilde Phillips house, 1901, rejected historicism and drew upon simple geometric form.

interest in the design of furniture and the decorative arts, the sinuous lines of Art Nouveau that adorned the surfaces of Bradley's work did not seem to interest the brothers. What was of greatest significance was that the Bradley articles demonstrated the concept that architects could be involved with the design and even making of furniture and furnishings and that these could be related to their architecture and interior spaces. This was an ideal already being espoused in the *International Studio* magazine by the English Arts and Crafts architects. A short time later Charles ordered back issues of the *International Studio*, which he had bound with his own library mark, then later received his subscription for bound copies from the publisher.

■ Gustav Stickley's simple forms and forthright joinery so impressed Charles that his own first attempts at making furniture in his own shop would be drawn directly from Stickley's products. In similar fashion Henry's designs for a dining table and chairs for his own family in 1904 demonstrated his equal respect for Stickley's designs. Though this pure influence on the Greenes' furniture designs would not last long, their respect for Stickley continued throughout their careers, and Stickley pieces are found included in the furnishings of their ultimate Arts and Crafts designs.

■ By 1900 there was already a dramatic change surfacing in the work of the firm. With only a few exceptions, the historicism found in their larger commissions up to this time was not a part of the new designs, and the applied decoration found in earlier work remained a part of the past. While it would take another few years, the Greenes' work showed a distinct redirection. Simple, straightforward forms became the dominant element of their designs, with common materials composed carefully and giving a genuine wholesome and livable character to the work.

■ With this new design attitude emerging concurrent with other rapid changes in the firm at the end of 1901, the simplicity of the geometric forms of the Lorenz P. Hansen and Matilde Phillips houses clearly demonstrate the Greenes' complete rejection of the prevailing historicism and the depth of their convictions and search for a more rational and appropriate building language for the foothills and arroyos of the San Gabriel Valley. While Greene and Greene had not yet defined their own personal vocabulary, the new work was a significant step in that direction. Inspired by their embrace of the Arts and Crafts movement and a genuine feeling of the pace and quality of Southern California life, the ingredients were set in place for the origin of the style for which Greene and Greene have been recognized nationally as "formulators of a new and native architecture."[15]

■ The Greenes could appreciate Stickley's words in his foreword to that first issue where he discussed the establishment of his workshops as the United Crafts of Eastwood, New York:

The new association is a guild of cabinet workers, metal and leather workers, which has been recently formed for the production of household furnishings. . . . The United Crafts endeavor to promote and to extend the principles established by Morris, in both the artistic and socialistic sense.

In another article in that issue of *The Craftsman,* entitled "An Argument for Simplicity in Household Furnishings," Stickley's words must have been welcomed greatly by the Greenes: "Present tendencies are toward a simplicity unknown in the past. The form of any object is made to express the structural idea directly, frankly, often almost with baldness."

■ The following month the *Ladies Home Journal* began its series of articles and illustrations of the designs of Will Bradley that continued through August of 1902. The Greenes were so fascinated that they clipped the illustrations and inserted them into a scrapbook that they had started during their Boston days at MIT. While Bradley's designs appear to have inspired the Greenes'

15. From the text of the citation awarded to Henry Mather Greene and Charles Sumner Greene by the National American Institute of Architects in 1952.

2

PARK PLACE
1902-1907

Left, sidewalk vista along North Grand Avenue (formerly Reservoir Terrace).

Right, Greene and Greene designs for cobblestone and clinker-brick walls, brick sidewalks, timber pergolas, and ball trees in the parkways of the Park Place tract remain today, providing the genteel neighborhood ambiance of a century-old lifestyle.

Park Place is a small neighborhood on the bluffs of Pasadena's Arroyo Seco and distinguished by the number of houses designed by Greene and Greene. Of the original thirty-four parcels within its four blocks, eleven houses were by the Greenes and represent a microcosm of the evolution of the style by which the firm has come to be recognized. In addition. cobblestone and clinker-brick walls, articulated wooden fences, flower-covered pergolas, and the discipline of the brick sidewalks and parkway landscapes fronting each of the Greene-designed properties provided a distinct character and charm that carried out the same principles of the Arts and Crafts movement found in the architecture. Here there was both a great diversity and a strong unity of spirit growing easily out of the natural topography and environment. A few multifamily residential developments of recent years have brought about some change in the neighborhood; yet, the strength of the historic streetscape continues to convey the dreams and passions that brought the original owners, as well as Charles Greene, to settle on this land. Today those who stroll along the walks or down the adjacent park trails continue to appreciate the soft, easy sculptural forms that the Greenes brought to natural materials. Here there still remains a quality of life as valid in our contemporary society as it was a century ago.

■ The Park Place tract land dates back some thousand years, when it was inhabited by the Hahamongna Indians, who selected the bluffs overlooking the vast Arroyo Seco (meaning dry wash) valley and across to the San Gabriel Mountains. Around 1770 when the Spaniards took possession of Southern California, Father Junipero Serra wrote, "We have seen Indians in immense numbers living on seeds and fishing. All the males go naked but the women and female children are decently covered from their breasts downward."[1]

■ Known initially as Park Place Reservation, the area became Reservoir Hill following the settlement of Pasadena (an Algonquin word meaning crown or key of the valley) by the Indiana Colony in 1874. After the breakup of the Spanish land grants in 1883, the early population of health seekers were rapidly joined by midwestern farmers lured by stories of opportunities amidst vast orchards and a temperate climate. They adapted their skills in growing wheat to growing citrus groves, only to be overrun by the land boom of 1886 as developers cut the citrus groves and wheat fields into residential lots. Reservoir Hill was acquired by the Park Place Improvement Company with offices at the crossroads of Pasadena's downtown business center. To promote the Park Place

tract development, the syndicate installed a horse-drawn railway to lure potential land buyers. The West Pasadena Railway began at Colorado Boulevard and Fair Oaks Avenue and carried its passengers west to Park Place, following Arroyo View Drive (now Arroyo Terrace) around the northern bluffs of Park Place and continuing through the center of the tract on Reservoir Terrace (now North Grand Avenue). From there the two open horse-drawn cars departed from the southern end of Reservoir Terrace where the tracks led down across the Arroyo bridge, along the lake formed by the Scoville Dam, and northward along Park (Linda Vista) Avenue, thus promoting the Linda Vista properties, before ending at the Park Place Nursery, a company noted for having provided nearly all of the eucalyptus and pepper trees throughout the San Gabriel Valley.

■ Below Park Place the entire arroyo now became the focus for many activities, such as hiking the trails, following the streams, collecting bird eggs, riding horseback, participating in hayrides, and even going on wildcat hunts.

1. Beverly Wayte, *At the Arroyo's Edge, A History of Linda Vista* (Los Angeles: Historical Society of Southern California and LindaVista/Annondale Association, 1993). This provides a complete study of the Park Place tract and surrounding arroyo.

The Park Place tract, circa 1901-07.

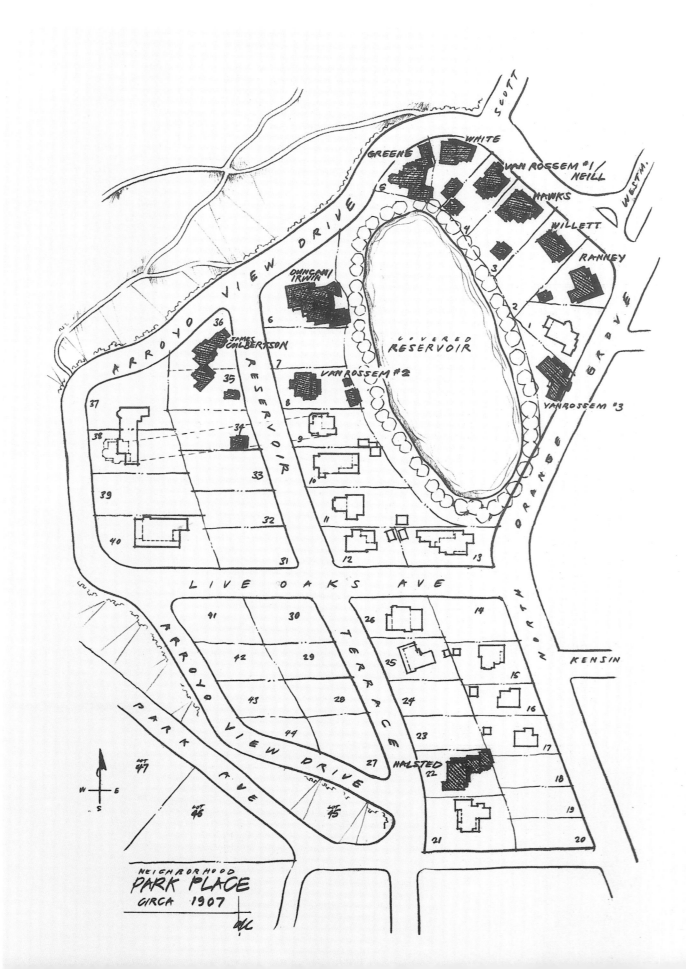

Below the residences of today's Park Place neighborhood, portions of the concrete foundation from the former Scoville Dam stand in sharp contrast to the serene waters in the arroyo's remaining natural terrain.

■ However, despite its spectacular views, the success of Park Place collapsed once the land boom was over. By the time Charles and Henry Greene arrived in Pasadena, real-estate developers had lost heavily, mortgages were being abandoned, and many houses were for rent. Even the rails for the horse-drawn railroad were taken up in 1892 and sold for use in the construction of the Mount Lowe Railway.

■ Little of record occurred in Park Place until the turn of the century. A few houses built by speculators remained, but there were many vacant parcels, some planted in wheat. In 1900 a large Victorian house with a third-level tower and a 270-degree view of the upper and lower arroyo occupied a prestigious location on the edge of the bluffs of the northwesterly point of the Park Place tract, but in a few years it was moved two hundred feet east onto Reservoir Terrace. A few larger residences began to rise along the westerly bluff soon thereafter, but the real building activity in Park Place began with the moving by Katherine M. Duncan in 1901 of a six-room house onto lot #6.

■ Katherine Duncan was a successful dressmaker who had maintained her business for a time in the Stowell Block down the hall from the office of Greene and Greene. By 1900 she had relocated in the Vandervort Block next to Dr. Greene's medical offices. In June of the following year she purchased one of the prime parcels of Park Place along the north rim of the subdivision

with a commanding view over the entire arroyo. She was probably encouraged by her father, a carpenter, and her brother, who dealt in real estate, to move a six-room house onto the Park Place site and at that time to make some alterations. While this modest cottage, with its arched porches along the street facade, was stylistically related to the Shingle style familiar to the Greenes during their years of apprenticeship in Boston, there are no records to suggest that Greene and Greene had any part in its original design or in its relocation and initial alterations. On the contrary, Charles Greene later expressed in writing a clear distaste for the all-cobblestone wall along the street frontage, a wall that, according to family lore, had some stonework laid by Katherine Duncan herself.

■ In 1903 Mrs. Duncan doubled the size of the house by adding another six rooms on the ground floor. While there is no hard evidence that Greene and Greene had a role in that work, there are strong reasons to think they did. They had known Mrs. Duncan for many years; the house was two doors from Charles's house; the interior detail and furnishing of the dining room in Gustav Stickley furniture are consistent with the Greenes' practice; and the building permit for the addition listed C. N. Stanley as the contractor, a man whom Greene and Greene used frequently. Another clue to their participation in this early work was the fact that work on both the Duncan additions and the construction of the first van Rossem house were going on simultaneously, and the large square tiles and details of the living-room fireplaces are similar.

This house of unknown design, moved by Katherine Duncan onto lot #6 in Park Place in 1901, was completely absorbed in the 1906 two-story redesign by Greene and Greene for Theodore Irwin.

Mrs. Chas. Sumner Greene House, 1902

Site-plan drawing of the 1902 design.

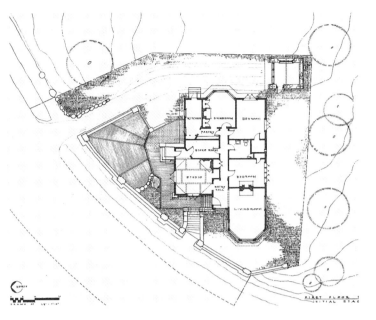

Above, Mrs. Chas. Sumner Greene house as originally constructed in 1902.

Left, the original color scheme Charles Greene selected for his own house has been an important part of the 1998 restoration of the house.

2. Greene and Greene Library, The Gamble House, USC.

The first documented design in the Park Place tract by the Greenes was for Charles's own home. Construction began in March 1902. This was the first of a series of commissions over the next five years, during which Greene and Greene built eleven residences and designs for the streetscape that stand today as the greatest single concentration of their work. These designs had such an impact upon the character and charm of the neighborhood that newspapers dubbed it "Little Switzerland," and it became a popular sightseeing attraction. Charles and his three sisters-in-law purchased lot #5, a pie-shaped parcel on the broad curve of Arroyo View Drive. He designed his own house, which he christened Oakholm, siting it under the large California live oak trees where, it was rumored, the Indiana Colony had met to found the City of Pasadena.

■ The decision to acquire the property and to build in Park Place was made wholly upon his return from England. No such plans existed prior to the trip, as evidenced by Henry's letter to Charles and Alice on June 26, 1901, wherein he wrote, "There isn't a house in town to rent. If you folks want to keep house this Fall, you had better advise some of us as to your plans so we can be on the lookout for you. It is going to be exceedingly hard to find a place."[2]

■ The Park Place property was purchased within weeks after Charles and Alice returned from England, and Charles quickly drew up the design. The brief set of working drawings were entitled "House for Mrs. Chas. Sumner Greene, Pasadena," but without the customary credit to the firm. Construction began on March 20, 1902, and on April 10 a newspaper story announced that the house was being shingled.

■ The plan for the two-bedroom, one-story house was a straightforward series of rooms clustered along a narrow central

Street-elevation drawing of the original 1902 house.

Mrs. Charles S. Greene

living-room colors, 1902.   *Bedroom 1 color scheme, 1902.*   *Dining-room color scheme, 1902.*   *Charles Greene studio color scheme, 1902.*

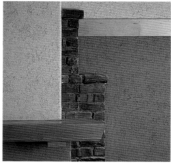

Charles's woodworking shop behind the house, circa 1904.

hallway. Particularly noteworthy was the eighteen-foot ceiling of the studio, the upper portion octagonal in shape and crowned with a magnificent open-timbered truss structure. The upper portion of this studio, accessed only by a removable ladder, was surrounded by a balcony for bookshelves. A solid railing to the balcony created a central shaft of space from the timber detail above to the studio below. From there a separate entrance for clients opened directly to the side terrace.

■ In the living and dining rooms, the full bay windows forming the ends of the spaces echoed the octagonal forms of the studio and related this design to other work by the firm. This was a further example of the Greenes' efforts to explore geometry as a basis for form, as they had attempted to do a few months earlier in the designs for the Matilde Phillips and Lorenz P. Hansen houses. In Charles's house the angular forms were further enhanced by the faceted planes of the low-pitched shingle roof, contrasting with the natural sand color of the dash-coat, plaster-clad exterior walls. The upper octagonal portion of the studio was differentiated by its unstained machined shingles.

Archive view into living room,

circa 1904.

Site-plan drawing of the
completed 1916 design of the Mrs.
Charles S. Greene house.

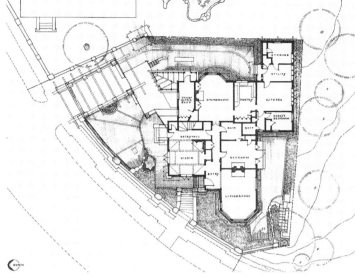

■ The treatment of the interior walls and color established this
house as Charles's experimental laboratory. Plaster walls bypassed
the final coat, utilizing the texture of the generally smooth brown
coat with the inherent porosity and texture of the wood float
finish. To this a thin coat of paint was applied, allowing the texture
of the brown coat to remain. In some areas a two-step system was
used with two colors, the first being revealed through the second
coat, thus adding to the texture of the wall. Charles's lifelong
interest in the chemistry of finishes was asserted in this house, and
through the six additions and alterations, he continued to explore
the ideas that would then appear in the designs for later clients.
■ At the rear apex of the lot and tucked up against the tall deodar
trees surrounding the covered reservoir adjacent to the property,
Charles built a small shop with thick salvaged-stone walls
and a low-sloped, almost flat roof. This was where his serious
interest in furniture making was carried out. Encouraged by
the publications of Stickley and by Bradley's furniture designs, he
built a desk and flat files for himself that were more closely aligned
to Stickley's linearity than to the sinuous lines of Bradley. The
next year the first Greene and Greene furniture designs for others
appeared and were carried out by Charles for his sisters-in-law,
Martha, Violet, and Jane White. For his own living room he made
a library table with tilting top that drew from the functional
characteristics of the construction to determine the aesthetic
character of the design.
■ As his family grew, there was one addition after another, each one
stretching the limits of new ideas a little further. Today as one
moves up through the five levels of the house, one can trace the
evolution of ideas springing from Charles's imagination. At every

turn is found a design or detail used later as an element of the
Greenes' building vocabulary in some client's house.
■ A three-room addition of 1906 literally created a complete second
floor, raising the entire roof, which was now carried out with
exposed rafter tails, timber outriggers to support the long
overhanging eaves, and the soft sculptural roll of the Greenes'
unique composition roof material detailed with integral gutters.
A short time later two more bedrooms were added that were
reached by a narrow twisting stairway connecting at the two-and-
a-half-story level, and after that a third story was nestled among the
gnarled branches of the oak tree outside. The occupant, stepping
through the low casement window of this "tree house" to a railed
roof terrace, could look out on one of the finest views of the arroyo
and San Gabriel Mountains to be found in this part of town.
■ In 1910 when Charles and his wife and their five young children
returned from another visit to England that had lasted for nearly
nine months, the household included a governess and servant. This

Street elevation of the 1918 completed
design. The wood pergola atop the garage
columns was designed by Charles Greene
but was not constructed prior to the
family's move to Carmel. The pergola was
completed in 1998 as part of the complete
restoration of the house by new owners.

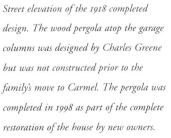

Right, second-floor stair landing,
1906 addition to the Mrs. Chas. Sumner
Greene house.

*Above, the cobalt blue walls of the
dining-room, like other strong colors in
the 1902 palette, relate directly to H. H.
Richardson's Trinity Church.*

*Overleaf, street view near the completion
of the 1998 restoration, featuring Charles's
design for the garage pergola.*

necessitated another quick addition to the ground-floor level, and
Charles's shop was sacrificed for the new wing with a larger kitchen,
laundry and storage rooms, and a nanny's bedroom and bath.

■ During the most distinguished years of the Greenes' practice,
neither Charles nor Henry stopped working for clients long enough
to design furniture for their own homes. But in the early teen years,
with much less work in the office, Charles began to take the time to
design several significant pieces for his personal use. These included
an unusual writing desk in rosewood derived from a similar design
for the Gamble house, several chairs from designs for Mrs. Bush,
and a dining-room suite composed of a sideboard and china cabinet
to complement a dining table made earlier. Each of these later
pieces, along with a large bookcase for his office, were simpler and

more direct than those for recent clients and represent the most
refined work designed by the firm and crafted by the Peter and John
Hall craftsmen.

■ By 1914 Charles had decided to build a garage to house his new
Hudson automobile, a purchase that drew the ire of his friend and
client Earle C. Anthony, who owned the Packard franchise in Los
Angeles. This garage, designed in clinker brick and cobblestones
with great plaster-coated brick piers on top to support a wooden
pergola, took up the last of the land on the site except for a broad,
brick side terrace overlooking Arroyo View Drive. When Charles
moved to Carmel in 1916, he had not yet built his pergola. It was
not until 1998, when the present owners consulted the original
sketches, that this last segment of Charles's vision for his Park Place
property was carried out.

James A. Culbertson house as
originally built in 1902.

James A. Culbertson, Esq., House, 1902

Before Charles had completed his own home, James Alexander Culbertson, a lumber industrialist from Kenilworth, Illinois, purchased lots #36 and #37, directly across from Katherine Duncan, facing the bluffs and trails leading down to the parkland and arroyo below. He then engaged Greene and Greene as architects and provided them with a budget considerably larger than that for Charles's own house. The design for James A. Culbertson resulted from a variety of factors that converged at a particularly important time for the Greenes. Significant were their years in Boston, where they had been surrounded by those close to H. H. Richardson and through them had had opportunities to witness the works of leading Boston architects of the period. Equally significant were three other major factors: a clipping of a related design by William Ralph Emerson, whose work they seem to have admired; the impact of Charles's recent return from his honeymoon trip to England; and the Greenes' reacquaintance with the principles of William Morris and the Arts and Crafts movement, including the publication of *The Craftsman*. It is also worth noting that while in England Charles had taken excellent photographs of country houses and, though no direct connection has been discovered, was likely to have been impressed with the prevailing English Tudor design.

■ When construction of the house started in October 1902, Charles wrote to James Culbertson at his home in Kenilworth, "The suggestion enclosed in your letter for the living room pleased me very much, as I am in thorough sympathy with the William Morris movement, in fact the whole inside of the house is influenced by it in design."[3] While this statement in his own words is most important, it still did not indicate whether the full realization of these principles was a result of the introduction of Morris beliefs into the curriculum of the Manual Training School or from Charles's trip to England or from Stickley's first issue of *The Craftsman*, which could have just arrived. The large amount of Stickley furniture illustrated in the magazine and selected for the house certainly suggested that both the architects and the client paid careful attention to these early issues.

3. Charles Greene's letter to James A. Culbertson, Kenilworth, Illinois, dated 7 October 1902, Greene and Greene Library, The Gamble House, USC.

The redwood carving over the redesigned James Culbertson dining-room mantel was given greater expression by Charles's use of soft watercolor and gold leaf applications.

Watercolor applied to the redwood carving for the living room produced a composition of extreme subtlety.

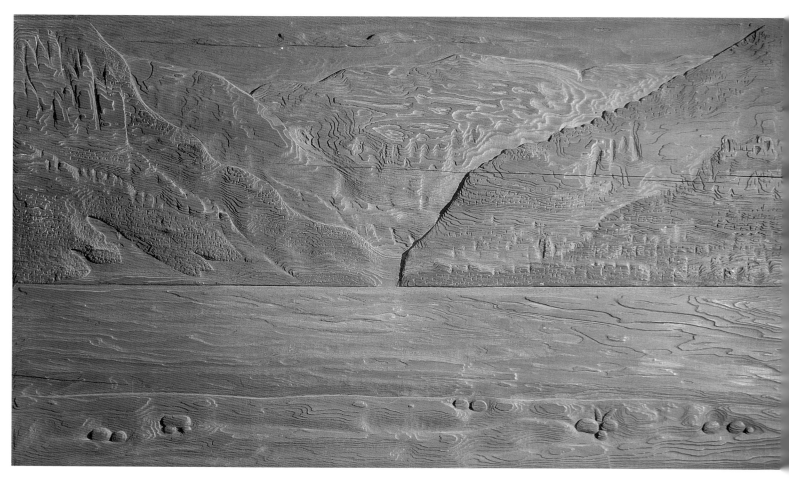

Overleaf, the James Culbertson house following the addition of the living room and dining room bay windows in 1914. The entire second floor was removed in the 1952 remodeling.

Additions and alterations to the James Culbertson dining room in 1906 included the paneled wooden ceiling and the leaded-and-stained-glass central chandelier.

■ Charles's statement that the whole of the interior of the house was influenced by the Morris movement was somewhat of an understatement. A study of the living room alone demonstrated a large amount of Stickley pieces and an embrace of the Orient, of the culture of the American Indian, of art pottery, Tiffany lamps, etc., all of which together became somewhat of a Craftsman "aesthetic movement" on an accelerated taste scale.

■ The Culbertson house, like so many of the Greene and Greene designs in Park Place, underwent as many as nine alterations and additions by the architects, each furthering the evolution of the Greene style. Placing the autobarn in the front yard opposite the entry to the house was one example of garden sculpture-trellis unsurpassed in scale, proportion, and detail. The major additions and alterations of the following years wove the finely tuned philosophy and craft of their most sophisticated era with the detail and expressions in the original design of the house. This was revealed most clearly in the interiors in the richly carved wall paneling of redwood, left raw, with touches of watercolor toning and gold leaf; in the simple but elegant wood detailing of the new dining room; in the wispy yet disciplined compositions of the mahogany and leaded-and-stained glass lanterns; in the graceful yokes of the pergola along the brick sidewalks; and in the two large, faceted bay windows that were completed in 1914, a year before Mr. Culbertson's death. While the original house had been constructed by C. N. Stanley, who had built much of the early Park Place work, the later alterations speak clearly of the hand of Peter and John Hall, Emil Lange, and their respective master craftsmen.

The original design for the Misses
Martha, Violet, and Jane White house
(Charles's three sisters-in-law), 1903,
built adjacent to Charles's own house.

Misses Martha, Violet, and Jane White House, 1903

Early in 1903 construction began on the modest one-story house for Charles's three sisters-in-law, Martha, Violet, and Jane White. According to Charles, the house "was designed for three unmarried sisters, and embodies their own personal ideas of convenience."[4] A curious statement but one that, remembering Dr. Greene's admonition about the health benefits of natural light and ventilation, may have arisen from his own discomfort with the windowless, skylighted central position of the bathroom.

■ The house shared a portion of lot #5 with Charles and Alice Greene and was positioned along the front bluff ten feet above the road, where it commanded a spectacular view of the valley and mountains. With its triangular apex at the rear of the site, the modest but intimate garden incorporated a small pool, which Charles described as "a little pool of lilies and lotus, with grasses overhanging the edges where gold fish lazily seek the shadows." Between the two houses was a wooden gate with a modest *torii*-like timber structure connecting the two properties, which in later years allowed easy access for the Greene children to play in their aunts' garden.

■ The roof structure and materials of the White sisters' house introduced ideas that were to become major elements of the Greenes' personal design vocabulary. To prevent any obstruction to the view from Charles's house, the pitch of the roof was kept low. This necessitated the use of a composition roof covering of overlapping strips thirty-six inches in width, which the Greenes capped with a redwood rib covering the joints, offering interesting rhythm and scale elements to the inexpensive roofing material. As a shield from the hot sun, the eaves were extended, necessitating timber outriggers for support. Here, for the first time, the Greenes shaped the ends of the outriggers at an angle cut, with a notch taken out of the bottom, thus altering the visual impact of the heavy beams. The exterior wooden timber work and roof rafters were treated with a transparent brown stain, contrasting with the natural quality of the shakes that, prior to installation, had been dipped in a transparent green-colored Cabot stain.

■ The first Greene and Greene furniture designs for others were those for the White sisters. Charles's own words speak of the brothers' enthusiasm for the totality of their architecture:

The dining room is wainscotted in deep toned redwood to the height of doors, and hung with a few old prints. . . . At the east end of the room there is a broad window ledge containing a little aquarium specially designed to accord with the room and its furniture of birch. The top of the table is finished to use without a cloth, and neither heat nor water will damage it. The rest of the furniture was designed to fit the room.[5]

The table was a reference to the dining set and side tables, which the family recalls as being very similar to the tea table of oak and cedar for the nook in the living room. While strongly influenced by the designs of Gustav Stickley, the Greenes' furniture was already gaining its own identity by further expressing the pegged joinery and by breaking linearity with the varying dimensions of the wood parts that dance in or out along the edge of the top — a conscious effort to acknowledge the expansion and contraction characteristics of the wood parts in the design.

■ In order to expand the rear garden in later years, the White sisters' garage was demolished, and Charles devised an unfortunate two-car tandem garage under the house by breaking through the high cobblestone retaining wall along the front of the property.

This oak-and-cedar tea table for the White sisters elaborated on the details of the furniture of Gustav Stickley.

4. Charles Sumner Greene, "Bungalows," *The Western Architect,* July 1908.

5. Ibid.

The van Rossem family along Scott Place circa 1903, at the time of the construction of the first of the three van Rossem houses. The area to the right would later become the rear yards of the Cole and Gamble houses.

The Van Rossem family in front of their nearly completed house #1, 1903.

Mrs. Josephine van Rossem House #1, 1903

One of the most active of the Greenes' clients in Park Place was Josephine van Rossem, a widow who, with her two young sons, had come to Pasadena in 1895 and purchased the hillside slope on the northern curve of the Park Place tract. When Charles built his home and studio on the bluff directly across the street, a friendship and business relationship developed between him and Mrs. van Rossem that would involve several commissions in the neighborhood. Her son Jack claimed that Mrs. van Rossem had the highest regard for Charles's talents and "believed he was tops, a virtual tin Jesus himself."[6] Although much admired for her personal drive and business acumen, she was difficult to get along with because, according to her family, she "believed in two things—her way and the wrong way." In Pasadena she first worked in the Kohler Photography Studio as a retoucher and was a fairly good artist. Then, over the years, she dabbled in speculative building, lost considerably in several mining ventures, followed a Shakespeare company across the United States as a costume designer and wardrobe mistress, and later returned to Pasadena where she engaged in the development of several business blocks, each with book establishments or library facilities.

■ In several interviews Jack (Walter Johannes van Rossem) indicated that the Greene family presence was felt strongly in Park Place. Alice Greene, in her housedress and apron, was very much involved with her five children and their friends, including the sons of Myron Hunt, who lived around the corner, and like Alice, the White sisters seemed like aunts to the neighborhood children. Charles was well respected but seldom seen and too busy to stop and talk. Jack recalled that "Mr. Greene seemed so totally absorbed [with his thoughts] that if he walked by you on the street he did not see you."[7]

■ The first of the three commissions in Park Place for Josephine van Rossem was Greene and Greene Job No. 100, a rental house built just east of the White sisters' property. A one-room house built on lot #4 in the early days of the Park Place subdivision was

6. Authors personal interviews with Walter Johannes (Jack) van Rossem.

7. Ibid.

42

Right, Mrs. Josephine van Rossem house #2, 1904.

demolished and replaced by the two-story, seven-room cottage that had a tight box plan with horizontal clapboard siding, wood-shingle roof, and double-hung windows, and featured two dramatic square bay windows, one enhancing the front elevation, living room, and dining room on the side of the house. Set on a slightly lesser bluff up some five feet from the street, the house was constructed on the Greenes' typical cobblestone foundation but possessed none of the articulated timber structure and detail being explored next door, where the White sisters' house was not yet completed.

■ The first van Rossem house is significant for its refinement of lighting and interior finishes and for the Greenes' growing building vocabulary. Integrated into the vertical, natural redwood, board-and-batten paneling were wall sconces finished to match the walls. Each sconce was composed of a simple three-inch-square block mounted to progressively larger back panels and supporting a socket mounting for a glass shade. These were finished smooth, as were the wall surfaces, in contrast to what was then the much-discussed, labor-intensive wire brushing of the heavy timber beams and plank ceilings of the living and dining rooms. This unusual technique became another element of the Greenes' personal style.

Mrs. Josephine van Rossem House #2, 1904

In mid-1904, a few months after the completion of her first house by the Greenes, Mrs. van Rossem commissioned a second house around the corner on Reservoir Terrace (now North Grand Avenue), a speculative venture for her eastern clients Mr. and Mrs. Walstein Root. Though following the first van Rossem house by less than a few months and similar to it in many ways, this simple two-story, seven-room cottage, however modest, represents in its design and detail more of the concepts and ideas that were emerging in the Greenes' new work. The speed with which the brothers were developing their ideas was assisted greatly by the encouragement and confidence of their extraordinary clients.

■ This second van Rossem house was the first to be built on Reservoir Terrace, the principle inner street of the Park Place tract. The site was just two parcels south of the Duncan house and had a less spectacular view than the parcels located along the bluffs. In

spite of its modest scale, the compact plan provided both light and air circulation and, through careful juxtaposition, the living room was spacious and featured many of the qualities of the Greenes' larger houses, including a partial inglenook with a large hearth, built-in seating, and book cabinets carried out with the same attention to articulated wood detail found in the home's entry, landing, and stairway designs.

■ In the excitement of the rapid development of their new architectural vocabulary and the flood of work in the office, the Greenes' zeal may have been more than three of their clients in Park Place could bear. In each of the initial designs for C. J. Willett, Louise T. Halsted, and F. W. Hawks, the concept, scale, and cost were rejected, and in each case more modest plans were worked out and accepted.

Louise T. Halsted House, 1905

The lengthy relationship between the Greenes and the Halsteds began in 1900, shortly after S. Hazard Halsted, a great-grandson of the first U.S. postmaster general under George Washington, arrived in Pasadena. Halsted surrounded himself with distinguished investors, many of whom later became significant clients of the Greenes. In 1901 he founded the Pasadena Ice Company and engaged Greene and Greene frequently over several decades to design a number of its buildings. His own residence, which started out modestly enough, was also expanded time and time again, until Greene and Greene were called in for at least eight additions. Such alterations were not at all unusual. Over half of the Greene

The Louise T. Halsted house, 1905

Louise T. Halsted living room.

Greene and Greene combined commercial lighting panels with their own wooden wall lighting fixture for the Halsted living room.

and Greene job numbers identify alterations or additions to earlier work either because of growing families or because of a client's wish to upgrade an early design by incorporating the exciting new features of the developing Greene and Greene style.

■ The Halsted bungalow, a more restrained scheme than the one originally proposed, was constructed on the southernmost parcel of land at the end of the Park Place subdivision, looking west over the lower Park Avenue bridge to the San Rafael Hills. The principal differences between the two schemes involved the deletion of a second floor over half of the house as well as diamond-paned windows that, in the drawings, would have given an excessively dramatic character to the otherwise modest bungalow. Both designs developed around the large living room, where examples abound of the Greenes' concern with every detail. The attention to light and air circulation was evident in the long banks of casement windows opening to the south and to the views across the valley. The new electric lights had taken an enormous leap forward with the linear composition of art-glass lanterns and the selection of

similar wall sconces with glass panels suspended from the bracket, creating a slight shimmer when someone walked about the room. As in the White sisters' house, the positioning of a long, high-backed settle adjacent to the hearth created the intimacy of an inglenook within the spacious openness of the room. The brickwork detail on the large fireplace offers this bungalow the warmth and charm often associated with larger-budget projects. Furniture of simple lines and a scattering of oriental rugs supplied all the ingredients for a comfortable Arts and Crafts environment.

■ But it was the exterior that caught the eye. This small, modest bungalow, hugged to the ground by a long, single-story front roofline, was articulated by its timber outriggers supporting long, low eaves that provided shelter from the hot sun. Open wood stairs across a simple rolling green lawn led to an entry sitting terrace banked by a foundation of brick-capped cobblestone piers. Nothing was fancy or costly, yet the overall effect was one of quiet charm made all the more elegant by its lack of pretension.

C. J. Willett House, 1905

Judge Charles J. Willett had owned lot #2 of Park Place since the turn of the century, and when he became aware of the growing number of bungalows being built along Arroyo View Drive, he commissioned Greene and Greene to design a speculative or rental house. The first scheme was large, dramatic, and spacious. A cruciform two-story plan contrasted octagonal and rectangular forms. Like the early scheme for the Halsted house, this, too, featured the diamond panes in the upper-window composition, a concept that in both houses was deleted. The contrast between the two Willett designs is monumental. The Willett house, as built, had a basic one-story rectangular plan with a servant's room in the gabled attic. It had all the elements of the Greenes' style and demonstrated how extremely effective that style was on even the most modest of houses. The house is best described in Charles's own words from an article on Park Place in *The Western Architect,* published in 1908:

(This) is a small cottage designed for renting purposes. The outside materials are Oregon pine timbers and white cedar shingles without stain. As the house is several years old, the whole has weathered into varying tones of brown and grey. The retaining wall in front and the foundation and chimneys are finished in rough pebble dash cement

toned slightly darker than the wood but approaching it in color. . . . The front door opens directly into the living room which has a large fireplace of dark brown bricks. The wood work is of Oregon cedar toned brown. The plaster of walls is stained on sand finish a soft brown that is slightly mottled while the ceiling is lighter in the same general tone. The electric fixtures were specially designed here as well as in nearly all of the other houses [by Greene and Greene in Park Place] and the same general color tones were used in glass of the front door as in the fixtures. Even the curtains and portiers with their fixtures were designed by the architects. It is impossible to describe the harmony that may be obtained when the furniture and fittings are all designed with the house. [8]

Photographs show the interiors furnished in Mission oak furniture, Indian rugs, and Greene-designed leaded-glass box lanterns suspended from swagged chains and a straightforward built-in dining-room buffet, a prototype to that which would be built for the John Bentz house a few months later.

■ The complete remodeling in 1927 left little of the original character of the Willett house, which was undoubtedly the finest example of the Greenes' principles applied to the one-story bungalow.

8. Charles Sumner Greene, "Bungalows," *The Western Architect,* July 1908.

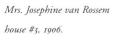

Mrs. Josephine van Rossem
house #3, 1906.

Mrs. Josephine van Rossem House #3, 1906

During the early 1900s one or another of the Greene houses or additions was constantly under construction in the Park Place complex, and early in 1906 Josephine van Rossem again called on the Greenes to design her own residence on an unusual triangular site defined in the rear by a tall stand of deodar trees and at the front by a bluff down to the street level. The Greenes, responding to the site, placed the house high above the dirt and dust of North Orange Grove Boulevard and the noisy clang of passing horse cars. The winged plan challenged the highly articulated natural-timbered structure with high-pitched gable roofs turning one on another. The main rear gable reached across the short span of the plan, producing a high attic and a third level. The forward wing perched on top of cobblestone walls, separating the house from the busy thoroughfare by walled stairs rising from the walk up to the high entry terrace. With its balconies, overhanging eaves, and shake siding, the composition lent a Swiss character to the house and provided a dramatic architectural statement near the northernmost entrance into Park Place. The sheer drama of the architectural forms and timber-and-stone vocabulary must have drawn considerable comment.

■ The interior treatments and another new furniture exploration demonstrated continued strides forward for owner and architect alike. The Greenes had scoured the timber sources of Northern California for the full two-by-twenty-inch clear redwood planking for the living-room ceiling and left it rough. As a finish, they preserved the wood with a volatile chemical that first turned the wood a bright yellow green and then a soft, natural wood tone when rubbed out with oil. So volatile was the preservative that the rags had to be stored outside at night as they were prone to spontaneous combustion. The floors, walls, and ceilings were completely of wood.

■ It is clear when studying this design that Josephine van Rossem gave her architects a great deal of latitude. From plan to mass to structure to interiors and furniture, the design is rugged, raw, powerful. Here in one of the few instances where the Greenes designed furniture for the Park Place houses, the pieces revert in concept to earlier Arts and Crafts designs found both in the United States and England. The forms were linear, almost brutal, with exposed cleats put together with a pattern of expressed screws with such honesty, it was startling. But the sensitivity of the proportions

F. W. Hawks house, 1906.

The driveway design of the Hawks house flowed through the site as though it were a dry stream in the nearby arroyo.

and the quality of craftsmanship hinted at the works of Voysey, Mackintosh, Bradley, and Stickley; yet, there is also a freshness that is disarming. This approach to furniture was rarely a part of the Greenes' vocabulary and appeared for but a short time in such commissions as the Willett and Bentz houses of the same period.

■ Progress is not always exercised with wisdom and foresight, and fifty years later North Orange Grove Avenue was widened. This resulted in the demolition of the last van Rossem house and the loss of one of the unique achievements of Greene and Greene.

F. W. Hawks House, 1906

The third commission along Arroyo View Drive to undergo substantial changes in design was that for Frank Winchester Hawks, a recent arrival from Wisconsin. The earlier scheme proposed a long U-shaped plan on the narrow site, embracing a central garden anchored by the two-story clinker brick chimney of the living room that stretched across the street facade. Massive timber trusses were developed to allow an unobstructed view of the valley beyond from a covered porch spanning the entire front of the house. Section drawings depict a two-story-high living room of open-timber truss structure strapped together with wrought iron, balcony railings of articulated wood joinery, and door-paneling detail generated by its exposed screw patterns. In the development

of its external structure, the design was related to the Robert Pitcairn house constructed a few months earlier, as well as to the truss structure of the Theodore Irwin house going up around the corner. This large design was too much for the Hawks and was never built, although some of its elements emerged in later commissions.

■ In response to the Hawkses' request for a redesign following the form of the John Bentz house under construction a few blocks away, the Greenes planned a simple two-story rectangular form under a broad gable roof with ample attic space. But the grand covered porch of the earlier design was retained, now with a roof terrace above that offered an equally spectacular view of the valley and mountain range.

■ The distinguishing feature of the Hawks design was the brick-and-cobblestone drive that wound up the side of the house, rising and turning as a dry stream to the garage in the rear. Entered through two cobblestone piers capped by brick and supporting art-glass lanterns, this sculptural drive conveys something of the charm of the trails winding down the nearby arroyo.

47

Archive photograph of workmen in front of the nearly completed major additions and alterations to the Katherine Duncan house for Theodore Irwin, 1906.

The Duncan/Irwin House, 1906

Duncan/Irwin house, 1906.

The Duncan/Irwin house viewed from the air reveals the central courtyard, contained by a wooden trellis overhead, allowing light and air softly into the central portions of the interior.

One of the most dramatic and challenging of the Greenes' works in Park Place was the Duncan/Irwin house. There is some question as to when the Greenes first became involved in this property, but, as previously indicated, there is some evidence of the Greenes' hand in the 1903 addition for Mrs. Duncan. There is little question, however, about its history once Theodore Irwin took over.

■ Irwin had been renting Katherine Duncan's house for some months before purchasing it in early 1906, and he was well aware of the rapidly changing expression of the Greene works in progress all around him. With his decision to double the size of the twelve-room house, to have a second story, and to have it carried out in the Greenes' new articulated-timber style, he provided to the brothers both an enormous challenge and the opportunity to stretch their abilities to the fullest.

■ The small central courtyard's problems were dealt with so brazenly that it became one of the major features of the redesign. By setting back the second-level walls and thus creating balcony levels on three sides of the upper court, and by containing the vertical space with a bold red timber trellis, the space was transformed into one that responded to the changing light patterns throughout the day. Its detailing celebrates the emerging structural vocabulary that the Greenes were quick to refine and for which their so-called "ultimate commissions" are so noted. In like fashion the dramatic timber trusses studied in the early Hawks project are carried out here, making possible the unobstructed views of the valley from the living and dining spaces. Setting the theme of the wooden structure, the post-and-truss structural systems support large second-level porches and define secondary and tertiary spaces within the extensive tiled terraces embracing the two street facades. A massive clinker-brick-and-cobblestone wall makes the transition to the broad lawn that extended to the original cobblestone retaining wall at the sidewalk that was developed by Mrs. Duncan in 1901. According to Charles, this retaining wall "should be covered with vines; as it stands, of course, [it] is out of harmony with the general scheme." The exterior materials of the Irwin house were similar to that of the White sisters' house, with timber structure of a transparent brown stain and the wall shakes dipped in a transparent deep green stain, the combination of colors blending in with the colors of the eucalyptus trees prevalent in the neighborhood.

■ No two spaces were the same. Each had a particular character rising more from the exigencies of multiple alterations than from any deliberate purpose. In spite of this, the Greenes' brusque use of similar materials and the thread of detail and structural gymnastics correlated these disparate elements into a harmonious yet exciting whole.

The central courtyard and second-level
balconies of the Duncan/Irwin house, 1906.

■ The dining room of the Irwin house represents one of those rare moments when the genius of the Greenes brought together philosophy, art, ingenuity, and exquisite craftsmanship. The fireplace of deep green Grueby tiles was framed by a Port Orford cedar mantel, the design of which was so direct and honest to the joinery detail that it takes you aback. At the same time it was so sensitively proportioned that it blended gracefully with the abstract linear composition of wood trim on the walls that became, in effect, a remarkable abstract painting. Suspended from the ceiling trim is the light chandelier, a free-spirited but highly disciplined series of swag chains and etched-glass bell shades giving soft light throughout.

■ There is nothing fancy here. The woods are common and the joinery straightforward. Craftsmanship is present, yet there is no pretension. There is an elegance in unity but no call for the precious. The house evokes the furniture of Gustav Stickley, craftsman rugs, and the earthiness of pottery.[9]

■ Greene and Greene had honored the integrity of the original house. For Irwin they had created a large living environment befitting the client's needs; yet, they had responded to the pace of life overlooking the natural arroyo that lay before them, and had absorbed all prior additions and alterations into one unified architectural statement. In so doing they had expanded their own vocabulary and produced one of the truest expressions of the principles of the Arts and Crafts movement. In meeting the articulated structural challenges of the Duncan/Irwin design, they had found the tools of the future. They were now ready for the "ultimate commissions."

9. For further material on the Duncan/Irwin house, see the exhibition catalogue by Janeen Marrin and Randell L. Makinson, *Greene and Greene Interiors '83* (Pasadena: Friends of the Gamble House, USC, 1983).

The high-ceilinged second-floor master bedroom.

Duncan/Irwin dining room.

View of the reception hall in the Duncan/Irwin house.

The van Rossem/Neill house, 1906, celebrates the sculptural genius of the Greenes' use of arroyo boulders and clinker brick.

There is a discipline in the hierarchy of the disorder of the Greenes' masonry art.

designed furniture, incorporating the green tiles within the wooden detail of benches. Particularly interesting is the narrow gate through the massive front wall, the subject of many photographs and preserved on film by Howard Hawks's *The Goose Girl*.[10] Brick caps on the wall expressed at points of change provide platforms for ceramic pots planted with cascading azaleas and other flowering plants.

■ By enclosing the entry porch, the Greenes created one of the largest living spaces of their career. However the most striking structural change was the complete conversion of the exterior to the Greenes' new style. Long overhangs were supported by massive outriggers, the shiplap-siding walls were clad in shingles, casement windows replaced double-hung bays on the ground floor, and the addition of a new entry portico and pergola across the drive turned the once-modest design into a rich addition to the Greenes' legacy along Arroyo View Drive.

■ At the break of 1907, the Greene and Greene practice had grown enormously, particularly around Pasadena, and other architects and builders were attempting to emulate their designs and details with varying degrees of success. Now, with most of their work centered in the Pasadena area, the brothers decided to move their Los Angeles office back to Pasadena and into the Boston Building immediately behind the Kinney-Kendall Building. It was from this location that their ultimate commissions and furnishings would emerge.

The van Rossem/Neill House, 1906

Late in 1906 Mrs. van Rossem sold the first of her Greene and Greene houses to Mr. and Mrs. James W. Neill, owners of a shop on Colorado Boulevard dealing in fine Oriental imports, including the now-famous green Chinese tiles used on the walls, trellises, and gateways in many a Greene and Greene house. Like so many others who were captivated by the new building vocabulary, the Neills commissioned Greene and Greene to design major alterations and additions to the van Rossem house #1. The most dramatic change was the high clinker-brick-and-cobblestone wall and rail to provide privacy for a new outdoor terrace above the sidewalk and with a magnificent panorama of the mountains. By a careful massing of large boulders from the arroyo and graduation to smaller ones, and becoming more dominated by clinker-brick laid with a random yet disciplined quality, this wall became a major sculptural element along Arroyo View Drive. Its eight-inch square pavers of the terrace were set loosely on sand to provide a disciplined yet still-natural ground surface for which the Greenes

Mary L. Ranney house, 1907.

Mary L. Ranney House, 1907

The last of the Greene and Greene designs in Park Place was the Mary L. Ranney house, built in the early months of 1907. Possibly because of the amount of work on the boards at that time, the chores of moving the offices, and the Greenes' high regard for Mary Ranney, a draftsperson in their office, she was allowed to design and carry out the working drawings for her own home under the watchful eyes of the brothers. The Ranney house, though a small rectangular dwelling, commanded attention because of the detailing of its design and its prominent location on a portion of lot #1 of Park Place near the entrance to the tract at Orange Grove Avenue and Arroyo View Drive. It sits lower on the site and farther back from the other Greene and Greene houses along the sweeping curve of the road. Because of the rising grade, independent designs, and different construction periods, there is a rich variety in this enclave of Greene and Greene houses.

■ By this time Greene and Greene had fully refined their new style, and in this house they showed how easily it could be adapted to even the most modest of structures. Here again the Greenes expressed the natural qualities of their architectural vocabulary by leaving the Douglas fir timbers and redwood shingles raw, allowing them to age to varying shades of brown, grey, and black. Unusual was the crisp line of the white painted-wood trim of the eaves, a contrast to the subtle earth tones of the rest of the structure. With a so-called outdoor living room on the quiet side of the house under a timbered pergola, a service yard and carefully articulated wooden gate off the kitchen, and a second-level screened sleeping balcony, the Ranney design evoked a charm and comfort normally found in larger commissions.

■ Mary Ranney made substantial additions and alterations to her house in 1912, but there are no records suggesting the involvement of Greene and Greene in these changes.

■ During the work in progress on the Ranney and van Rossem/Neill houses, Charles Greene, supported by a number of the clients in Park Place, petitioned the city in February 1907 to allow the installation of brick sidewalks fronting the Greene and Greene houses along Arroyo View Drive and Reservoir Terrace. Construction of these sidewalks took place over an extended period of time and consequently resulted in differing patterns and techniques of installation from one house to another. This enhanced the character of the Greenes' designs developed between 1901 and 1907.

Entry hall and stairwell of the Mary L. Ranney house, 1907. The lighting fixture is a contemporary addition.

leading from the top of the bluffs opposite the Charles Greene, Duncan/Irwin, and James Culbertson houses were defined with cobblestone walls, and the connection to the Brookside Park below became more a part of Park Place.

■ The second and most significant writing about Park Place and its architecture was by Charles Greene himself. In a major article in *The Western Architect* in July 1908 entitled "Bungalows," he set forth, in the first few paragraphs, the beliefs and conditions that established the architectural vocabulary we now identify with the work of Greene and Greene. Brushing aside the reference to the Greenes' work as "bungalows," Charles wrote:

There is a suggestiveness in the word bungalow that makes it interesting. Just now it is a popular catchword—all the more because few of us have seen a real one. There is a play for the imagination. We have never called our houses bungalows but we cannot shake off the appellation however removed it may be from a semblance of anything Anglo-Indian.

The wondrous climate of California and the freedom of the life one may lead here have much to do with the development of the style of house illustrated in this issue.

There is a charm about it all that tempts one to try the new. Some people come here to enjoy a few months of the year, others come for rest and pleasure after a life of hard work. Even when one comes with a host of traditions one is apt to find it "so different" that one hesitates—and at last stops to listen, most often to be convinced.

In the beginning there are three things the prospective builder should know by heart.

First—*Good work costs much more than poor imitation or factory. There is no honest way to get something for nothing.*

Second—*No house however expensive can be a success unless you, the owners, give the matter time and thought enough to know what you want it for. By success I mean all things necessary to your comfort and happiness in the life you are obliged to lead.*

Third—*you must employ someone who is broad enough to understand and sympathize with you and your needs and yet has the ability to put them into shape from the artist's point of view.*

■ That Park Place had been drawing considerable attention for several years is documented by two major articles devoted to the development and written in 1907. The first, published in the *Pasadena Daily News* on March 16, 1907, was entitled "Little Switzerland, Pasadena's Boast for Homes," and was responsible for the continuing reference to Park Place as "Little Switzerland." The lengthy article spoke of the "many artistic adaptations of this quaint foreign architecture to be found among residences of Crown City" and acknowledged the importance of the surrounding neighborhood landscape as an important "feature." While "Little Switzerland" is not an appropriate descriptive term, it did represent the perception of large numbers of people who made the effort to travel to and picnic around the area. Eventually the rough trails

This latter is hearsay so far as schools are concerned, but is history so far as art makes itself. Furthermore if one tries to do these things one will have accomplished something of permanent value in the world for others as well as oneself. If after trying one succeeds in all these three things one will have a lasting pleasure.

The style of a house should be as far as possible determined by four conditions:

First—climate.

Second—Environment.

Third—Kinds of material available.

Fourth—Habits and tastes—i.e. life of the owner.

The intelligence of the owner as well as the ability of the architect and skill of the contractor limit the perfection of the result.

As to environment—in such a place as Pasadena with people in easy circumstances and willing enough, it is plain to see how the California architect of "bungalows" must be what he is—for better or worse—a man dependent upon his own power of expression rather than that of rigid custom.[11]

11. Charles Sumner Greene, "Bungalows," *The Western Architect,* July 1908.

Despite the other styles of architecture that were a part of the early development of Park Place and the changes brought about by the more recent contemporary development within its initial tract, the gradual restoration of the Greene and Greene houses preserves for us the spirit and charm of a place and time as well as a sense of history. Although Park Place was developed during the years that brought forth the Greenes' personal language of building, these designs benefited equally from the creative explorations taking place in the other works of the firm during this same period that, each in its own way, contributed to the emergence of the distinct Greene and Greene style.

Charles and Henry Greene developed a distinct architectural vocabulary through which they were able to express their beliefs in the fundamental requirements of design. There had to be a valid reason for everything they did. By applying logical principles to their designs and combining their individual talents as artists, engineers, and craftsmen, they were able to bring to their work a sense of genuine purpose that today we identify as their particular style.

■ That the young architects believed deeply in this concept is borne out in a statement Charles wrote in a letter to Charles M. Pratt in defense of certain costs: "The work itself took months to execute and [the] best years of my life went to develop this style."

■ The most significant analysis of the misuse of the word *style* and the many variations on its meaning was that of Eugene Emanuel Viollet Le-Duc (1814-79), who discussed the subject in his independent lecture series in 1864 in Paris, and published as *Entretiens Sur L'Architecture:*

In the present day we are no longer familiar with those simple and true ideas which lead artists to invest their conceptions with style; I think it necessary therefore to define the constituent elements of style. . . . Let us therefore take one of the primitive arts . . . the art of the coppersmith, for example. . . . We take the art at the time when he discovered that by beating a sheet of copper in a particular way he could so model it as to give it the form of a vessel. . . . He leaves a flat circular bottom to his vessel, so that it may stand firm when full. To hinder the liquid from spilling when the vessel is shaken, he contracts its upper orifice, and then widens it out suddenly at the edge, to facilitate pouring of the liquid. There must be a means of holding the vessel; the workman therefore attaches handles with rivets. But as the vessel must be inverted when empty, and has to be drained dry, he makes the handles so that they shall not stand above the level of the top of the vessel. Thus fashioned by methods suggested in fabrication, this vessel has style; first because it exactly indicates its purpose; second, because it is fashioned in accordance with the material employed and the means of fabrication suited to the material; third, because the form obtained is suitable to the material of which this utensil is made and the use for which it is intended. This vessel has style, because human reason indicated exactly the form suitable to it. . . .

This history is typical of that of style in all the arts. Arts which cease to express the want they are intended to satisfy, the nature of the materials employed, and the method of fashioning it, cease to have style.[1]

Throughout the Arts and Crafts movement theorists and practitioners alike have spoken out clearly on the subject. A. W. N. Pugin wrote:

The two great rules are: First that there should be no features about a building which are not necessary for convenience, construction and propriety; secondly, that all ornament should consist of enrichment of the essential construction.[2]

These concepts are much the same as those found in various writings of the Greenes throughout their career, many having developed during their days at the Manual Training School. Henry van de Velde could have been talking of the Greenes' work in his statement "Style results from the general connections arising between all the manifestations of creative thought in a given period."[3]

■ Thus, when understood properly, the particular architectural language the Greenes chose to express their regional designs should indeed be acknowledged as their own and unmistakable style. However, without an understanding of the principles upon which that style was based and the talents required to bring it forth, those who attempted to imitate their style often contributed to the diminishing favor of their work during the years immediately following the most sophisticated designs of their career.

■ The evolution of the elements that constitute what we now identify as the Greene and Greene style occurred in the houses constructed between 1902 and 1904. The ideas that they felt made sense in the Southern California landscape progressed even more rapidly. The development of plan forms, structural systems, detailing, interiors, lighting, furnishings, and landscaping not only had individual integrity but at the same time became part of one total and complete thought. In house after house, these new elements of their style began to appear.

■ Charles and Henry Greene frequently attributed the turning point in their career to the Arturo Bandini house. This may have been true of their floor-plan concepts and the relationships between indoor and outdoor space. But, perhaps unconsciously, the seeds of their style had already been sown with the shaping

1. Viollet Le-Duc, lecture notes published as *Entretiens Sur L'Architecture*, Paris, 1864.

2. A. W. Pugin quotation from lecture notes of architect and educator Arthur B. Gallion, dean, School of Architecture, University of Southern California, 1948-60.

3. Ibid.

The courtyard planning concept used in the Arturo Bandini house introduced a new era in the Greene and Greene organization of spaces.

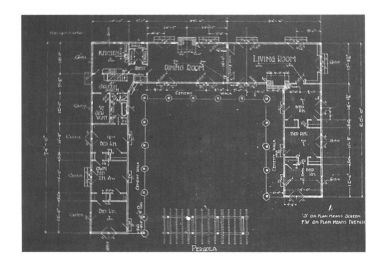

of the timber outriggers and the furniture designs for the White sisters' house and in the open flow of interior spaces and wooden interior details of the Darling house, with designs that had their origins on the drawing boards in late 1902. Earlier the James Culbertson house and Charles's own home had opened the door, but in all of these designs the floor plans were essentially tight, with groupings of rooms around inner hallway spines. What the Bandini commission introduced was an open plan, free of constraints, embracing and defining exterior spaces and allowing for the sunlight and vistas to be included in the planning process.

■ The firm had now been in business for nine years. With a considerable amount of work on the drawing boards, their second decade of work opened with a significant change in operations, which was officially announced in the newspapers in January 1903:

Messrs Greene and Greene, Architects, announce that on and after February 1, 1903, their office will be in the Grant building, N.W. corner Fourth and Broadway, Los Angeles, rooms 722 and 723. The Pasadena office will be discontinued. Mr. Charles Greene will be found at his studio, Arroyo View Drive, Pasadena, Monday, Wednesday and Friday afternoons.

Thus, Charles, having just completed his own house, with special attention given to his two-story studio with separate entrance, was able to maintain his artist-patron relationships with clients at his new residence on the bluffs of Reservoir Hill. It was here that Arturo Bandini presented the firm with the commission that freed the Greenes from the tight formality of traditional plan forms.

Don Arturo Bandini, the son of one of the old Spanish dons, was from a family whose roots lay in the life, government, and environment of early California. He and his wife, Helen Elliot, daughter of one of the original founders of Pasadena, respected the natural character of the early Spanish way of life and the old Spanish haciendas scattered about the southland. They asked for a simple bungalow with the charm of the early adobe structures, taking its form from the central courtyard plan and constructed of the most modest of materials. They wanted their house, which was to be named El Hogar (The Hearth), to express an unhurried and unpretentious life yet evoke a cultured background. This concept appealed to the Greenes as evidenced by Charles's letter to Mrs. James A. Garfield in June of 1903: "We are just beginning a house on the old mission plan that is to have a court about 60-feet square. It is all of wood and very simple—not in the so-called mission style at all."[4]

■ The plan deleted internal hallways and was composed of a series of spaces one room deep, arranged around three sides of a spacious central court. Each of the rooms opened directly to the covered veranda, which, along with a flower-covered pergola, defined the court with its flower beds, foot paths, fountain, and a hammock

4. Letter from Charles Greene to Mrs. James A. Garfield, Greene and Greene Library, The Gamble House, USC.

61

5. Kenneth Glendower Darling, "Our New Home," *My Early Life in California and My First American and European Tours* (1890–08), Honnold Library, Claremont Colleges.

6. "American Domestic Architecture, House at Pasadena," California, *Academy Architecture, 1903— America*. The Darling house was built in Claremont, several miles east of Pasadena.

The simple wooden wall sconces designed for the Mary Darling house, 1903, was the Greenes' introduction to lighting design.

Above right, Mary Reeve Darling house, 1903.

suspended between trees. Cool breezes flowed across the courtyard and through every room, each capturing views of the surrounding countryside and at the same time opening to the verandah and the sounds of water. There was an easy embrace of indoor and outdoor spaces, and the garden became an integral part of everyday activities. Intimate sheltered interiors provided an escape from the midday sun and the dry air. Ample doors and windows allowed for cross circulation in all rooms, which were opened each afternoon to catch the evening breezes.

■ Here indeed was a planning concept responding to the healthy criteria of light and air circulation so frequently prescribed by Dr. Greene. In this simple courtyard plan, linking interior and exterior spaces in the most subtle of ways, were the principles so fundamental that they would appear in one form or another in both large and small designs throughout the Greenes' career.

■ The Bandini house was constructed primarily of redwood, rough and lightly stained on the exterior, and smooth with a light oil finish on the interior. The walls were board-and-batten natural-wood paneling. The firm's continued exploration of furniture provided rustic designs for benches and bookshelves. Along the verandas, straightforward wood columns were set on a stone at the base, unusual for hacienda construction but inspired by the Greenes' interest in Japanese vernacular designs.

Mary Reeve Darling House, 1903

In dramatic contrast to the openness of the Bandini house, the plan for the Mary Darling house in Claremont, California, is compact, focused around a central stairwell that developed a strong bilateral symmetry for the second-floor sleeping quarters. An unusual element of this design was the turning of the roof ridge to the short dimension of the plan, making it possible for natural light to enter each of the four bedrooms from two orientations and, due to the height of the ridge, provide ample sunshine in the second-floor balcony toggle above the entry. Also unusual was the concern given to developing living, entry, and study spaces to allow for either an easy flow from one to the other or for privacy and independence in each. This option was offered by great sliding doors, which also brought a feeling of vastness to an otherwise modest house.

■ The interiors, however, were similar to the Bandini house in their rustic craftsman character. This quality is best described in Kenneth Glendower Darling's memoirs, entitled *Our New Home:*

On the northern outskirts of the town, ensconced in an entire block of orange, lemon and grapefruit trees, laborious planning, consultations with architects, and like activities, to which Mother had dedicated many a weary month. Designed by an eminent California Domestic architect, in a modified Swiss-chalet style, it was so distinctive in certain of its external features and interior appointments and furnishing that it was later accorded space, together with several illustrations in the London Architects Journal.[5]

Darling was referring to the English publication *Academy Architecture, 1903, America,*[6] in which Charles's watercolors and pen-and-ink sketches illustrated the landscape as well as the complete furnishing of the interiors. This, the first publication of the Greenes' work overseas, demonstrated clearly through the illustrations the close attention the Greenes were giving to Gustav Stickley's magazine, *The Craftsman.* Their designs for furniture and the selection of accessories here related closely to Stickley's designs and the work of other Arts and Crafts artisans featured in the magazine.

F. F. Rowland, M.D., House, 1903

Other work on the drawing boards in 1903 included ideas previously explored, but the Greenes were also experimenting with variations on the newly emerging style expressed in the design for Dr. Francis F. Rowland. They retained the short-ridge-gable principle from the Darling house but reversed the facade and entry, giving the street-facing elevation a modest and gracious low profile. Openings were designed in the front and rear roofs, allowing light into the interiors. Here, as in the Swan and later the Longley houses, the Greenes relied heavily on the power of the long sloping rooflines to give the design a quiet dignity despite the large scale of the two-story structure.

Samuel P. Sanborn House, 1903

The Sanborn house was built at the same time as the Rowland house, but, while exhibiting aspects of the articulated structural detail evolving in the Greenes' work, it still revealed their fascination with geometric forms and angles as the dominant design factor. Dramatic timbers and long projecting rafters and roof outriggers provided a flamboyant flair to the junctures between the bold octagonal forms and the rectilinear composition. The playful three-dimensional character of the two flying roofs embracing the drama of the octagonal tower belie the tight plan and long hallways within. What was attempted with the winged floor plan of the Sanborn house on a rectilinear lot along Colorado Boulevard would turn out to be very different when developed for Edgar W. Camp on the open slopes of the foothills of Sierra Madre.

Above, in the F. F. Rowland house, 1903, the roof ridge was turned the short direction of the plan, inviting morning and afternoon light into the upper bedrooms and putting balconies on the north and south to capture the breezes. This feature presented a modest scale to the street face of the house.

Below, the second house built for Samuel P. Sanborn, 1903, explored an angular plan and geometric room forms.

With the addition of a second floor to the Camp house, the linearity of the board-and-batten lower wall treatments was carried uninterrupted in full lengths up the open, naturally lighted stairwell.

Edgar W. Camp house, 1904. Initially a very simple single-story winged design, its most notable feature was the sculptural massing of boulders from the Sierra Madre foothills for the rugged chimneys, which were treated just as boldly on the rustic interiors.

Edgar W. Camp House, 1904

Closely allied to the Bandini design by the rough board-and-batten detailing of the exteriors and interiors, the Camp house spread the wings of the plan open wide, welcoming the paths of the sun and courting the breezes from the canyons above. The more modest central courtyard, with its view over the San Gabriel Valley, was here only a small terrace opening directly to Camp's vast property, which featured a wide variety of natural plant materials, trees, and citrus groves.

■ On the interiors, the Greenes took their ideas for furniture another step forward, designing not only benches and shelving but also tables, picture frames, and patterns of applique for the Camps' daughters and nieces to sew into the window curtains. These patterns consisted of dancing squares reminiscent of the designs of the European practitioners of the Arts and Crafts movement, Voysey, Hoffman, and Mackintosh.

■ But it was the powerful use of native materials and the sculptural mountains of boulders and cobblestones in the exterior chimney and interior fireplaces that caught one's breath. In these masonry achievements was another new element of the Greenes' emerging style.

Above, the Camp living room features the Greenes' continued effort with furniture, shelving, and curtain designs.

Left, the upper-hall closet door latch demonstrated a refined composition made up of common hardware parts and fine craftsmanship.

Mrs. Lucretia R. Garfield house, 1904.

Mrs. Lucretia R. Garfield House, 1904

At this point in the evolution of the Greenes' designs, the articulation of the wooden timber construction began to take on a presence of its own and became a signature of their more mature work. The scale and proportion of the timber became an imperative in the sculpting of its joinery as well as space, and was sized not just by structural necessity but, more importantly, by their visual engineering; the timbers looked as though they were structurally sound, and their sizes were carefully selected according to the hierarchy of their interrelating elements. This overengineering of most of the beams, timbers, outriggers, and rafters of most Greene and Greene designs was thus a function more of the perception of support than of actual engineering standards at the time.

■ As one design after another progressed through the office, there began to be more and more attention given to the shaping of the ends of the timbers—-softening their visual scale, tapering them to lighten the visual weight of projecting cantilever beams, sculpting the ends as a clear expression of terminus—and the rounding of all edges, a detail as important to the curtailment of splintering as to aesthetics.

■ In time, however, there emerged quite naturally a third criteria for the extraordinary attention given the post-and-beam vocabulary—that of the impact of the sun, best expressed in an exchange during the design of the Pasadena house for Mrs. James A. Garfield. Writing from her home in West Mentor, Ohio, in early June 1904, she asked, "Will it interfere with the effect you are striving for to let the girders in the gables of the roof extend only to the edge, instead of reaching beyond? I prefer that treatment."

■ Charles Greene's terse response left little room for discussion. "The reason why the beams project from the gables is because they cast such beautiful shadows on the sides of the house in this bright atmosphere." The projections remained.

■ Mrs. Garfield, widow of the assassinated president, was related to the Greenes through General Nathaniel Greene, and had become friendly with Charles and Alice Greene during her periodic visits with friends in Pasadena and, as their guest, had taken tea with them on the brick terrace under the oak tree overlooking the entire Arroyo Seco and the San Gabriel Mountains. Her site in South Pasadena would command just such a view over the entire San Gabriel Valley. When she decided to build her own house, she chose the Greenes as her architects over her son, Abram, a

distinguished Cleveland architect in his own right.[7] His presence, however, was sometimes helpful and frequently felt in some of her letters. The correspondence leading to the designs for the house reflect a cordial and willing rapport between architect and client. The letters, which began early in 1903, provide a clear perspective of this delicate relationship. They demonstrate that the Greenes refused to compromise their artistic convictions but worked instead to fuse their client's point of view with that of their own. Mrs. Garfield had been pleased with the original design, which proved to be too costly; thus, with the aid of her son, she became intimately involved in the project through the mail. She questioned roof forms, made suggestions for window alignments, for various adjustments and for changes of materials that would help to bring costs in line.

■ Another exchange in the correspondence is indicative of the strong will of the brothers. In early June she had written, "What do you think of omitting the skylight? Cannot ventilation be arranged without the light and still look well?"

■ Charles responded by return mail, "Retain skylight. Reason will follow."[8] In the final construction of the house the skylight remained, though the reason never appeared in subsequent correspondence.

■ The Garfield house, unlike several preceding commissions in the office, retained a tight two-story rectangular plan with a gabled roof, a concept that the Greenes continued to use when the site or the client's needs dictated such compactness. It was their various uses of this form that prompted many a writer and member of the public to liken the Greenes' work to the Swiss chalet, a comparison not totally warranted.

7. Further information on architect Abram Garfield may be found in *Encyclopedia of American Biography*, New Series, vol. A-37 (New York & West Palm Beach: The American Historical Society, 1934-70).

8. Letters between Mrs. James A. Garfield and Charles Greene, Greene and Greene Library, The Gamble House, USC.

Charlotte A. Whitridge House, 1904

Although the firm felt the office location in Los Angeles to be a wise choice, Henry Greene and his family, including his mother-in-law, Charlotte Whitridge, were lured back to Pasadena by the poppy fields of the Pasadena foothills as well as social interests in the area. Because of Henry's wife's lifelong problems with deafness and, as a consequence, her strong bonds with her mother, he designed a special plan with one central entry but two independent living quarters within the two-story structure.[9] A strong central hallway bisected the plan, which provided dual facilities throughout, though giving over a smaller amount of space for Henry's young family. In time, portions of the second-floor attic were developed to provide additional bedrooms as more children came along.

■ The Charlotte Whitridge house was incorrectly identified as the Henry M. Greene house in prior publications. Its design clearly demonstrated Henry's comfort and confidence in the firm's explorations and experiments at the time. The plan was a frank response to the two-family needs and was stepped to provide each with views over the valley. It is in the composition of the exterior that Henry's disciplined touch provided a powerful and straightforward statement. There was no hint of frivolity to be found in the entire composition. The chimneys were pure vertical stacks, and the horizontal siding accentuated the crisp forms of the roof. The volumetric composition of the elements revealed the absolute control of the architect. Exterior lines of the elevations

moved in and out with purpose and integrity, and there was a distinct unity about the overall composition. Roof planes were strong, an expression of overlapping and interrelating low gables woven together with a quiet grace reminiscent of the nearby hills. Though compact in plan, Henry's design tucked, extended, and adjusted to its internal needs while constantly maintaining the richly varied yet simple thrust of its external statement.

■ Through the variety of commissions throughout 1902 and 1903, the Greenes explored different elements that contributed to their evolution as craftsmen-architects and that would appear in one structure or another. But as early as 1904, in two Long Beach commissions, they brought together the full range of their new architectural vocabulary for the first time. With these two designs—one a tight central plan and the other a winged open plan—the brothers found clients who offered them the opportunities they had been seeking. Here were strong ladies, Jennie A. Reeve and Adelaide Tichenor, who, as clients, both caused the Greenes to stretch their talents to the fullest and yet embraced and encouraged their experiments in structure, planning, interiors, furnishings, and the decorative arts. The Greenes' work in Long Beach not only advanced the development of the firm's style but also made clear how important it was to find the artisans with the gifts to meet the exacting standards Charles and Henry had set for themselves.

9. Information on the Whitridge/Greene household is derived from the author's personal interviews with the children of Henry Greene: Isabelle Greene McElwain, Henry Dart Greene, William Sumner Greene, and Elbert Greene, 1955-97.

The Charlotte A. Whitridge house, 1904, frequently known as the Henry M. Greene house, was designed by Henry to house both his own family and his mother-in-law, Mrs. Whitridge.

The Jennie A. Reeve house, Long Beach, California, 1904, brought together for the first time in a single design the essential elements that would define the Greene and Greene style.

Joinery detail from the bedroom bureau designed for the Jennie Reeve house.

The Jennie A. Reeve House, 1904

Jennie Reeve, the mother of Mary Reeve Darling, whose house just east of Pasadena was nearing completion, commissioned the Greenes to design her house on a tight corner site in Long Beach and introduced them to Adelaide Tichenor. The Reeve design brought together for the first time most of the architectural elements that were becoming readily identified with the Greene and Greene style. This simple two-story shingle-clad house is the pivotal structure acknowledging the brothers' complete embrace of the principles of the Arts and Crafts movement. Here were the articulated timber structure; multiple-gabled overhanging roofs with projecting outriggers now more softly shaped on the ends; open sleeping porches; vertical slit windows for closet ventilation; horizontal bands of casement windows; sensitive combination of cobblestone with brick masonry; leaded glass for door and lantern designs; the coordination of landscape, walks, fencing, and garden gates; and a full development of interior furniture and lighting.

■ Though open patio ideas were much on the Greenes' minds, they responded to the Reeve corner ocean-front site and the chilly, sometimes foggy, environment with a compact plan that paid special attention to the seaside climate. Three massive fireplaces formed the axial core of the plan, and the living room and a flexible bedroom on the ground floor were oriented to the ocean view and featured great bands of glass window-walls and window seats to catch the rays of sunshine and brighten the detail of the interior wood paneling. In contrast, the corner inglenook of the living room provided a cavelike quality and was an invitation into a smaller protected space with corner seating built into a hearth.

■ Imaginative attention was paid to every aspect of the house. On the interior the Greenes' imprint was easily recognized in the carefully detailed paneling and built-in cabinet work, where the expressed pegs were softly rounded and the finish of the wood had a waxed patina. Leaded-glass designs coordinated the panes of doors and windows with the china cabinets and interior storage units. Here evident were craftsmanship and design quality anticipating the masterworks of 1907-09.

■ Lighting received more attention than in any previous design. Leaded opalescent-glass lanterns covered with copper hoods were suspended from the low ceilings by brass chains. Wall sconces became quite playful, with major areas combining gas lighting with electric light lanterns. An elaborate wooden wall bracket held two lanterns to each side and the gas light between, its flame protected by a special hood suspended from the ceiling. The leaded lanterns were of similar design, whether for interior or exterior use.

■ Here also was an opportunity to design more furniture. Although these pieces were still indebted to the works of Gustav Stickley, the wood was ash, and, as in the White sisters' furniture, the pegs were expressed off the surface of the wood and, with the mortise-and-tenon detail, constituted an honest expression of function as the dominant decorative element.

Carved-wood screen separating the entry hall from the stairwell of the Reeve house.

The first Greene and Greene design for a suspended interior lantern was carried out in metal and art glass for the Jennie Reeve house.

The Main Pavilion in the Imperial Japanese Garden at the
Louisiana Purchase International Exposition in Saint Louis, 1904,
was the direct inspiration for the elegant and simple roof forms
of the Tichenor house. Charles designed the Tichenor roofs
immediately following his and Mrs. Tichenor's visit to the fair.

Adelaide Tichenor House, 1904

Charles Greene original watercolor rendering of the Adelaide Tichenor house, Long Beach, 1904.

Unlike the limited site and restricted funding for the Jennie Reeve house, her friend Adelaide Tichenor's substantial budget afforded the Greenes opportunities for even further advancement in the structure of her house, and the design of superb gardens, outdoor living areas, interiors, furniture, and accessories.

■ Adelaide Tichenor was born in Ravenna, Ohio, was educated at Oberlin College, studied art in Boston, and taught there and later in Redlands, California. In 1885 she married Lester Schuyler Tichenor and was active in the civic life of San Bernardino until her husband's death in 1892. She then moved to Long Beach, where she was a founder of the Ebell Club, participated in the establishment of the public library, and was appointed to the commission to develop the vast shipyards and port facilities. Her long involvement in social, business, and cultural affairs gained her the reputation as the "Mother of Long Beach." In 1902 she and her friend Jennie Reeve embarked on a two-year world tour, during which she became fascinated by the arts of China and Japan.

■ By the time of the Reeve house, the Greene and Greene practice had grown steadily. The Long Beach houses were a substantial distance from the Greenes' main office in downtown Los Angeles and were just two of the more than two dozen jobs in various stages of production at the time. Client demands were becoming more than they could handle together, making it necessary for them to divide the work.

■ Adelaide Tichenor's house fell to Charles Greene. Their mutual interests in the arts of China and Japan immediately drew Adelaide and Charles together, and her genuine respect for his talents further enabled Charles to continue exploring his ideas with an unprecedented freedom. As the initial concepts of her house were developing, Adelaide traveled to Saint Louis to attend the Louisiana Purchase International Exposition. In a letter dated June 10, 1904, and addressed to Mr. C. S. Greene, she wrote:

We arrived here only yesterday, but the more I see of it, the more I feel that I do not want to go on with my home until you see this. . . . I really think you will never regret it if you arrange your affairs to come at once. . . . Please consider this: as I have said before, I am anxious to have you use the knowledge you may gain here on my own house. . . . There are things I would like to buy too, but I dare not until I know what you are going to do.[10]

10. Letter of 10 June 1904, courtesy Robert Judson Clark, from the Tichenor correspondence file, Documents Collection, College of Environmental Design, University of California, Berkeley.

11. Clay Lancaster, *The American Bungalow, 1880–1930* (New York: Abbeyville Press, 1985).

12. Clay Lancaster, "Metaphysical Beliefs and Architectural Principles, A Study in Contrasts Between Those of the West and Far East," *The Journal of Aesthetics and Art Criticism*, vol. xiv, no. 3 (March 1956).

It was virtually a command, and considering the fact that the firm had on exhibition three of their projects at the fair, it is easy to understand Charles's immediate decision to make the trip.

■ Just how far the Tichenor design had progressed before this trip is unclear. The half-timber construction, the faint Tudor cast of the ground floor with its infill of clinker bricks, seem to be a carryover from Charles's 1901 visit to England. A study of the final drawings, however, shows that his visit to the Imperial Japanese Garden at the fair had a significant impact on the design. As Clay Lancaster observed in his book on the American bungalow:

That the Greene brothers got details for their work from authentic Japanese sources is evident from the forms themselves. . . . The most distinct Japanese motif [in the Tichenor house] was not the rear courtyard, even with its arched bridge, but the main mass of the house. Its bank fenestration, horizontal balconies, corner accents . . . and tile irimoyai roof, were it not for the chimney, present a convincing Japanese impression.[11]

In an earlier writing, Lancaster summed up the importance of the work of the Greene brothers with this statement:

Nowhere in Western building have the architects identified themselves with their work so completely as have Greene and Greene, in the selection of every tile and brick and pane of glass, and in the shaping of every timber that went into their houses. Although never in Japan themselves, their high standards for quality were the nearest to those of the Far East of all the American builders whose work I have examined, style similarities resulting as a natural consequence.[12]

Indeed, a comparison of features in the Imperial Japanese Garden with the final design of the Tichenor house shows many similarities. The principal roof form was remarkably like that of the Main Pavilion. The second-floor galleries, which wrap around the front and west elevations, and the character of the reflecting pond evoke imagery from the Kinkaku, or Golden Pavilion. In addition Charles and Adelaide spent considerable time selecting various items to furnish the house, including several large Grueby pottery urns for the living room.

■ Charles's design responded to the 60-by-260-foot corner lot that stretched between Ocean Boulevard and the bluffs overlooking the sandy beach. A short cul-de-sac street ran along one side of the property. The front of the house faced the bluff. The rear garden turned its back on the boulevard. The primary living space stretched laterally on both levels, across the narrow portion of the site facing the bluffs. The graceful roof line, highly influenced by the Japanese Pavilion at the fair, became the single most significant element of the overall design.

■ With the Tichenor house being located far from the relatively arid climate of Pasadena and the San Gabriel Valley, the garden courtyard was adapted to the cool temperatures and breezes of the beach environment. The narrow court was defined by two single-story wings of the house, and while accessible for outdoor use, it served more as a visual transition from interior spaces to the reflecting pond. Beyond and on the visual axis of the living-room view was a teahouse constructed of clinker-brick columns, with its back wall to the noisy street and sheltered by a timber-and-tile roof similar to that on the house. This small structure provided the garden with a strong visual and physical conclusion.

The ocean-facing facade of the Tichenor
house, nearing completion, was
dramatically disfigured by the client's
demand that the upper balcony be
enclosed, an act that destroyed the
integrity of the roof design as well as
Charles Greene's creative spirit.

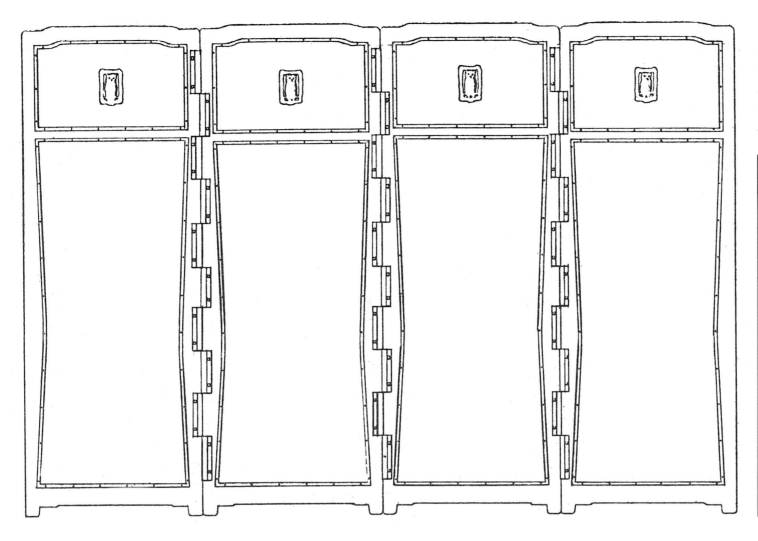

With the encouragement of Mrs. Tichenor, Charles stretched his repertoire in lighting design, advancing the Greene and Greene decorative arts seemingly overnight.

The four-part folding screen for Mrs. Tichenor, constructed of ash, drew its character from the leather hinge detail and responded to the client's fascination with the owl. This detail was carried out on several of the furniture designs.

13. Tichenor correspondence of 27 September 1905, Documents Collection, College of Environmental Design, University of California, Berkeley. Additional information may be found in chapter 12 in the book *Toward a Simpler Way of Life: The Arts and Crafts Architects of California*, ed. Robert Winter (Berkeley, Los Angeles, London: Norfleet Press Book, University of California Press, 1997).

■ Because of the large number of commissions in the Greene office, the relatively long distance to the Tichenor site, several major design changes during construction, and Adelaide's strong need for more personal attention, there continued a succession of letters, first to Charles and then to Henry and Charles, delineating her displeasure with delays, costs and various facets of the design. In one she wrote:

Can you leave your Pasadena customers long enough so that I may hope to have my house during my lifetime? If you wish me to make a will who is to have the house if it is ever finished. . . . These little book shelves you have made will hold about 1/5 of my books. Do you wish me to put the others in the fire? I suppose I am to burn all my pictures too. I see no place to hang any except in the bedroom, and I do not believe that bedrooms should have them.[13]

In the most damaging disagreement, Adelaide insisted on the enclosure of the second-floor roof terrace overlooking the ocean, an argument that would have broken Charles's spirit completely had it not been for their mutual fascination with the designs for the furniture, lighting, and accessories. As it was, the enclosure of the roof terrace so destroyed the integrity of the roof form, which Charles had adapted so lovingly from the Japanese Main

Pavilion, that he lost all passion for the project upon its final completion. On the contrary and in spite of all her frustrations during the construction of the house, Mrs. Tichenor was completely enchanted with her home throughout her life, hardly changing the arrangement of the furnishings.

■ The one area where architect and client were in complete agreement was in the development of the furnishings. Adelaide provided Charles with the broadest opportunity he had had to stretch his skills in the areas of interior design, furniture, lighting, and accessories. Where his prior furniture had drawn inspiration from the linear designs of Gustav Stickley, the Tichenor creations introduced soft sculptural nuances drawn from the client and architect's interests in the arts of the Orient.

■ The single most significant piece of furniture demonstrating a stylistic transition from the severe linearity of Stickley's influence to the soft sculptural character of their own furniture style was the upright writing desk for the bedroom, which makes careful use of the "lift" in the side panels, the drawer handles, and in the cleats of

Charles's design for the upright secretary for Mrs. Tichenor represents the pivotal turning point in the Greenes' furniture designs. Thereafter, the Greenes departed further and further from the linearity of their earlier works and followed a path of refinement of materials, artfully crafted in soft subtle sculptural forms.

A straight-back chair designed for Mrs. Tichenor was not made to their design detail, substantially weakening the structure of the back of the chair. This alerted the Greenes to the need to seek more-skilled craftsmen for future work.

the door details. In the dining table and other pieces, similar forms are combined with joinery of mortise-and-tenon construction that employ expressed pegging. Incised slits in the backs of the dining chairs hinted at elements of the Greenes' work that would become highly refined during the following two years. Charles's drawing for the desk chair shows a clear understanding of the construction needed for back and leg support. But in the workshop where the Tichenor furniture was made, the seat rails were incorrectly cut into the back leg, weakening the back of the chair and causing fractures that required later owners to make clumsy repairs using common metal angles. What now became perfectly clear was that, although Charles Greene had found his mid-career furniture design vocabulary, the firm had yet to find the craftsmen who could express the designs to meet the increasing demands of the brothers. However, this dilemma would soon be resolved back in Pasadena by the association of the Greenes with wood and glass artisans during work on the Henry M. Robinson house.

■ The original design for the Tichenor house was vitally important to the development of the Greenes' work. The concept of unifying site, gardens, structure, interiors, lighting, and furnishings was here accomplished on a scale they had never before had the liberty to

explore. Though there were delays, conflicts, and frustrations in both design and construction, the final product is nonetheless one of the most important residential designs of the Greenes' career and of the international Arts and Crafts movement.

■ Because of the rapid development of Long Beach properties near the ocean, the Reeve house was moved twice, making more difficult the tasks of those documenting its history. Both moves were made by Dr. V. Ray Townsend, son of one of the original Indiana Colony founders of Pasadena, who had been living in Long Beach since 1907. In 1916 he purchased the Reeve house, which was then up on blocks ready to be moved. He relocated it seven blocks inland and rented it out between 1919 and 1927, during which time he and his family occupied the Darling house in Claremont. In 1927 he again moved the house, this time for his own use, and sought out Henry Greene to design the additions he desired as well as the landscaping, fencing, and furniture to coordinate with the original pieces.

Henry M. Robinson House, 1905

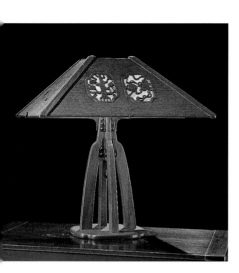

Library writing-desk lamp,
Henry M. Robinson house, 1905.

Previous page, Henry M. Robinson
house, 1905.

14. Rockwell Hereford, *A Whole Man and a Half Century* (Pacific Grove, California: The Boxwood Press, 1985).

The Henry M. Robinson house was another milestone. Its scale, external forms and use of materials set it apart from prior Greene and Greene work. Dramatic changes in the Greenes' philosophy, expression, and craft can be traced throughout the design, construction, and furnishings of this house. Here they polished their concepts, assembled excellent artisan-craftsmen to work on furniture and leaded glass, and developed the confidence to undertake their most sophisticated work.

■ Henry M. Robinson, like Adelaide Tichenor, was born in Ravenna, Ohio, in the same year as Charles. As an adult he practiced law in Youngstown, Ohio, where he represented major coal and steel corporations before moving to New York to become involved in organizing the United States Steel Corporation. There he remained until his retirement at the age of forty and his move to Pasadena in 1906, where, over the years, he was associated with such figures as the astronomer George Ellery Hale, Henry E. Huntington, the Albert Einsteins, Herbert Hoover, George Patton, Robert L. Milliken and Edwin Hubble. He became very active in community affairs, engineered the conversion of Throop Polytechnic Institute into the California Institute of Technology, was largely responsible for establishing the Huntington Library and Art Gallery in San Marino, and became a member of the advisory council of the Federal Reserve Board. He was a close personal friend of four presidents, served in four administrations on various commissions here and abroad, and was offered cabinet positions as secretary of the interior and secretary of the treasury by Presidents Wilson, Harding and Hoover. His wife, the former Laurabelle Arms, was the daughter of Charles D. Arms, whose estate comprised vast holdings in mining throughout the country. With Henry Robinson's many interests keeping them continually on the move, Laurabelle yearned for a permanent home. In this she was encouraged by her brother-in-law, Tod Ford Sr., former president of Youngstown Iron and Steel Company, who had been her husband's mentor during the early days of his law practice. At his urging, the Robinsons bought several acres on the bluffs of the Arroyo Seco just north of the Fords' new property on South Grand Avenue in Pasadena.[14]

■ Several months earlier Ford had engaged the Greenes to make some alterations to an 1895 house on his property, and although his own house was by another architect, he was to be responsible for some of the Greenes' most remarkable commissions, including the Henry M. Robinson house.

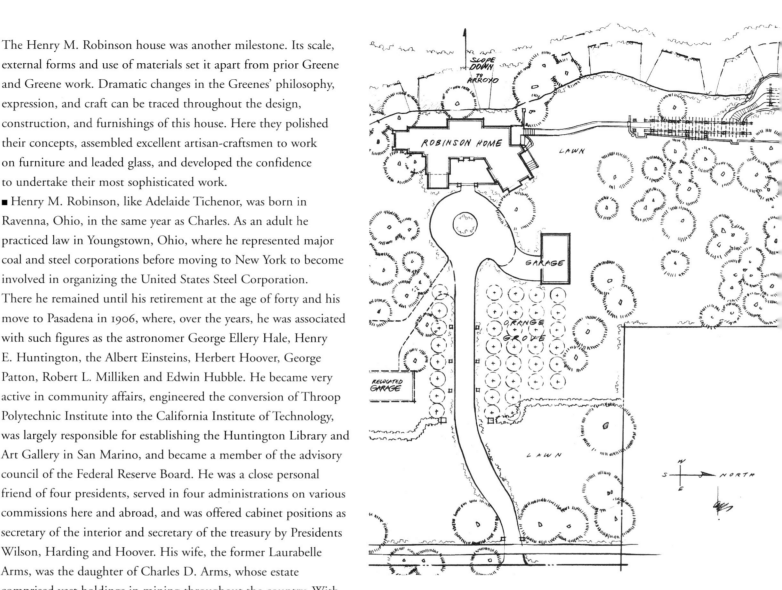

The Henry M. Robinson house, 1905, was sited on the bluffs of the Pasadena arroyo and represents the first of several large estates carried out by Greene and Greene.

The tapered buttress detail and the dash-coat exterior stucco finish of the Robinson house were the first of the Greenes' designs to reflect the inspiration Charles must have gained from the works of C. F. A. Voysey in and around London, likely experienced on the trip to England in 1902.

■ The Robinson design placed the house on the edge of the bluff with a commanding view of the arroyo and the mountain range beyond. The plan resembled the slightly winged composition of the Camp house with its small entry terrace, but there all similarity ended. The ground floor was of brick, and the half-timber frame of the second floor was clad in a stucco exterior with a rough dash-coat finish. The roof construction and the expressed timber structure of porches and pergola followed the Greenes' evolving wooden expressions.

■ It was the scale of the house that offered opportunities for the Greenes to explore ideas that had been simmering on their minds since Charles's trip to England in 1901. The use of the half-timber expression on the second level is an obvious connection to the work he had seen in and around London. But it is the use of the massive buttresses at the corners that dominates the design and suggests Charles's likely interest in the buttress designs of C. F. A. Voysey. This was one of the clearest and most direct connections between the English Arts and Crafts movement and the Greenes' work. These concepts were used again briefly in the designs for a reinforced concrete bridge and pylons the following year but seem to have been dropped from their vocabulary thereafter. Here, however, the buttresses are powerfully carried out and the massive forms and fluid qualities of the stucco materials gave the Robinson estate a distinct, soft sculptural quality and added a new spirit to the Greenes' work.

■ Important as was the exterior of the house, it was in the interiors, furniture, and lighting that revealed the speed with which the Greenes were refining their skills. They contrasted the interior materials of brick, paneling, and plaster with a symphony of wood detail and joinery. New authority is given to the volume of the entry-stairwell space, which is punctuated by the subtle feather patterns in the leading of the upper windows, the sophistication of the advanced design for wall sconces, and the drama of the polished-wood and stained-glass lantern suspended from the high ceiling.

■ But the greatest change was in the furniture. The earliest designs for the Robinson furniture recalled the Greenes' previous work carried out in cedar, with linear lines, expressed mortise and tenons, and projecting pegs. But the dramatic escalation in the quantity and quality of the furnishings in the Robinson house resulted from the Greenes' search for master craftsmen, leading them to Peter Hall, his brother John Hall, and Emil Lange. These

men's associations with the Greenes and their skills in the crafting of furniture and glass sparked an excitement that was exhibited with each new piece. In the den the material was ash, and in the table lamp and writing desk the lines were further softened. The living and dining rooms were dominated by the influence of four-hundred-year-old Chinese household furniture. The wood was now mahogany and the joinery and detail highly sophisticated. When the large movable chandelier for the dining room was completed, the design, detail, and craftsmanship had achieved the degree of excellence identified with the Greenes' masterworks. Without question it was the talents of these newcomers combined with those of the Greenes that made possible the refined work that today is the signature of the Greene and Greene style.

Entry hall of the
Henry M. Robinson house.

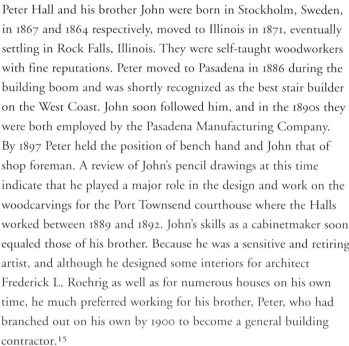

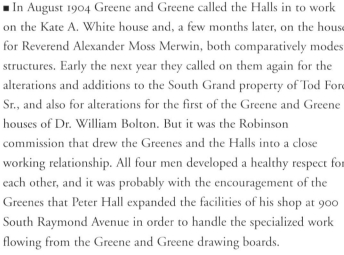

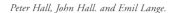

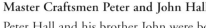

Peter Hall, John Hall. and Emil Lange.

Emil Lange and an associate in
the Lange art-glass studio.

Master Craftsmen Peter and John Hall

Peter Hall and his brother John were born in Stockholm, Sweden, in 1867 and 1864 respectively, moved to Illinois in 1871, eventually settling in Rock Falls, Illinois. They were self-taught woodworkers with fine reputations. Peter moved to Pasadena in 1886 during the building boom and was shortly recognized as the best stair builder on the West Coast. John soon followed him, and in the 1890s they were both employed by the Pasadena Manufacturing Company. By 1897 Peter held the position of bench hand and John that of shop foreman. A review of John's pencil drawings at this time indicate that he played a major role in the design and work on the woodcarvings for the Port Townsend courthouse where the Halls worked between 1889 and 1892. John's skills as a cabinetmaker soon equaled those of his brother. Because he was a sensitive and retiring artist, and although he designed some interiors for architect Frederick L. Roehrig as well as for numerous houses on his own time, he much preferred working for his brother, Peter, who had branched out on his own by 1900 to become a general building contractor.[15]

■ In August 1904 Greene and Greene called the Halls in to work on the Kate A. White house and, a few months later, on the house for Reverend Alexander Moss Merwin, both comparatively modest structures. Early the next year they called on them again for the alterations and additions to the South Grand property of Tod Ford Sr., and also for alterations for the first of the Greene and Greene houses of Dr. William Bolton. But it was the Robinson commission that drew the Greenes and the Halls into a close working relationship. All four men developed a healthy respect for each other, and it was probably with the encouragement of the Greenes that Peter Hall expanded the facilities of his shop at 900 South Raymond Avenue in order to handle the specialized work flowing from the Greene and Greene drawing boards.

■ The production of leaded-and-stained-glass designs was also an integral part of the Greenes' vocabulary. In their early works, they relied on the Los Angeles Art Glass Studios or the Judson Studios in nearby Garvanza, where there were many glass artisans who had formerly been employed in the Tiffany Studios in New York. But as Charles grew more and more concerned with subtle colorations and better ways to introduce texture and scale into the leading process, the Greenes began to look to the glass artisans themselves. In this search they made the acquaintance of Emil Lange, secretary and treasurer of the Sturdy-Lange Company, "Manufacturers of Art Glass and Decorators," situated at 1500 East Ninth Street in Los Angeles.

Emil Lange, Glass Artisan

Emil Lange, of German descent, came to Pasadena from Burlington, Iowa, where he had established his own glass business. There his geometric designs, complemented by the subtle shadings of his glass selection, were noticeably progressive in an era dominated by the Victorian aesthetic. He was doing well until domestic problems prompted his move to Los Angeles in 1904. After going into partnership with Harry Sturdy in California, Lange was reputed to have the best supply of Tiffany's iridescent art glass in the Los Angeles area. This may have caught the attention of the Greenes, for Charles had been enamored with Tiffany's glass when he was in New York in 1901 and was particularly interested in its iridescent qualities. Although it has been mistakenly claimed that Lange worked for a time in Tiffany's studios, he did not, and more recent research indicates that his experience came from his own activities in and around Burlington, Iowa.[16]

■ Because of the wide variation in composition, technique, and coloration of glass designs for the Robinson house, the exact date of Lange's first work for Greene and Greene is a matter of speculation. The linear geometric feather designs crafted with rigid brass cames in the clear glass windows of the library and upper hall contrast dramatically with the flowing composition, color, and soft leading in the entry glass. In the lanterns Charles incorporates soft, changing color tones using iridescent glass; and, finally, in the late design for the elaborate movable chandelier for the dining

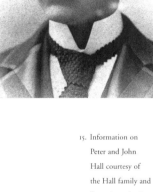

15. Information on Peter and John Hall courtesy of the Hall family and from the author's interviews with Leonard W. Collins, senior draftsman for Greene and Greene.

16. Information on Emil Lange courtesy of Lange's granddaughter, Joan Kaas, and from the author's interviews with glass artisan Claus Willenberg, who worked for a time in the Sturdy-Lange art-glass studios in Los Angeles.

Dining room in the Henry M.
Robinson house.

room, the lights of the lantern feature cherry vines weaving
through curved surfaces in a mosaic pattern calling for the most
expert crafting.

■ The chandeliers and major lighting fixtures for the Robinson
house marked a new era for the Greenes. Lighting design no longer
dealt with the mere housing of lightbulbs. Instead it became a
sculptured art form and took on a major role in the development
of the Greenes' interior spaces. So dramatic were some of these
lighting designs—such as the dining room chandelier in the
Robinson house, which could be moved up and down—that it
drew on the very best from artist and artisan. In the hands of
people less sensitive than Charles Greene and Emil Lange, such
a complex concoction of forms and elements could have been
disastrous. But in their hands it became a beautiful work of art.

■ Without question, the Robinson house was a testing ground for
a number of innovations relating to the scale of the project, the
study of exterior forms, the exploration of furniture aesthetics,
the use of citrus groves in landscaping, and the common effort
of artists and craftsmen behind the architectural legacy of Greene
and Greene.

■ By the beginning of 1906 there were more than fifty jobs going
through the office, some in the form of alterations or additions
but over 60 percent for new structures. The Greene and Greene
staff in the Grant Building in Los Angeles was increasing rapidly,
and this required Henry to devote more and more of his time to
management. With Charles's attention concentrated on such
time-consuming projects as the Tichenor and Robinson houses,
the careful balance of the brothers' roles was changing. Although
still actively involved in new design concepts, Henry had, of
necessity, to take on the responsibility for coordinating the
operations of the office.

■ In early 1906 Henry moved the firm from the smaller quarters in
the Grant Building to the recently completed Pacific Electric
Building, a few blocks away. This building was designed by
Thornton Fitzhugh for Henry E. Huntington as an office building
and terminal for his streetcars, which wove together the areas
around Los Angeles. The new location was more convenient for
both Henry and Charles, as they were commuting to and from
Pasadena almost every day. It also made their communication
much easier with Carl Leonardt, the contractor of the building,
with whom they were associated in the construction of the
Oaklawn Bridge later in the year.

South Pasadena Realty and Improvement Company
Gates, Bridge and Waiting Station, 1904-1906

Late in 1904 a small commission for the South Pasadena Realty and Improvement Company for portals and fencing at the entrance to the Oaklawn subdivision gave the Greenes an opportunity to try out their new ideas more playfully in nonresidential work. The sculpture of irregular boulders capped with the disciplined timber-detailed roof that sheltered the handcrafted wrought-iron gates provided a powerful but welcoming point of entry to the new subdivision. Charles's drawing for the portals appeared in the newspapers on New Year's Day 1905 and included the design for the stone pylon and wood fencing that was to define the entire tract development.

■ Now, less than a year later, came the commission for the design of the reinforced concrete bridge at the southern end of the Oaklawn tract, spanning two railways, a cycleway and a private road connecting Fair Oaks Avenue, just opposite the foot of Raymond Hill and the famous Raymond Hotel. Henry was thrilled, and the brothers' various designs are well documented by the series of small sketches remaining among their effects. They rejected one scheme featuring a series of pointed arches and finally decided on five graceful arches increasing in size toward the center of the 380-foot length, the longest arch being 88 feet long and rising 30 feet above the railroad tracks. Pylons with electric lanterns were designed for each end of the bridge. A handsome waiting station similar in materials and detail to the entrance portals at the opposite entry to the tract development was built along Fair Oaks Avenue. The

Greenes selected Michael de Palo as consulting structural engineer. He had a fine reputation and had just completed the first reinforced concrete bridge on the West Coast, a long single arch across the lagoon at Playa del Rey. The contractor was Carl Leonardt, whose offices were just down the hall from the Greenes in the Pacific Electric Building.

■ The Oaklawn Bridge received considerable press coverage at the time and the Greenes were lavishly praised for the design. But when the contractor's shoring was removed, cracks appeared in the crest of the longest arch and the Greenes' pride in the graceful engineering feat turned into the most disillusioning project of their career. Henry never got over his disappointment and in later years frequently commented that "we really went through hell over that bridge."[17]

■ Eventually it was determined that the steel had been misplaced in a section and the consulting engineer and the contractor were held responsible for the disaster, but the reputations of all involved suffered. Although tests determined that the cracks were not serious and the construction was stable, the railroad demanded that an additional pier be placed in the center of the longest span, an unnecessary precaution that completely destroyed the grace and integrity of the overall design.

Lucy Wheeler House, 1905

Henry's strong belief in the efficiency and economy of the two-story rectangular plan is evident in the wonderful little house for Miss Lucy Wheeler, a stenographer and notary who had purchased a typical corner lot in the vast spectrum of tract developments surrounding downtown Los Angeles. The Wheeler house revealed Henry's commitment to an architectural vocabulary that would provide quality for the everyday man or woman with a modest budget, and in it, as in those going up along Arroyo Terrace in Park Place, were some of the experiments that led to the new style. The roof made use of the rolled edge with integral gutter, while the rafters were uniform and the line straight. Not yet

Lower left and right, South Pasadena Realty and Improvement Company entrance portals for the Oaklawn Park tract development, 1904-05.

17. Author's personal interview with Henry McElwain, about 1957.

Isabelle (Greene) Greene's daughter,

was there a slight lift to soften the visual appearance and allow the water in the gutters to drain naturally to the downspouts. Not yet would the lines of the roof rise slightly, not only for function but also for what some would misinterpret as an oriental influence, a detail often taken by lesser designers of the day to such extremes as to become satirical. But on the interior colors were strong, like those used by Charles in his own house, and recalled the rich, deep color palette the brothers had witnessed in H. H. Richardson's Trinity Church in Boston.

■ Several of the firm's designs through 1905 and 1906 illustrate Henry Greene's belief in the wisdom of the compact two-story house. In the designs for the Bentz, Phillips, De Forest, Picairn and Cole houses, this was the dominant format. Yet each of these designs reached out beyond that simple form and demonstrated that within the Greenes' expressed-timber building language there was opportunity for infinite variety. While the fundamental plan forms are similar, each house has its distinct character.

John Benz House, 1906

In 1906 John Benz, a longtime friend and former client, joined with Nylles Eaton and J. C. Brainard in the purchase of thirty-two acres located two blocks north of the Park Place tract, where much of the Greene and Greene work was under construction. In an effort to encourage the sale of the new land parcels, Benz and his wife, Louise, called upon the Greenes to design for them a house that would set the standards for development within the "Prospect Park Tract." According to Mrs. Benz:

It was decided that we build on the least expensive lot there. Mr. Greene was called on to draw the plans and specifications—Henry Greene being the engineer. He thought he couldn't possibly be able to do so for he was so very busy with five major jobs in Pasadena

The Oaklawn Bridge, 1906.

Below, detail of the Oaklawn Waiting Station.

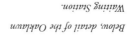
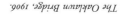

were commanding.

■ Beautifully proportioned and sensitively detailed, the Benz house remains today the Gamble House of the Greenes' smaller two-story designs. Though on a more modest scale, its gardens, terraces, pergolas, interiors, and furnishing received the same consideration from the Greenes' office as the increasingly larger commissions

Ironically the Benz house, set on what may have been initially the least desirable site, has matured into one of the most popular in the subdivision, sharing honors and common boundaries with Frank Lloyd Wright's famous La Miniatura, built for Mrs. George Madison Millard a decade and a half later.

at the time, but considering our friendship he did as we wanted, a very simple one. My mind was quite set upon the Swiss Chalet type of house of which he approved heartily, saying square or nearly square houses give the most room and are more economical—he also advised the use of hallways for the same reason.[18]

18. Letter to the author from Mrs. John C. Benz, dated 30 November 1958.

The John Benz house, 1906, represents the classic Greene and Greene two-story house design.

Right, the John Benz dining room and sideboard. For several years, Greene and Greene created furniture designs featuring the detail of the wood cleat attached to the panels with express screws carefully installed such that the slots in the screw heads were all of a like direction. This sideboard is similar to furnishings designed for the Willett and the third van Rossem houses.

John Bakewell Phillips House, 1906

Under construction at the same time as the Benz house, the John Bakewell Phillips house, on a slightly larger footprint, achieved an abundance of space due to the centralization of the circulation and stair pattern, and the utilization of the vast attic space created by the long, broad central-gable roof ridge. Also explored here was the breakup of masses by overhanging the second floor, thus casting decisive horizontal shadows across the front elevation, which was enhanced by the power of the roof overhang and the drama of the structural duplicity of the outriggers.

Dr. William T. Bolton House #3, 1906

For the Bolton house, the Greenes turned the roof gable opposite to the Phillips design, running it the width of the two-story house and thus accentuating its horizontality. This resulted in greater space being devoted to long hallways connecting the string of lateral spaces. The distinguishing characteristic of the Bolton house, however, was the furniture.

■ In July 1905, shortly after work had begun on the Robinson house and a month after Peter Hall had taken out the building permit for his carpentry shop, construction began on the third house by Greene and Greene for the Bolton family. As Dr. and Mrs. Bolton were aware of the Greenes' growing fascination with interiors and furniture, they commissioned the design of furniture for the entry hall, foyer, living room and dining room.

■ As was the house itself, the furnishings were the product of both Charles and Henry Greene, working closely together, although the unique qualities of their individual talents speak clearly in certain pieces. Here, prior to its use in the Robinson house, is the first use of mahogany in their furniture and the first experiments in the use of the expressed square ebony peg now so identified with their furniture designs of 1907-11. Here the peg is larger, the face almost flat, and the relief off the surface less than that in later use.

■ Each of the brothers was experimenting with a number of ideas at the same time. As with the Robinson dining-room furniture

of the same period, some of Charles's entry-hall designs for the Bolton house are literal references to his profound interest in traditional, four-hundred-year-old Chinese household furnishings.[19] Successful as these designs were, they represented the last of the furniture designs to draw so directly from that historical source. However, the use of the "lift," or abstract cloud pattern, would continue to be a signature of the Greenes' work, whether in their architecture, furniture, or imagery of the fabric or other graphic design.

■ The entry-hall furniture was an interesting combination of images; yet it all hung together handsomely. While the sophisticated hall table and taller pedestal are evocative of Chinese tradition, Charles's playful concepts and forms of the mirror, complete with candlesticks, was flanked by Henry's two tall-back chairs, highly linear in composition and made all the more elegant by his careful attention to scale and proportion. In the foyer writing desk, the forthright handling of the legs and drop-front support is bold and powerful, yet the detail of its interior compartments is as delicate and refined as in the later work.

■ The dining-room furniture speaks again of each of the brothers. The careful proportioning of the secondary verticals of the linear leg and lateral strut composition of these extremely simple designs were representative of Henry's disciplined hand and produced the most progressive linear designs to come from the Greenes until Henry's dining-table design for Walter L. Richardson in 1927. However, the inlay detail and the dining sideboard and server are from the hand of Charles Greene.

■ Dr. Bolton died unexpectedly before the house was completed, when only the dining furniture was in production. Instead of taking occupancy herself, Mrs. Bolton rented the house, including the dining-room furniture, to Mrs. Belle Barlow Bush, who immediately commissioned the balance of the Bolton furniture.

19. Charles Greene's library included the Edward S. Morse book *Japanese Homes and Their Surroundings* (Franklin Square, New York: Harper & Brothers, 1885).

Above, the John Bakewell Phillips house, 1906.

Below, the Dr. William T. Bolton house #3, 1906. The over-scaled bay window was an addition to the house in later years by architect Garret Van Pelt, formerly a draftsman for Greene and Greene.

The three-panel mahogany screen for the Bolton house is one of the most progressive designs to emerge from the Greene and Greene office, and is likely the design of Henry Greene, who designed several other pieces for the house for its first occupant, Mrs. Belle Barlow Bush.

Chair designed for the Bolton house #3. The Bolton house furniture represents the first Greene and Greene designs to be carried out in mahogany and their first use of the square ebony peg. Charles so liked this design that he had several made for his own home with seats in both wood and cushion.

Mrs. Belle Barlow Bush

Soon after moving into the Bolton house, Mrs. Bush asked Charles to design several small curio cabinets, a clock, a small table, and picture frames, some of which were inlaid in ebony with small bees representing her initials. While most of this furniture was completed by the Halls, two of the curio cabinets were made by a nephew of Mrs. Bush, Walter A. Gripton, who had a cabinet shop in Pasadena. His sister, Ethyl Gripton, carried out Charles's abstract folded-ribbon patterns for appliqué work on the living-room and foyer curtains.

■ Mrs. Bush, like a number of the Greenes' other clients, became absorbed with Charles's interest in the total design of interiors and related furnishings. Her close association with the brothers lasted many years. The last piece of furniture for Mrs. Bush was a large couch for the foyer, the eventual delivery of which was an event vividly recalled by members of the Bush family because it took four years to complete due to the extraordinary amount of furniture being produced by this time at the Hall shops for other Greene clients.

Above, brick walk along the side of the Caroline De Forest house, 1906, leads to the entry porch at the rear of the house.

Above right, the rear gardens of the De Forest house slope away from the house, allowing an uninterrupted view over the San Gabriel Valley from the rear living room and sun porch.

Robert Pitcairn Jr. house, 1906.

■ Years later, after Mrs. Bush had moved to Boston, she commissioned Charles to design bookplates for herself and for at least one of her daughters.

■ With the completion of the furnishings for the Robinson and Bolton/Bush houses, the Greene furniture vocabulary had been established. Certainly the close working relationship between Charles and John Hall had been cemented; the Hall shops were now fully developed, and the elements necessary for the enormous amount of work ahead were all in place.

Caroline De Forest House, 1906

One of the more charming of the smaller houses of this period was designed for Caroline De Forest on a narrow sloping site with a view of downtown Los Angeles in the far distance. Here Henry turned the rectangle's short side to the street and placed the living room at the rear to capture the views. The entrance to the house, located near the rear, came from the large, covered side terrace with a commanding view of the San Gabriel Valley. Noise and activity from the street were minimized and a high degree of privacy was achieved.

■ As in the Rowland house, the long single gable was turned to ridge across the short axis of the plan, giving a subtle low profile to the front elevation of the two-story structure, with roof openings to balconies allowing light into the second-level bedrooms.

Robert Pitcairn Jr. House, 1906

A short distance from the earlier Libby house, the Robert Pitcairn Jr. house again broke new ground for the Greenes. Though a simple two-story rectangular plan with an adjoining service wing to the rear corner, this large but modest commission demonstrated that the Greenes' style could adapt equally well to their large structures as to their smaller bungalows. It is a clear demonstration of the inaccuracy of an article by Arthur C. David in the October 1906 issue of *The Architectural Record* in which he claims that the Greene vocabulary did not adapt itself to larger structures and was, in the Libby house for instance, awkward and inept or, as he put it, "looks like an overgrown boy who had clung to his pinafores." It seems unlikely that Mr. David had seen the Pitcairn house a few blocks away, for its design exhibited the exciting opportunities that lay ahead for the architectural firm of Greene and Greene.

Chimney detail of the Mary E. Cole house. Wire-impregnated glass was used in the long roof overhangs to allow light into the windows of the second-floor bedroom.

The majestic trees behind the Mary E. Cole house, under construction, are on the property acquired by David and Mary Gamble a year after the Cole house was built.

Mrs. Mary E. Cole House, 1906

Conceived in late 1906, though not constructed until mid-1907, the Mrs. Mary E. Cole house was the final precursor to the great masterworks through which Greene and Greene would interpret the principles of the Arts and Crafts movement.

■ Here in the Cole house was the most highly articulated, bold timber detailing yet to emerge in the Greenes' work. They had developed a remarkable system of building wood upon wood that could be adapted to any situation emanating from a design. It was a system allowing infinite variation and a flexibility that provided enormous opportunities for plan forms and a direct and honest expression of post-and-beam stick construction described by architect and architectural critic Ralph Adams Cram in 1913:

Structurally it is a blessing: only too often the exigencies of our assumed precedents lead us into the wide and easy road of structural duplicity, but in this sort of thing there is only an honesty that is sometimes almost brazen. It is a wooden style built woodenly, and it has the force and the integrity of Japanese architecture. Added to this is the elusive element of charm that comes only from the personality of the creator, and charm in a degree hardly matched in other modern work.[20]

20. Ralph Adams Cram, *American Country Houses of Today* (New York: Architectural Book Publishing Co., 1913).

Cram is indeed correct and in the forefront of architectural thought with his reference to the works of the Arts and Crafts movement in America as "modern work."

■ The Cole house is an interesting amalgam of early and late Greene imagery combining the rugged quality of the massive sculptural cobblestone chimneys and supporting piers with the first use of the massive porte cochere on the front face of the house and the soft color and patina of the wood paneling and joinery on the interiors. With this refined articulated structural vocabulary, it was possible to create the gentle lift of the roofline desired for the drainage of the integral roof gutters and at the same time inherently soften the horizontal lines of the overall structure.

Anonymous oil painting of the
Shelter for Viewlovers, 1907.

Shelter for Viewlovers, 1907

Concurrent with the construction of the Cole house was that of the Shelter for Viewlovers built upon the crest of Monk Hill, with a panorama of the entire San Gabriel Mountains, foothills, and surrounding valleys, a panorama of a land that had made possible the evolution of the Greenes' most personal architectural and artistic expression. Between 1903 and 1907 Charles and Henry Greene developed their interpretation of the principles of the Arts and Crafts movement, applied those concepts to the California landscape, and surrounded themselves with extraordinarily gifted craftsmen. In so doing they developed a following and influenced other architects and a broad spectrum of architectural thought. Their works appeared in significant national architectural publications. With their designs they had created an architecture that endowed the inexpensive house with grace and dignity and gave a new direction to domestic architecture. It was this appropriateness, simplicity, and quality that appealed to those of taste and wealth who would soon be providing the unlimited budgets and artistic freedom to make possible the extraordinary artistry of the masterworks. But while attention would always be focussed on the exceptional commissions of the next few years, the source of the Greenes' inspiration lay in these four preceding years, when they were encouraged by an enlightened clientele to experiment with new ideas, new materials, and new methods.

4

THE MASTERWORKS
1 9 0 7 - 1 9 0 9

Entry hall stairwell,

Robert R. Blacker house, 1907.

1. Author's personal
interviews at The
Gamble House with
master woodcraftsman
David Swanson, 1967.

They have been called the ultimate bungalows, the five large commissions designed and built at the peak of the Greenes' career. While the size of the Blacker, Ford, Gamble, Pratt, and Thorsen houses may raise questions about their being designated bungalows, they were clearly founded on the principles of the English workers' houses constructed in Bengal, India, from whence the term bungalow was derived.

■ By the end of 1906 Charles and Henry Greene were already distinguished for having developed some of the most charming small wooden dwellings around the San Gabriel Valley. The Robinson house was attracting much attention. National publications were frequently featuring their designs. They had refined their architectural vocabulary and surrounded themselves with the very finest of master craftsmen. With earlier clients returning to them for additions and alterations and these large new commissions starting to come into the office, the amount of work around Pasadena made it necessary for them to move their office from the Pacific Electric Building in Los Angeles back to Pasadena and into the Boston Building, immediately behind the Kinney-Kendall Building. It was from this location and from Charles's new octagonal studio on the second level of his residence that the Greenes' ultimate commissions and their furnishings would emerge.

■ The next three years would be the most intensive of the Greenes' architectural career. As 1907 began they were employing as many as fifteen draftsmen. Several of these, headed by Leonard W. Collins, spent most of their time on furniture drawings. As a result of the great increase of furniture, Peter Hall was required to add space and equipment to his own shops in 1907 and 1908 and put his brother, John Hall, in charge of the mill and the making of furniture. This was to have a decided impact on Charles's designs and the quantity of work produced. John Hall's long experience in cabinetmaking clearly distinguished the work under his supervision. Charles's first conceptual freehand drawings were carefully studied by both before the final detailing and construction drawings were done. Charles's pencil sketches for furniture found among John Hall's papers indicate the close professional rapport between the two men. There developed an equally close rapport between Charles and many of the master craftsmen working in the mill on his furniture, carvings, or lighting fixtures.

■ David Swanson, a young master craftsman from Sweden who joined Peter Hall in 1908 and later became shop foreman, recalled both of the brothers. Henry was so involved with engineering, construction, and the operations of the office, he said, that he rarely had time to visit the mill. Charles had a completely different personality. He had long flowing hair and would don a smock every morning when he came to the mill and work right along with the men, moving from one project to another, offering subtle refinements as he went. He would often work with the tools himself. The craftsmen had a great deal of respect for Charles and got along with him well as long as they did not differ with him.[1] Although extremely mild and soft-spoken, Charles commanded the greatest respect from the workmen and was equally able to induce clients to spend the money required to produce such fine and intricately fabricated furniture.

■ The association with Peter and John Hall and with Emil Lange was essential, and these five masterworks testified to the exceptional teamwork of the construction crews and the craftsmen in the mill and furniture shops. With the Greenes' high standards of performance, it was not unusual for work to be ripped out and done over. Under some circumstances this might have lowered the morale of the workers, but, according to David Swanson, "there was such a high regard for Charles and Henry Greene that there was a competition between the most skilled craftsmen to work on their projects."

■ It is also important to recognize here that the budgets provided by the five clients who commissioned the masterworks were what made these larger achievements of the Greenes possible.

The Oak Knoll subdivision had just been developed along the southeastern boundaries of Pasadena, bordering on fashionable San Marino. Designed to offer the finest real estate in the area, its picturesque rolling terrain, formerly filled with grazing sheep, now afforded potential buyers with views across the San Gabriel Valley to the south, a canyon to the east, and the panorama of the mountains to the north.

■ One of the first to purchase property in Oak Knoll was Robert R. Blacker and his second wife, Nellie Canfield Blacker. Blacker had retired a few years earlier, following a successful career as a lumberman in Manistee, Michigan. Having decided to build in Pasadena, he selected a prime 5½-acre parcel near the entry point of the center island of the subdivision, a parcel that, by virtue of its position and size, became the flagship property of the Oak Knoll neighborhood.[2]

■ Early in 1906 architects Myron Hunt and Elmer Grey had been commissioned to design the Blackers' new home. Plans had been developed and renderings completed when reports of the San Francisco earthquake alarmed Blacker and he called in his architects. Dissatisfied with their discussion of foundation designs and earthquake safety, he dismissed them and a short time later

engaged Greene and Greene as his new architects. The Hunt and Grey plan was already scheduled for publication in the *Architectural Record* of October 1906, as designed for Blacker. It was published again in *The Craftsman* in October 1907 but only as a Pasadena house. The Hunt and Grey design had therefore been completed early in 1906. The earthquake was on April 18, 1906, and the Blacker land survey for Greene and Greene was dated in early November of 1906.

■ A review of the Hunt and Grey plan suggests that the Blackers were satisfied with the basic arrangement of the floor plan, for it was adopted with minor changes by the Greenes. Not so with the site development or the uninspiring Mission Revival character of the house depicted in the Hunt and Grey renderings.

■ The Greenes disagreed with the Hunt and Grey siting of the house and repositioned it toward the corner of the site, forsook the formal gardens for the natural Oak Knoll countryside, and brought

2. Information on the Blacker family has been through personal interviews and correspondence with Blacker great-grandson John Boothby and with Steve Harold, Curator, Manistee County Historical Museum.

The mastery and sophistication of the Greenes' handling of line and form in the composition and detail of the teakwood and fir entry hall of the Blacker house is unsurpassed in the Arts and Crafts movement. The brothers' respect for the temple structures of the Orient is here expressed more literally than in their other designs.

forward the full thrust of their new and refined timber style to create the largest and most elaborate of their masterworks. Here they demonstrated the fundamental concepts of their Arts and Crafts philosophy—the provision of shade and shelter in a hot, arid climate, free cross circulation of air, and an open relationship between house and garden, which applied equally well to the large estate and to the modest bungalow. The repositioning of the house allowed for entry at the principal intersection in the subdivision and for a freer, more natural garden setting. To break further from the formality of the Hunt and Grey plan, the Greenes designed an enormous, heavily timbered porte cochere, which angled from the central entry and was supported by a massive clinker-brick pier in the island of the grand circular drive. By enhancing the existing natural swales of the site, they developed a large lake and took advantage of the undulating terrain to join interiors and garden from both the main floor and the basement level.

■ The Blacker house was the largest property and most elaborate commission that Greene and Greene developed in their wooden-bungalow style. Built upon rugged clinker-brick foundations and broad terra-cotta-paved terraces, the powerful post-and-beam timber structure, with its brazen exploitation of

metal-strap and wooden-dowel joinery, broad roof overhangs, projecting outriggers, and rafter tails, provided a constant ballet of silhouettes and shadows as the sun moved through the day. Equally effective under the evening lighting from the lanterns of brass and iridescent glass, the 12,000-square-foot structure sat as quietly upon the 5½ acres as a kiosk in a Japanese garden. So effective was this combination of natural materials and lyrical forms that the Greenes kept the parklike landscaping minimal to retain, as much as possible, the soft contours of the rolling Oak Knoll Ranch.

■ Little of the Hunt and Grey plan remained following the Greenes' skillful weaving of the interior with the garden. The essence of the landscape design emanated from the heart of the house, from two opposing axes, which provided the order necessary to the otherwise natural undulations of the site. The axis of the large entry hall carried the eye through the rear courtyard and on through to the most formal element of the garden at the far points of the property. In so doing, it provided the spine, the point of reference between the order of the house and the undulating topography leading down to the edge of the lake. To one side, off the westerly dining-room wing of the house, the garage, keeper's house, and greenhouse continued the domestic linear order along Wentworth Avenue. On the opposite side of this axis, the site was allowed to roll naturally to the long, gentle curve of Hillcrest Avenue as it embraced the easternmost borders of the property. The Greenes had allowed the topography of the site to provide the inspiration for its organization.

Site plan of the original five and one-half acres comprising the Blacker estate.

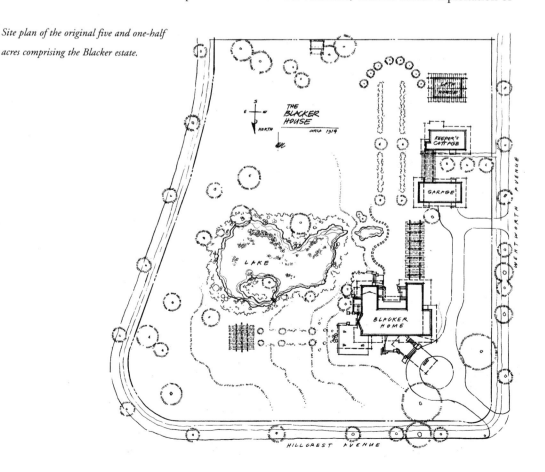

Rear elevation of the Blacker house shows
the Greene's shaping of the landscape
to gain access to the basement level and
billiard room.

Rear and side elevations of the Blacker
house prior to the 1912 addition of the
pergola to the left, and the 1914 enclosure
of the sleeping porch, upper left.

Right, staircase, upper hall, and chandelier of the Blacker house.

■ Off the living-room terrace, a second strong axis paralleling the front of the house led through open, rolling lawn to the timbered pergola beside the lake. Vines climbed over the open joinery, providing respite from the warmth of the day, a place for quiet reading, or a spot for entertaining guests for tea. From here as well as from the various terraces and balconies that the Greenes had added to the original plan, one could choose a view of the mountains or the San Gabriel Valley or the ravine to the east.

■ Greene and Greene, by their careful analysis of the site, had made a remarkable gift to the Blackers' neighbors by retaining the rich natural qualities of the Oak Knoll Ranch in the form of a quiet park and lake in the center of the tract. They had indeed approached the design of the landscape with logical principles commensurate with the Arts and Crafts movement.

■ The construction of the garage, keeper's house, and greenhouse began in April 1907. Progress photographs reveal that these structures were nearly complete before ground was broken for the house. This adjusts the perceived historical timeline, placing the construction of the Blacker house almost concurrent with that of the Gamble house.

■ Dawson and Daniels, beginning contractors for the Blacker house, carried out the basic framing and exteriors before new permits were taken out by Peter Hall in late April 1908 for completion of the house and the interior work. In July, drawings for the considerable amount of furniture and lighting fixtures were finished, and by the end of September 1908, the house was completed. The billiard room was added on the basement level and pergolas added in the garden in 1910; and the major enclosure of the sleeping porch was completed in 1914.

■ While the site development and the dynamics of the Greenes' wooden timber/joinery vocabulary were carried out to the fullest in this enormous project, it is the interiors and the furnishings that take their imagination to even further heights. Perhaps it is the scale of the spaces, the high degree of the subtle joinery and detail, the loving attention to color and textures of materials, the magic of the lighting sculptures, and the absolute rightness of the furniture designs that bring about the extraordinary unity felt throughout. Structure and furniture were clearly one; yet each retained its inherent individuality. Within this totality there was infinite variation. To achieve this, the Greenes had developed a series of distinct principles and relationships but retained complete control over such systems. Strict order existed, though with a flexibility that allowed the Greenes to remain in command. So they pushed, pulled, tucked or turned when called upon to do so, without sacrificing either structural integrity or visual continuity. And this flexible system is felt at every turn throughout the Blacker house, as well as in all of their later works.

Tinted archival postcard illustrates the rural environment surrounding the Blacker house at the time of its construction, with the magnificent panorama of the San Gabriel Mountains.

The living room of the Robert R. Blacker
house boasts a Grueby-tiled fireplace
and a fire screen designed by Greene
and Greene.

The six hanging lanterns of the
living-room continue the theme in the
freize, deliniating lily pads in
leaded-and-stained glass.

Lily pads echoing those in the garden lake were created in gesso relief on the canvas surfaces of the ceiling and living-room frieze and covered with gold leaf muted by the subtle toning of the finish glaze.

This teakwood, ebony, and leather armchair
was crafted for the entry hall of the Robert R.
Blacker house.

Left, dining-room chandelier of the
Robert R. Blacker house.

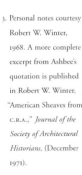

Above, wall sconce of bedroom #1 of
the Blacker house.

3. Personal notes courtesy
Robert W. Winter,
1968. A more complete
excerpt from Ashbee's
quotation is published
in Robert W. Winter,
"American Sheaves from
C.R.A.," *Journal of the
Society of Architectural
Historians*, (December
1971).

■ In response to the dry, warm Southern California climate, the Greene interiors were muted by color or selections of material where called for, yet they could be opened at will to light and air. The Blacker entry at first welcomes, then closes the out-of-doors; greets the visitor with the warmth of rubbed teakwood, then unfolds the long vista of the garden through the full bank of French doors leading to the rear courtyard. The hanging lanterns controlled the light, whether by day or evening, and despite the somewhat limited technology of the era became magical points of light casting a warm glow around the space and across the detail and grain of the hand-polished paneling.

■ The Blacker living room featured the brothers' only use of metal leaf around the frieze and in the floral corners of the ceiling panels. Subtle patterns of lily pads, depicting those in the lake, were carried out in gesso relief and then covered with gold-colored metal leaf that reflected a soft, warm glow from the six indirect lighting fixtures. Like the frieze, the leaded-and-stained glass of the light baskets also depicted the lily pads. Here, more than in any other Greene design, plant materials were used as a thematic relationship between the interiors and the gardens, and the plant species selected were carefully drawn from the landscaping outside.

■ In the large dining room and adjacent breakfast room, folding glass doors could be opened or removed, allowing for the placing of the dining and breakfast tables together, creating a large banquet room. Banks of clear casement windows surrounded the breakfast room on three sides to welcome morning and afternoon sun.

■ Throughout, interior paneling, furniture, and lighting fixtures featured teakwood, mahogany, Port Orford cedar, ebony, and an assortment of other woods, metals, and mother-of-pearl.

■ Over sixty pieces of Blacker furniture and fifty-three lighting fixtures—all in various stages of completion—as well as pieces for other clients, would have been on display in the Hall shops early in 1909 when Charles Robert Ashbee visited with Charles Greene. As one of the leading designers, craftsmen, and observers of the Arts and Crafts movement here and in his native England, Ashbee's account of his American tour may tell more about the Greenes, and particularly about the Blacker furnishings, than any other source:

I think C. Sumner Greene's work beautiful; among the best there is in this country. Like [Frank] Lloyd Wright the spell of Japan is on him, he feels the beauty and makes magic out of the horizontal line, but there is in his work more tenderness, more subtlety, more self effacement than in Wright's work. It is more refined and has more repose. Perhaps it loses in strength, perhaps it is California that speaks rather than Illinois, anyway as work it is, so far as the interiors go, more sympathetic to me. . . .

He [C. Sumner Greene] took us to these workshops [the Hall shops] where they were making, without exception, the best and most characteristic furniture I have seen in this country. There were beautiful cabinets and chairs of walnut and lignum-vitae, exquisite doweling and pegging, and in all a supreme feeling for the material, quite up to the best of our English craftsmanship, Spooner, the Barnslys, Lutyens, Lethaby. I have not felt so at home in any workshop on this side of the Atlantic. . . . Here things were really alive—and the "Arts and Crafts" that all the others were screaming and hustling about, are here actually being produced by a young architect, this quiet, dreamy, nervous, tenacious little man, fighting single-handedly until recently against tremendous odds.[3]

Freeman A. Ford House, 1907

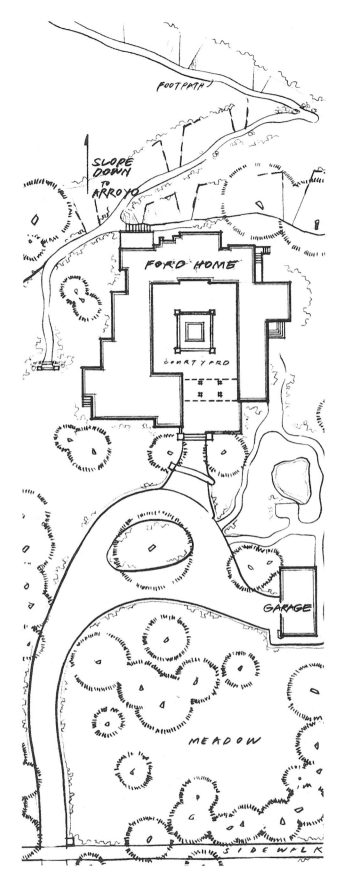

The site arrangement for the Freeman A. Fords placed the house on the bluffs overlooking the scenic arroyo vista, like that of their Robinson relatives next door to the north.

Freeman A. Ford house, 1907, adjacent to the Henry M. Robinson house to the north. The open front courtyard spaces of the Ford house achieved privacy with the configuration of the landscape plantings shielding the house entirely from the street.

Overleaf, central courtyard of the Freeman A. Ford house. There was a genteel ambiance to this early California plan that was enhanced by the soft roll and natural color of the original composition roofing, accented by the ever-changing shadows of the passing sun. In combination, these elements were essential to the Greene and Greene style.

The Freeman A. Ford house celebrated the Greenes' genuine fascination with the central-courtyard planning principles first explored in the Bandini design of 1903. Since then, with one client after another, they had continued to develop its principles until, in the Ford house, they were able to demonstrate the most refined evolution of their courtyard concepts. With the addition of the landscaping and the full development of the interiors and furnishings, this design certainly represents another of the Greenes' masterworks.

■ The Freeman Ford commission came into the Greene and Greene office in early 1906, when the Robinson house next door was well under construction. The selection of the stucco dash coat for the exterior, rather than the Greenes' general use of shakes or shingles, was apparently a carryover from the Robinson house and the influence of the Voysey houses around London.

■ The important courtyard scheme was not, however, the only design by the Greenes for the Ford property. First dated September 2, 1906, the fully developed drawings for the large, single-story courtyard design show a "revised date" of July 9, 1907. In the interim months, a totally different three-story design for the same property was carried completely through ink-on-linen drawings and dated May 16, 1907. Just what lay behind this rejection, redesign, and resurrection of the original courtyard concept is curious. Hardly six weeks later, on June 27, 1907, contracts were signed for the construction of the original courtyard design, just two months following the first work on the Blacker site.

■ The basic Ford site was a long rectangular property with a street face of 175.75 feet and a distance to the rear of 472.82 feet. The main plateau lifted slightly for some 360 feet to the crest of long sloping bluffs, providing a broad sweeping panorama of the San Rafael hills across the arroyo. The Greenes set the house atop this plateau at the edge of the palisades, affording the public areas of the house differing views of the vast natural arroyo. The house, which could not be seen from the street, was one of the most private of the Greenes' designs and yet took full advantage of the length of the plateau. Bringing the drive gently in from the south side of the property allowed for considerable use of the natural hollows of the land nestled between native California live oak trees. Enhanced by the additional rolling mounds, the design provided

both verdant valleys of ground cover and open, sunlit areas of grassy meadow. At the house, the drive swings completely around a central island, allowing for the discharge of guests at the broad steps leading to the entry court. To the right of the circular drive was the garage, carried out with the same deft detail as the house. Again, as in the forward yard, large, rolling mounds of earth and plant materials separate the Ford from the Robinson house. So meticulously have the Greenes taken advantage of the natural undulating terrain that the overall site feels natural and blends with the general neighborhood.

■ From the circular drive, the broad stairway rises to the entry forecourt. Here a narrow breezeway connects the side wings of the house, which constrict to prepare for the entrance into the large central court around which the activities of the house relate. In contrast to the rusticity of the Bandini court, the ground plane is paved in terra-cotta tiles bordered with blue brick, except for the drop of the square central fountain of stucco dash-coat set serenely amidst the cool natural green of a manicured lawn. Bay trees in planters were placed at the corners of the fountain, and other plant materials were arranged around the court in large, round terra-cotta pots. South of this central fountain was the wide wood-and-stained-glass entry door, placed directly on the central axis below one of the two two-story elements of the otherwise single-story design. Above the entry was a loft, and in the forward part of the south wing were a small tower room and roof terrace, offering either the privacy of the open, natural timbered wood of the interior or a view of the central court and beyond to the vast front gardens.

■ Shadows of the projecting rafters and outriggers dance about the court, changing with the sun. The roofs are low and hover over the house, allowing sunshine into the courtyard yet shielding the walls from the midday heat. Horizontal bands of casement windows provide for both the free circulation of breezes from the arroyo and the entry of the cheerful morning light. The roofing material is composition, with a natural, ground-slate surface. The roof lines are softened by the roll of the integral gutters and are in quiet harmony with the color and patina of the surrounding stately eucalyptus trees. Other than the natural texture and color of the stucco dash coat of the exterior, the detail of the Greenes' wooden style was clearly present and, in this elegant bungalow, conveyed the grace and pace of the early California hacienda.

4. Charles Sumner Greene, "Symbolism," unpublished manuscript, (November 1932), Greene and Greene Library, The Gamble House, USC.

■ While the central court is given great strength by the discipline of its geometry, the periphery of the plan moves in and out, seemingly at will; yet, the Greenes carefully calculated to allow every space along the two side wings to capture the spectacular views of the arroyo or surrounding vistas. In so doing, the plan and forms of the house are both playful and relaxing as they tuck and project, contributing to the casual sense of order.

■ In the interiors there is considerable variation, but at every turn there is a constant reminder of the oneness of the whole, demonstrating a statement made two decades later by Charles Greene in an essay on symbolism in which he talks about the "oneness of all that exists."[4]

■ While the entry was originally small and had a low ceiling in contrast to the height of the adjacent study, the living room was separated from the balance of the house, as well as from other Greene and Greene work, by being dropped. There was a graceful welcome that came from entering and then descending into the public space; but at the opposite end, where a hall led to the private wing of the family bedrooms, there was a step up, a clear signal of a change from a public to a private area. The living room, as in the other masterworks, was a symphony in wood. Walls were paneled and hand-rubbed beams spanned across the ceiling, seeming to suggest the structural order not only of the building process but also of the uses of the space. The handling of the trim in the frieze was a reminder of the corbel and timber structures of the Orient. Though isolated in the living room, this oriental touch was in complete harmony with the straightforward wooden joinery of the balance of the house and blended gracefully with the featherlike patterns of the leaded-and-stained glass of the doors and lighting fixtures and the refined Arts and Crafts furniture.

■ Here Charles seemed to be playing with the ebony pegs in the furniture, for some of them are no longer square or rectangular but rather like parallelograms with concave sides. Added to this, there was an irregularity about their order, though they did not stray from their place of function, as if to prove that absolute order was something to be defied.

■ As with the Robinson house, there was a broader range to the character of the various pieces of furniture. Rare for the brothers was the large upholstered living-room couch, simple of line, comfortable, and with the wood structural frame expressed just enough to relate to other furniture. The fabric was without pattern, leaving the grace and character of the design to rest with the form, scale, and proportion. Thus the piece had a timeless quality, fitting

Writing case for the living room library table of the Freeman A. Ford house.

The stepping of the south-side elevation of the Freeman A. Ford house allowed for individual views of the arroyo from each of the successive rooms along the bedroom wing of the house.

into various eras and environments—a quality that was very much a part of the Greene and Greene furniture aesthete. In contrast were the relative lightness of the variety of chairs for the living room, the delicacy of the inlay of the elegantly cantilevered writing tables, and the joinery and hardware of the letter case. Added to all this was one of the most unusual of all of Charles's furniture designs—the large wing-back living-room chair complete with ottoman. In a photograph it is perceived as awkward, uncomfortable, and out of scale with the balance of the pieces. In reality it was comfortable and fitted well into the Ford surroundings.

■ Each of the Ford interiors was richly enhanced by the luster of the hand-rubbed surfaces under the soft glow of the Greenes' lighting. Here, in an unusual move, Charles composed lighting fixture designs of glass and metal as well as glass and wood, and even went further by mixing both designs and materials in the

The classic simplicity and elegant scale of the dining room server for the Freeman A. Ford house was one of the most progressive of the mature Greene and Greene furniture creations.

same spaces. But in his masterful hands this not only worked but added to the fanciful mischief frequently found in his designs. Here, again, he seemed to be saying that "this should not be done but I'm going to show you I'm facile enough to pull it off."

■ It was in the design of the dining-room furniture that Charles charted new ground. There were purity and forthrightness about the oval top of the dining table and the hexagonal base, but it was the server that exhibited the progressive quality of the Greene and Greene furniture. Here was Charles at his best. The design relied solely on the furniture imagery for which Greene and Greene were noted, but there was also a restraint that was jarring. Devoid of any form of applied ornament, it was simply a statement of line, scale, and proportion; the beauty of the grain and finish of quality materials, and a direct statement of joinery. The familiar breadboard ends stabilized the top surface, and the use of ebony splines and the square ebony peg gave the table its superior design appeal. Aside from the slight inverted lift in the center apron, there was no hint of historical imagery. Altogether, this server design established the Greenes' furniture as timeless; it is as contemporary today as any modern design.

■ Through Arturo Bandini, the Greenes had become enamored with the concept of the early California hacienda. They had examined its possibilities in several smaller houses since 1903, conceived the first Freeman A. Ford design in 1906, and a year later in the Ford house presented their most sophisticated courtyard plan in another of their masterworks.

David B. Gamble House, 1908

Two weeks prior to breaking ground for the Ford house, David B. Gamble, a second-generation member of the Proctor and Gamble Company of Cincinnati, and his wife, Mary, purchased the property at 4 Westmoreland Place, which was a short block parallel to North Orange Grove Boulevard and connecting at the southern end to Arroyo View Drive in Park Place. At 2 Westmoreland the Greenes were beginning construction on the home for Mary and John Addison Cole and, at the entry juncture of Arroyo View Drive, had just begun construction of the Mary Ranney house. Within a half block of the Gamble property, the Greenes' bungalows around Park Place were already capturing the interest of the community, and the newspaper articles were now making reference to the Park Place tract area as "Little Switzerland," a misnomer difficult to shake.

■ The Gambles had been wintering in the Pasadena resort hotels since the turn of the century. In searching for a parcel of land for their own home in 1907 they were attracted by the quiet of Westmoreland Place and the privacy there provided by the forty-foot parkway between it and North Orange Grove Avenue, and by the distinct separation from the image of the fashionable Millionaires' Row and grand estates of South Orange Grove Avenue. On Westmoreland they could build well but unpretentiously, consistent with the progressive tradition of the family. They were probably aware that in the previous three years the charm and integrity of the Greene designs had been attracting more and more attention, and had no doubt noticed the work in various stages of construction in Park Place, and quite possibly the presence of Charles Greene's home-office around the corner. Family legend has it that the Gambles had lunch with Charles and Henry, during which the commission was awarded. What would transpire in the coming months would be a series of designs evolving from the close working relationship between Mary Gamble and Charles Greene and given extraordinary order and discipline from the office under the strong hand of Henry Greene. The designs for the Gamble house, as well as for the other masterworks, were conceived from the new second-level studio Charles had added to his Arroyo View Drive home. From his drawing table in the center of this octagonal space, he could look through the branches of the large, gnarled oak outside to the vast panorama of the Arroyo Seco valley and the San Gabriel Mountains, always a source of inspiration for his creative mind. From here he could also look out over the vacant terrain of the Gamble property and the excitement and the raw beauty emerging from the timber joinery of the framing of the Cole house.

■ The Gamble site and floor plan went through three fundamental concepts. In response to the topographical survey drawing, the first design paralleled a wing of the house and the separate garage along the south border of the nearly 240-foot parallelogram of the site and set at a distinct angle to Westmoreland Place. By wrapping the house around two large eucalyptus trees at the high point of the property and angling out to capture the views and breezes of the arroyo, the first Gamble floor plan was one of the freest form compositions yet to come from the Greene office. The plan was too casual for the Gambles, however, but its spirit remained in the Greenes' minds and emerged a few months later in the plan for the Pratt house.

■ The second plan for the Gambles was much more traditional and rectilinear, but in spite of its disciplined formality it continued to encompass the Greenes' earlier concerns for the interior relationships with outdoor living spaces. This scheme was again set at a distinct angle to capture the prevailing breezes, a principle found to be at odds with the criteria in the deed that required the house to be parallel with Westmoreland Place. Thus, the third and final plan rotated the house parallel to the street, and the garage was now positioned in the swale of the lower portion of the site along the north property line, discreetly tucking the sounds and activities of the new gasoline-powered vehicles at a distance from the house.

■ To counter the height of the three levels of the house and the relative compactness of the plan, the Greenes utilized the vast flexibility of their timber vocabulary to bring into the design the strength of the horizontal line as a function of the relationship of structure to site in somewhat the same manner as in Frank Lloyd Wright's prairie house designs. On the facade, a portion of the second level was cantilevered over the entry. The second-floor roof was low and broad, strengthened by the hovering quality of the smaller third-level roof and the elongation of the front elevation with the north terrace and sleeping porch. Its strong horizontal railings and broad, low roof were all accentuated by the scale and form of the massive structural horizontal beams and outriggers. To the south, the fence and gate structure screening the service yard further emphasized this horizontality.

Previous page, panorama of entry hall and living room of the Gamble house.

Right, dining room of the Gamble house.

■ The grounds were gently rolled to allow for the drive to sweep from side to side and on to the garage or the entry stairs without being visible from the street. As the automobile approached the entry, existing vertical cypress trees on each side of the brick drive contrasted sharply with the low horizontal lines of the house. The parkway was planned to create a strong physical and visual barrier to the dust, traffic, and trolley along the oiled-dirt paving of North Orange Grove Avenue. The balance of the landscape was a rolling green lawn, except for a rose garden behind the garage and simple plantings along the rock-edged dirt paths. At the rear of the property, Charles nestled sitting alcoves and stone benches on top of a bluff ten feet above Scott Place. Here the Gambles could pause and look out across Scott Place to the several acres of orange groves in the Bellmore tract that Mr. Gamble had purchased.

■ In 1908 there was considerable activity in the firm. On March 9, 1908, Peter Hall pulled the permit for the Gamble House. A week later newspaper reports cited the near completion of the Ford house. On April 20, 1908, Peter Hall took out the permit for the interiors of the Blacker house, having taken the job over from contractors Dawson and Daniels. Sketches for the Charles M. Pratt house in Ojai were beginning. Throughout 1908 furniture drawings were being completed, and construction began for the Blacker, Ford, and Gamble houses, dominating the time of artisans in the Hall shops under the watchful eyes of John Hall and Charles Greene. By September the Blacker house was completed and the Gamble house was very near completion.

■ The Gamble house plan was based on a careful analysis of the Gambles' needs and a clear understanding of the various functions, and a knowledge of the occupants of the house. The broad entry terrace was contiguous to the large covered side terrace, which was developed as a major outdoor living space. It also served as the separate access for David Gamble's business associates, who entered his den, adjacent to the entry hall, through a separate door from this side terrace. The bold silhouette and the richly articulated wooden structure and joinery for the broad sleeping porch above dominated the front and side elevations of the house and brought to mind the Greenes' appreciation and respect for Japanese temple structures. But, as Japanese architects have been quick to point out, it was not Japanese.

The asymmetrical composition of the master bedroom chiffonier drew inspiration from traditional Japanese tonsu chest designs.

Right, the writing desk for the Gamble master bedroom respected the client's interest in fine Rookwood pottery by adding similar decorative forms inlaid into elements of the desk design.

■ The spacious rear terrace, unlike the linear discipline of the front terrace and its construction of dash-coat stucco, was a free form with high retaining wall and balustrade carried out ruggedly in clinker brick and boulders. As it twisted around the lily pond and the two large eucalyptus trees, it was complemented by the gentle curve of the stair and landings down to the stone steps that saunter through the undulating roll of the lawn. Atop a similarly constructed pier on the edge of the terrace was a hooded lantern, again inspired by the Orient, which cast soft light on the stair steps as well as an ambient glow on the terrace and pond. The dramatic difference in form and materials of the front and rear terraces relate again to both the deed restrictions and to the Gambles' apparent desire to exhibit a more formal facade while letting Charles's rampant imagination run with more freedom on the rear of the house and in the rear garden.

■ On the interior the plan evolved from the special living pattern established early by the Gambles. It was decidedly zoned. A strong central entry and circulation area divided the living room and den from the wing composed of the dining room, pantry, kitchen, service, and bedroom created especially for nonfamily guests. The principal stairway is the primary feature of the entry hall, positioned to the side to allow a complete vista from the front door through the length of the hall to the rear terrace, a pond, and the rear gardens. On the second level the immediate family was situated to one side of the large central hall. On the other side was a suite for Mrs. Gamble's sister, Miss Julia Huggins, and guest room for relatives. On both levels the back stair is organized to serve as a sound barrier between the kitchen-service, or private areas of the plan, and the public areas.

■ The Greenes were never content to allow ideas to go unbuilt, and several features from the unexecuted interim house design for Freeman A. Ford were carried directly across the drawing board into the design for the Gambles. Details of the leaded-glass entry, the fencing and *torii*-structured gateway to the service yard, the splayed patterns of the roof rafters over the porches, garden pottery, and the third-floor concept for a billiard room were almost identical in the two designs. The Gambles had no interest in billiards, and this extraordinary space on the third level appeared on the final ink-on-linen drawings as "the attic." So beautifully articulated were the open-beamed, expressed ceiling detail, the peg-and-dowel joinery of the wall paneling, and the care given to the stair railing that this attic is one of the most exquisite rooms in the house.

*The bedroom for Mary Gamble's
sister, Julia Huggins, was furnished with
Charles's designs in ash and wicker.*

■ On the interiors as well as the exterior, the Greenes believed that a wooden structure should express the integrity and identity of each of the separate parts. Each member was treated as a design element and contributed to the enrichment of the whole composition. This belief was as much a part of the Greenes' philosophy as was their concern for craftsmanship, and it was expressed by Henry Greene in his discussion of the Pitcairn house when he wrote:

The whole construction was carefully thought out, and there was a reason for every detail. The idea was to eliminate everything unnecessary, to make the whole as direct and simple as possible, but always with the beautiful in mind as the final goal.

In the Gamble house as in the Greenes' other major works, no detail was left to chance. Be it structure, interiors, furniture, lighting, carpets, picture frames, or hardware, each had an artistic identity of its own; and, yet, each blended quietly into the harmony of the overall composition of which it was only a contributing part. Bold structure existed right next to a delicate element of furniture. There was harmony here that was seldom found in the relationships between architecture and furnishings.
■ The Gambles' hospitality toward guests was expressed in the design of furnishings. For the nonfamily guests, who were highly regarded, lighting fixtures were more delicate in form and scale and the furniture was in grey maple with subtle inlay of nickel silver. The beds were nickel silver over brass with relief patterns in the same configuration as the silver inlay of the wooden furniture. For the entry hall, living room, and dining room, Honduras mahogany was the principal furniture material, and throughout all was the familiar subtle "lift" form and detail of the square ebony peg. This was quite straightforward, and there was little use of applied inlay or other decorative motif depicted in the family pieces. The exceptions were the walnut drop-front writing desk and the chiffonier in the master bedroom on which an inlay of fruitwoods and mother-of-pearl carried out Charles's interpretation of the floral pattern from two favorite pieces of the Gambles' Rookwood pottery. For Julia Huggins's (Mrs. Gamble's sister) room, ash was chosen for the upright writing desk, a lighter finish to blend more easily with the subtle grey-green color given to the wicker furniture Charles designed for her personal suite.

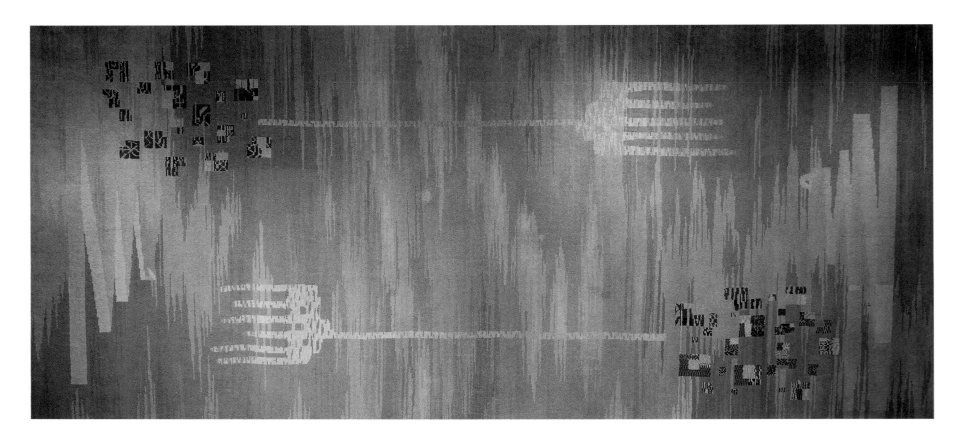

The living-room rugs crafted from Charles Greene's watercolor renderings are believed to have been handwoven in Austria. In color and in the abstract composition of the tree of life, they convey an imagery akin to the work of Gustav Klimt.

■ Unique to the Gamble house were the living-room carpets made in Austria, woven from Charles's watercolor drawings depicting an abstract rendition of the tree of life and a ribbon of cloud forms. When the carpets were delivered, Charles was dissatisfied with one of the colors woven into the pattern, and, typical of his exacting demands, he engaged the Iran Company of Los Angeles to make corrections. The company sent out some of their weavers, who sat on the floor of the Gamble living room for weeks, removing the offending color and reweaving with another yarn.

■ One of the most noteworthy elements of the masterworks and of the Gamble house in particular was the extensive use of leaded-and-stained glass. Charles's imaginative and sculptural designs carried out with and by Emil Lange produced some of the finest glass of the Arts and Crafts movement. The lighting-fixture glass presented differing qualities of color and light at different times of the day and could be called on at will by the flip of an electrical switch. In the extraordinary tripartite entry doors for the Gamble house, two layers of glass were laminated to give a greater latitude of color variations, and in Lange's own mind this was the most significant work of his long career. That same expertise was

evident in the workmanship for the interior windows, the book cabinet doors, and the many and varied lighting fixtures in the Gamble house, as well as the other Greene designs of this period.

■ From the outset, this was a house for people, for human enjoyment, for human response. It was flexible. It was timeless. There was a hierarchy of space, of place, of structure, of detail, of feeling. Each room had a sense of unity, of appropriateness. Many facets responded to the human mood. On a grey day, the stained glass of the entry cast a welcome light across the hall floor. On a sunny day, the dim interiors of the inglenook in the living room felt cool and comforting. In the spring, the solarium promised the wonders of a new season. Terraces, sleeping porches, gardens, boulder seats overlooking the arroyo—all offered places for contemplation.

■ The gift of the Gamble family home by the heirs of Cecil and Louise Gamble in 1966 to the City of Pasadena in a joint agreement with the University of Southern California has made possible the focus of scholarly interests of all the work of Charles and Henry Greene through public tours and the establishment of the Greene and Greene Library and Exhibition.

■ Because of this gift, a number of students and scholars have had an opportunity to live the experience the Greenes sought to create for their clients. That experience has been a continual unfolding of feeling and detail that only time can provide. Depending on the mood of the individual, there is always a spot either inside the house or out in the garden seeming to offer just the correct quality of the moment. Even in the larger spaces, there is a comfortable quietude for a person alone; yet, that same space serves equally well under the pressure of large numbers of people. The living room, in particular, has many spaces in one: a fireside inglenook, a solarium, a music area, a library, and a central gathering place, all functioning individually as well as collectively. At every turn one senses the love, the understanding, the deep commitment of owner, architect, and craftsman alike in producing a unified architectural statement, exemplifying the highest traditions and philosophies of the Arts and Crafts movement.

■ By January 1909 the Gamble house was nearly ready for occupancy. The first pieces of furniture had arrived on January 8, 1909, and in the Greene and Greene office, the construction drawings for the final two masterworks—the Pratt and Thorsen houses—were scheduled for completion in early and late March respectively. The Blackers and the Fords were already occupying their houses. The Hall mill and the Lange shop were producing at full capacity. Henry Greene was carrying out the other commissions going through the office while deftly maintaining a firm hand on the extraordinary amount of work on the masterworks and construction in the field. Charles Greene was beginning to buckle under the stress and pressure of his enormous responsibilities compounded by his personal desire to immerse himself fully in the creation of more than four hundred individual designs for furniture and lighting fixtures alone. The brothers were at the peak of their career. With so many demands on their time and their energy, it is not surprising that they were unaware that the ultimate bungalows had separated them from the affordable commissions of the years from 1903 through 1906. Now, with their large houses, high standards, exacting demands, and seemingly unlimited budgets, they were gaining a reputation for being very costly and time-consuming, a reputation that would soon undermine their architectural practice.[5]

5. Further information on The Gamble House is found in the following publications:

Bosley, Edward R. "Greene and Greene, Gamble House." *Architecture in Detail Series*. London: Phaidon, 1992.

Ford, Edward R. "The Arts and Crafts Movement: The Greene Brothers and Their English Contemporaries, David B. Gamble House." *The Details of Modern Architecture*. Cambridge, Massachusetts/London, England: The MIT Press, 1990.

Jordy, William H. "Progressive and Academic Ideals at the Turn of the Twentieth Century." *American Buildings and Their Architects*, vol. 3. Garden City, New York: Doubleday, 1972.

Makinson, Randell L. "Trip to Epoch-Making Greene and Greene, Blacker House—Gamble House." *Global Architecture, GA Houses 2*. Japan: A.D.A.EDITA, Tokyo Co., Ltd., 1977.

Makinson, Randell L. "Greene and Greene, David B. Gamble House." *Global Architecture, GA Houses 2*. Japan: A.D.A.EDITA, Tokyo Co., Ltd., 1984.

Thomas, Jeanette A. *Images of the Gamble House, Masterworks of Greene and Greene*. University of Southern California: The Gamble House, Pasadena, California, 1989.

Wolf, Tobias Arthur, "The Integration of Architecture and Landscape in Greene and Greene's Gamble House." Master's thesis, Cornell University, 1993.

The king-post detail of the structural truss in the Gamble house third-floor attic was given the same attention accorded the interiors throughout

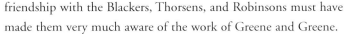

Charles M. Pratt House, 1909

Left, Charles M. Pratt house.

Below, the free-flowing plan of the Pratt house was nestled among the existing oak trees adjacent to a deep ravine on the fifteen-acre site. In this location, the Greenes were able to carry out a casual plan arrangement similar to their original plan proposed for the Gamble house the prior year.

Overleaf, Charles M. Pratt house in the foothills of the Ojai Valley.

The Pratt commission for a winter home in the Ojai Valley, a three-hour drive from Pasadena, came into the Greene office in early 1908 at a time when the Ford project was near completion, the Blacker house construction had just begun, and the Gamble house was preparing to break ground. Charles Millard Pratt, son of the cofounder of Standard Oil, remained in the family oil business throughout his life and served as president of the Pratt Institute. His wife, Mary Seamoor Morris, daughter of the governor of Connecticut, had become acquainted with Mrs. Blacker and her sister, Mrs. William R. Thorsen, while attending Vassar. The Pratts, known as the "lords of Long Island," owned a home consisting of 250 rooms on 1,000 acres on Long Island, but they had wintered in Pasadena for several years, staying at the Hotel Green, and their

friendship with the Blackers, Thorsens, and Robinsons must have made them very much aware of the work of Greene and Greene.

■ Their requirements for a modest winter cottage, which was to be called Casa Barranca, were very different from those of other clients. Pratt was a large shareholder in the Ojai Improvement Company that owned the Foothills Hotel, located on land adjacent to his own fifty-acre property and within walking distance of the Pratt homesite. Because of this, the Pratts intended to take most of their meals and do all of their entertaining at the hotel. With the house serving primarily as sleeping quarters, the criteria of the Pratt design was considerably less formal.

■ The sketch for the first plan, dated June 17, 1908, began as a simple L shape. However, as Charles began to respond to the rocky, undulating site, his imagination took off. Recalling the first plan for the Gamble house, the Pratt design angled in part to capture breezes and view, and made use of the curve and octagonal forms to give definition to the differing interior functions. In his first design, Charles hung a part of the house off the bluffs of the adjacent gorge, lifted the gentle gables of the roofs as he moved about the site, and contrasted the linear compositions of the terraces paved in tiles and brick with the curvilinear configuration of the natural stone retaining walls, creating lower glens and natural gardens along the precipice of the deep gorge.

■ The final plan was smaller: the wings were spread to embrace rear terraces; and the living room functioned as an all-purpose, flexible, irregular central space, handling entry, library, and fireside inglenook. The living room was also the principal connection between the two-story sleeping wing and the single-story dining, kitchen, and service wing.

■ The magnificent and lyrical plan spread its wings about the natural site, drew its axes and focal points from the mountain and canyon views, and gave order to its varying angles and curving elements by the strength and discipline of its structural system and imagery. It was distinctly different from any other Greene and Greene work, yet it was distinctly their own. Here there was the freedom to draw from the rugged terrain and vistas of an untamed land marked by differing species of plant materials and bold rock outcroppings that were the essence of the hot, arid California Ojai Valley. The casual but ordered exterior of the Pratt house showed a deep respect for the transitions between building and site.

■ Although the sensuous wooden interiors of Greene and Greene conveying the warmth and charm of an alpine ski lodge seemed at odds with the dry heat of the long summer season, somehow they were right. A popular favorite of the Greenes' designs, this tiny wooden structure, nestled beneath the powerful mountain range, belonged in Ojai. And in its planning it represented the freedom of form that Charles had attempted to capture at various times in his career. But this came at a very difficult period in his life. He was exhausted from the stress of work, and within a month of breaking ground, he departed for England, where he remained for the better part of a year, leaving the finishing designs and the construction to Henry.

■ Henry's creative hand was clearly evident in the final design. He converted windows to access doors between the main stair hall and the rear terrace, a highly significant move, for it was clear that the doors should have been a part of the original design. However, it was the linear composition that Henry designed for these doors that was cause for celebration. As though it were a painting by Mondrian, this pair of doors was a triumphant exercise in abstract composition and as much "Henry" as a portrait would have been. Henry's strength lay in his sensitive response to the mechanics of windows and doors—their structure, the hinging, the hardware needs—and his development of a carefully organized hierarchy of these linear elements.

■ Henry's designs for the exterior lanterns were equally straightforward and, again, enriched by virtue of his exquisite handling of the scale and proportion of the linear struts and planes of the brass fixtures so that no pattern seemed necessary in the diffused glass panels.

■ In each of these designs was a unity of spirit with the overall structure, allowing for the intricacy and fluidity of Charles's compositions to work with the highly sophisticated discipline of Henry's linearity.

■ The interiors of the Pratt house were magic. The low ceiling of the living room was intimate, juxtaposed in major contrast to the high ceiling of the relatively small dining room adjacent, one of the Greenes' very few uses of vertical space in their career. The living room was the virtual circulation center of the house, connecting the two wings and serving also as entry hall. Its rear wall opened immediately to the broad, partially covered rear terrace overlooking the canyon and the mountain range. The cabinets and lighting were enriched by the restraint and elegance of the design. In the dining room the verticality was emphasized by the long, octagonal lighting fixture suspended by leather straps and so positioned as to cast its down light specifically on the small dining table. Designed without leaves, this table was intended for the immediate family and served primarily as a breakfast table.

■ There were two master suites, complete with bath and sleeping porch—one on the lower level executed with plaster walls and ceiling and the other directly above, carried out exclusively in wood. In the upper suite, the rich board-and-batten paneling familiar to Greene designs wrapped into the ceiling and was given further character by the use of open timber trusses and the cant of the ceiling being clipped by the angle of the low roof rafters. At every turn and detail there was the softness of hand-rubbed Port Orford cedar blending with the rolled edges of the Douglas fir structural members.

■ There was less furniture in this smaller bungalow than in the other masterworks, but there was a classic quality about each piece; in addition, there were a number of designs that were never executed, including a daybed for the den, an upright piano and bench for the living room, and rolling tea cart for the dining room. Charles's design for the upholstered leather armchairs and the rocking chairs are quite possibly two of his most classic furniture designs. They both represent the Greenes' straightforward response to structural considerations, a careful analysis of the human form, the restraint of textural enrichments, and an extremely sensitive composition. In essence, they are beautiful examples of wooden sculpture.

■ The dining-room table had a charm that set it apart from all the other Greene tables. While it had the top form of the Japanese *tsuba*, or sword guard, as the principal shape, as in the Robinson and Gamble tables, it was the simplicity of the leg structure and the almost miniature quality of the scale that worked so well. The

Rear view of the Charles M. Pratt house.

*Above, dining room of the
Charles M. Pratt house.*

*Above right, this dining-room wall
sconce is one of the most classic of the
Greene and Greene style.*

gentle curve of the top contrasted nicely with the crisp, octagonal geometry of the living-room library table, which had been inlaid with an undulating line of thin silver in the long, narrow pulls for the two side drawers.

■ The most ornate piece of furniture in the Pratt collection was the upright writing desk for the living room. Its form was basically clean, with a subtle natural-mahogany grain and square ebony pegs. The two doors were edged in ebony. These framed Charles's abstract of gnarled California live oak trees that were carefully inlaid on the front and side panels in the various shades and colors of fruitwoods.

■ The Pratt furniture was completed and delivered to the house just before the summer of 1911, and a letter by Charles to Pratt on June 26, 1912, expressed his concern how the furniture had withstood its first summer weather.

■ The Pratts would call on the Greenes frequently over the years to make various additions to the house, many of which they had rejected in the earlier scheme. However, as time passed, they had seen the wisdom of the initial design. As Henry had finished the designs for the house and seen to its complete construction, the Pratts had complete confidence in him and spared little expense to make sure that anything he recommended was done. He inspected the property every few years and took charge of any maintenance needed either to the exterior or the interiors, often requiring an entire crew of Peter Hall's craftsmen to take residence on the property for as much as six to eight weeks.

*The low wood-paneled and timbered
ceiling of the Pratt living room is
accented by varying forms of the Greenes'
creative lighting vocabulary.*

The second-level master bedroom of the Pratt house is a symphony in wood, evoking the warmth and charm of a ski lodge yet completely at home in the hot arid foothills of the California Ojai Valley.

■ Correspondence revealed that there was also a cordial and warm relationship between the Pratts and Charles, with the brief exception of a difference of opinion dealing with the degree of personal supervision required on-site and the resulting costs. The nature of these differences was documented in the form of drafts of letters to Pratt from Charles in 1913, and these documents have provided an understanding of Charles's inner thoughts about his work and the sources and strengths of his convictions.

■ The Pratt house was a wooden house built woodenly. There was little here that had not been refined earlier within the language of the Greene style. However, the intimate scale of the spaces, the completeness of the wooden detail, and the appropriateness of some of the most exquisite furniture designs were here so simple and honest that it was one of the clearest and most unaffected of the brothers' best work. Perhaps this was the result of the greater equality of participation by both brothers, perhaps the freedom and nature of the owners' needs, or possibly the natural environment. Whatever the cause, this extraordinary craftsman bungalow was testimony to the genius of Charles and Henry Greene.

William R. Thorsen House, 1909

6. Correspondence with
   Steve Harold, Curator,
   Manistee County
   Historical Museum.

7. Theodore Turak,
   *William Le Baron
   Jenny, A Pioneer of
   Modern Architecture,*
   (Ann Arbor, Michigan:
   UMI Press, Architecture
   and Urban Design,
   Ann Arbor, Michigan.
   1967-86).

8. William Le Baron
   Jenny, architect
   (1832-07), was educated
   in Paris, began
   architectural practice in
   Chicago in 1868, and
   trained many young
   architects, including
   Martin, Roche, and
   William Holabird, all
   instrumental in the
   development of the
   Chicago skyscraper.

9. Early information on
   the Thorsen family
   courtesy Robert Judson
   Clark. Additional
   information may be
   found in Edward R.
   Bosley, Exhibition
   Catalogue, *Last of the
   Ultimate Bungalows,
   The William R.
   Thorsen House of
   Greene and Greene,*
   The Gamble House,
   USC, 1996.

William R. Thorsen, a brother-in-law of Robert Blacker, was the son of John Thorsen, who had incorporated the Stronach Lumber Company in Manistee, Michigan, in 1872 with John Canfield as president and his able and conservative young son, William Thorsen, as secretary and treasurer. Canfield had been a pioneer of Manistee, purchasing land formerly held by the Indians, and came to be regarded as the most successful and best financier lumberman in Michigan. Along with Blacker, the Canfields and Thorsens were the leading lumbermen in Manistee; in addition, all were involved in salt mines, shipping, and railroads.

■ The associations of these giants of the Michigan lumber industry were bonded even tighter by the marriage of Blacker and Thorsen to two of the Canfields' three daughters, Nellie and Carolyn Mae, who had attended Vassar together with the daughter of the governor of Connecticut, Mary Morris, who married Charles M. Pratt.[6]

■ The progressive architectural interests among these families was remarkable. William R. Thorsen's grandfather was a noted architect in Christiansand, Norway; William and John Canfield awarded the commission for their large Manistee residences to William Le Baron Jenny, distinguished for his design of the Home Insurance Building in Chicago, which was the first use in the United States of steel-frame building-construction technology.[7] Jenny had paved the way in Chicago for the advances in the evolution of the skyscraper by a variety of architects, including Holabird and Roach, who were engaged by Robert R. Blacker for his Manistee home.[8]

■ In the late 1890s, Thorsen, like Blacker, left his Manistee lumber business interests when the forests had been played out, finally settling in California. After first purchasing the Westside Lumber Company in Tuolomne, in California's historic Yosemite Valley, he acquired two extensive pear orchards, all of which he later administered from offices in downtown San Francisco. For two years beginning in 1908, the Thorsens rented houses located near the University of California in Berkeley from several traveling professors.[9] In late 1908 they acquired the modest corner property on Piedmont Avenue just two blocks off campus, and like the Blackers, engaged Greene and Greene as their architects. Charles Greene visited the site for the first time in October 1908, and the following month the Thorsens spent a week and a half with the

Blackers in Pasadena and conferred with Greene and Greene, during which time a second scheme for the Thorsen house was sketched by Henry Greene, dated November 16, 1908, a proposal nearly identical in concept with the final design.

■ At the beginning of 1909, the work in the Greene office and at the Hall shops was at a fever pitch, with at least twenty-four projects in process, including three of the five large masterworks along with their complements of lighting and furniture, and fifteen draftsmen busily developing the construction drawings for the designs of both Charles and Henry and completing the drawings for the Pratt and Thorsen houses.

■ Construction drawings for the Thorsen house were dated March 27, 1909. Once the construction contract had been awarded to Peter Hall and W. I. Ott (Hall & Ott, Contractors), Charles Greene departed for England with his wife and children.

■ The Thorsen site differed substantially from the sites of the four other masterworks and was considerably smaller than the Blackers' 5½ acres. The corner property sloped dramatically up from its west-facing frontage and was bounded on the north by the steep grade of the side street. Because of the busy traffic at the intersection and the small amount of land, Charles's initial sketch positioned the house along the two street frontages, creating a buffer to noise and embracing an internal rear yard for a modest garden. The plan, a fundamentally basic **L** shape, is given considerable variation by the very nature of the Greenes' personal style and by the varying grades and levels of the grounds, terraces, and interiors. This is a polished Southern California Shingle-style

William R. Thorsen's discomfort with the hanging lanterns in the Blacker house prompted the recessed stained-glass ceiling lighting in the living room. The forms of the mahogany library table, its unique detail, and the inlay work of the oval top ascribe its design to Henry Greene.

house in the foothills of Berkeley, vastly different from the eclectic traditions or rusticity then prevalent in the Berkeley Hills, where the exceptional works of Bernard Maybeck, Julia Morgan, and Louis Mullgardt, among others, were establishing their own presence.

■ Taking advantage of the topography, the design for the Thorsen house lifted the main floor high along Piedmont Avenue, allowing for a naturally lighted full basement and panoramic views of the entire Bay Region from both of the upper floors, including one through the straits that would be later connected by the Golden Gate Bridge. The entire massing of the house and the dramatic roof forms responded to the steep slope of the side street to the north. The resulting complex arrangement of gable roofs interacting with each other in varying relationships was one of the most dramatic and unique features of the design. The higher the rise, the farther each gable end was allowed to project, so that each roof became a great prow, reaching out to shelter the spaces below. From the second-floor gable, the slope continued along the side line of the property, fully sheltering the entire third floor and attic area and producing long overhangs from the far-reaching prows that now seemed to be protecting the complete 3½ stories of the north and south elevations. Slipping out from under these roof lines, the walk to the garage is sheltered by a timber bridge structure providing direct access from the second level of the house to the apartment over the garage. By virtue of its articulated timber vocabulary, blending of columns, corbel detail, fencing, gate, and expressed peg-and-strap joinery, this bridge structure was a powerful element in the overall mass, allowing light and air to flow through and around the house and garage. Here the scale and proportions were so skillfully handled that the entire bridge became a large, timbered symphony in wood.

■ Contrary to the other masterworks, little emphasis appears to have been placed upon the advantages of outdoor living. This may have been due to the Thorsens' wishes, the climatic conditions of the Bay Area, the site restraints or the combination of all three. There was, in fact, almost a pointed effort to divorce the living room from the garden by both the placement and enormous scale of the living-room fireplace and chimney. The plan did not encourage free movement in and out of the house nor even visual connection from window to garden. Here the relationships of the plan and spaces within the house reflected a more formal lifestyle than the bungalows of Southern California.

Living-room detail of the William R. Thorsen house. Grueby tiles, inlaid steel, mahogany paneling, and stained-glass lanterns provided Carrie Thorsen with a Greene and Greene interior like that of her sister and brother-in-law, Nellie and Robert Blacker.

All the details of the Thorsen interior contribute to the refined craftsman quality of the home: the harmony of line and soft patina of mahogany woods; ebony spline and peg detail; finger-lap joinery; leather seating; the subtle iridescence of clear glass; the luster of mother-of-pearl inlay; and the glazes of Fulper art pottery.

Detail of the dining room fireplace and inlaid side chair of the Thorsen house.

10. Letter to William R. Thorsen from his sister, Mrs. L. W. B. Purchas, sent during construction of the Thorsen house, Documents Collection, College of Environmental Design, UCB.

■ Evidently the Thorsen house was still on Charles's mind when he went to England, for when he returned he brought back a sketch for two long curving stairways sweeping up from the corners of the lot toward a mutual landing from which more formal steps arose. These led to an entry terrace sheltered by a low gabled roof and flanked by two brick platforms, upon which sat two of the square planters the Greenes had designed for the Gamble house, except that here they were carried out in a light terra-cotta clay as opposed to the grey of those in Pasadena.

■ In direct response to the sun conditions of the Bay Region, the Greenes here made greater use of large panes of plate glass, allowing light into the interior and opening it to the wide range of spectacular views. To do this, they featured two second-level roof terraces off the primary bedrooms, with angled prowlike railings that added to the nautical theme pervading the house and reflecting the Thorsen family's interest in sailing and the sea.

■ This was an extremely bold composition of masses on a steep and modest site. The house, although acknowledging the differences from the Southern California environment but carried out in the Greenes' distinct Southern California style, continued to be a strong and imaginative Arts and Crafts expression in the hill area of Berkeley. While very unlike its indigenous northern neighbors, it seemed to fit in perfectly. This was just what Carrie Thorsen wanted, a wooden house like that of her sister, Nellie Blacker, and her brother-in-law, Robert, on whom she frequently called for advice.

■ There were, however, differences between the Thorsen and Blacker houses, a few of which came about late in the construction of the house and quite possibly as a result of a comment in a letter of December 17, 1909, from William Thorsen's sister, Mrs. L. W. B. Purchas, following her visit to the Blacker house. She wrote:

I find the outside of the house and grounds very attractive—but my impressions after moving through the various rooms was that the architect has let his fancy run riot in wood. There is so much wood about the outside that when one finds oneself encased in wooden forms, wooden walls, wood ceilings, wood floors, wood furniture, wood fixtures for light—well, one has a little bit of the feeling of a spider scrambling from one cigar box to another. . . . I find the hall is excellent. . . . the porches—portecochere etc. most attractive. . . . All Mr. Greene's woodwork is a delight for the softness of its finish, it is like fresh butter . . . so soft are the surfaces and corners. . . . Don't let

the Greenes light your rooms with lanterns of stained glass. They are very artistic in shape and coloring perceived in the daylight but as points of illumination they are rather negative and one finds oneself in a "dim religious" light everywhere in the house. . . .[10]

The impact of this letter had little to do with the final designs of the Thorsen house, as its construction was already well along. Mr. Thorsen had his own feelings about the hanging lanterns. He disliked those suspended by leather straps in the Blacker house and limited them in his own house to the entry hall, having the Greenes change those in the living room to flush ceiling lighting, although in stained glass, which did nothing to elevate his sister's feelings for the amount of light produced.

■ Though fewer in number than in the other masterworks, the Thorsen furniture was superb, particularly Charles's designs for the dining room. There was such a clean, straightforward discipline to the basic forms of the sideboard and the server that the designs could as well be representative of contemporary work. Charles was so clear about the clean, progressive character of the sideboard that the inlays desired by Mrs. Thorsen to emulate those in the Blacker pieces were separated from the overall design of the cabinet by their placement, like a painting, on the door panels, which were framed in ebony. A late design was that for the remarkable living-room library table, distinguished from Charles's other Thorsen pieces by the different nature of materials and the dimension of its inlay and structural detail. Consequently it is believed to be one of the several furniture designs of Henry Greene. Several years later, the work of each of the brothers could be identified in the designs for fireplace andirons and fire screens for the Thorsen home.

■ The Thorsen furniture, unlike any of the Greenes' other decorative arts, was crafted on-site in the basement room beneath the dining room by Jack Peterson, also a craftsman trained in Scandinavia, though not believed to have been formerly associated with Peter Hall's Southern California shops.

■ The Thorsen house was to be the last of the Greenes' wooden masterworks. There would be other highly articulated designs, but none that would approach the spectrum of land, building, interiors, and furnishing designs of the years 1907 to 1909. Charles's fatigue and departure for England early in 1909, just as construction was beginning on the Pratt and Thorsen houses, foretold far more about the future of the firm and Charles's personal interests than anyone understood at the time. He was ready to move in other directions, explore new building materials that offered new challenges, and return to his interests in writing and painting. And he was also disenchanted with the growing number of bad emulations of their own work, the poor quality of such imitation beginning to tarnish the integrity of their own creative style. The most revealing source of Charles's inner feelings about the business, his architecture, and his artistic presence was set out in the drafts of two letters written in 1913 to Charles M. Pratt in response to charges for furniture, questions about the necessity for Charles's personal on-site supervision, and the subsequent costs for such personal attention. In one letter dealing with the itemization of costs for furniture and fixtures, Charles attempted to shift the blame to others, saying:

All of this figuring was done by our accustomed rules and by the office. I did none of it. These figures prove themselves. Nor is there a discrepancy of any moment between them and mine as I gave them to you in my last letter. . . . I know that the items of the list were incomplete contrary to your order as I understood it. My brother and I had some words about the way the list was to be made out. It was made according to our usual custom, not as I ordered it. . . . If you believe that I tried to deceive you I declare now and always that I had no such intention. . . . I still think that your sense of fairness must outweigh the contempt you might have for my business ability.[11]

Certainly Charles was not a businessman and had no interest in those aspects of the practice. His art had little patience for the mundane aspects of professional responsibility. His reference to "words with my brother" and the shift of the fault to the office were indicative of his frustrations with such responsibilities, of his unhappiness with the architectural scene in Pasadena in the early years of the second decade of the 1900s, and of the resurgence of his desire to pursue other artistic endeavors. His second letter to Pratt, also a draft, illuminated his deep belief in his own value:

11. Handwritten draft of letter, undated (about 1913), by Charles Greene to Charles M. Pratt, Greene and Greene Library, The Gamble House, USC.

Of the trips I made to Nordhoff [Ojai] last summer—two were for the servants room addition—one for some trouble about the roof and the other was for color matching. The other seven trips were for the walls and grounds and were not for a day but for several days each. I did not think it advisable to make plans of the walls and terraces because it would be impossible to take advantage of the natural contours and trees, etc. So . . . personally directed the work and carefully selected and placed the largest stones to harmonize with the surroundings. In some cases I made corrections in the work done when I was not on the grounds.

Of course this could have been done cheaper, in the common way, and by sending a man from the office instead of myself. But does not the result justify the expense?

. . . I can not find anything to reproach myself with nor have I any regrets. This to my mind approaches the ideal of a transaction between artist and patron, and would be near ideal if you could but share my view.

Art reduced to a commodity of course can not argue so. . . . But living art never can be so reduced. It must have become a curio in the hands of a dealer before it can be bartered without injury to the art.

This is one good reason why living art scarcely ever can compete with the old. Once exploited it ceases to be art. You say that you have never before paid so high a price for this kind of work: to which I reply that you misjudge the character of mine. [On the back side, Charles has reworded this to read "to which I reply that I believe that you are mistaken."] In other words, is the comparison fair? Knowing what I do of the architectural practice of today I can not be very far wrong. Furthermore there is no one to my knowledge who has the temerity to limit the number of their commissions to a personal supervision.

It is too much to expect that anyone may see the excellence of this kind of thing in a few days. The work itself took months to execute and [the] best years of my life went to develop this style. . . . My plea is not so much for the fact as for the principle—not so much for the artist as that art may find expression.

I do not claim for my management the strictest economy and I believe that I understand how you must feel when for the greater part of your life you have laboured to bring to perfection, the greatest of enterprises; how those great undertakings could only be perfected by a systematic and rigid restraint. How no saving could be too petty and order must be absolute.

*Entry hall window of
the William R. Thorsen house.*

My work is none of this. It is impossible that it should be so. Art and Commerce are divided and must ever be. . . . If one can afford to have these things, does it not argue as well for you as for Art that one should have them? I do not speak on my own authority alone as to the intrinsic value of my work, though I could never have produced it without knowing that. But do you know what a former President of the American Institute says of it and also connoisseurs who travel the world over in search of the rare and beautiful [most likely here referring to the visit from Charles Robert Ashbee]. I can not find reason for flattery in this, because for the most part they are unknown to me, or of only slight acquaintance. This sounds a bit egotistical. . . .

Into your busy life I have sought to bring what lay in my power of the best that I could do for Art and for you. How I wish I had the power to look into your soul to more fully understand not what you think but what you feel. . . . I have known many people that love the beautiful but it is beyond their reach. For you all these things are possible and, believe me, I have given what I could personally because I thought you would like it and because I felt sure that you would, in the end, appreciate.[12]

C. SUMNER GREENE

While it is not yet known whether these two drafts were ever sent to Pratt, Charles provided in these letters an insight into his very intimate thoughts and the depth of his belief in his art. At the same time, he revealed his personal insecurities and vacillated between blaming others at one moment and then accepting full responsibility at another.

■ One thing is clear: Charles was absolutely right on the necessity of an on-site design and supervision of elements that related to the topography of the site and, when necessary, the correction of elements done by others. Without that absolute control and the supervision of both Charles and Henry in the execution of their work, the so-called Greene and Greene style and their masterworks could never have been achieved. That work was and is, as Charles later titled one of his writings, architecture as a fine art.[13]

12. Ibid.

13. C. Sumner Greene, "Architecture As a Fine Art," *The Architect,* vol. XIII (April 1917).

145

PRELUDES TO CHANGE
1909-1917

There was a refreshing quiet about Henry Greene's designs. The thoughtful restraint, the logic, and the sensitive attention he brought to both the organization of plans and the three-dimensional development of his houses link his independent work to the modern movement. He was generally admired, more for the exquisite scale and proportions of his linear compositions than for the sinuous lines in his many freehand sketches. These sketches, particularly those in soft pencil, reveal a relaxed confidence, which allowed him to express the humor and passion that frequently surfaced in the company of family and friends. Henry was a quiet, soft-spoken man respected both for his work and for his personal integrity. He also had a particular sense of order and composition, which was an essential element of the Greene and Greene style and of all the work emanating from the office.

■ He called his brother, Charles, the artist. Indeed, in his mannerisms, his dress, his long flowing hair and his temperament, Charles presented the consummate image of the young visionary architect whose charm persuaded some clients to let him soar with new ideas. Henry, with his suit and tie and punctual decorum, provided the balance necessary for a successful practice. Without question, it is the yin and the yang of the brothers that imbued their joint projects with such undeniable spirit. Even in their later years, when Henry continued the practice in Pasadena and Charles in Carmel, they constantly drew upon each other's talents and expert knowledge.

■ Henry not only kept a firm hand on the five masterworks moving through the office between 1907 and 1909 and on the large amount of work still in process from previous years, but also assumed the responsibility for new commissions after Charles departed for England. A great number of projects were coming in, and while some did not progress beyond the drawing board, they represented a wide variety of designs. Henry was also often called upon by former clients wanting additions and alterations to their homes, as well as by architect G. Lawrence Stimson requesting designs for partial interiors for a number of his residential commissions within the Oaklawn tract and elsewhere in Pasadena. These designs for entry halls, stairwells, and living- and dining-room spaces were probably turned over to draftsmen in the office with occasional overview from Henry. His primary concern was for the new designs for Spinks, Crow, Bradley, Drake, Anthony, Neumeister, Smith, Blacker, Merrill, Spalding, and Nathan Bentz. Of these, the Spinks, Crow, and Anthony houses offer scholars the best opportunity to examine his work.

Mrs. Margaret B. S. Clapham Spinks House, 1909

The house for Judge William Ward Spinks and his wife entered the office in mid-1907, but somehow construction was delayed until April of 1909, just as Charles was leaving for England. This house, another of Henry's basic two-story rectangular designs, was distinguished by the grace and elegance of its sweeping but restrained landscaping. It was situated a block from the Blacker house in the rolling Oak Knoll neighborhood, set substantially farther back than its neighbors, and screened from Hillcrest Avenue by a tall stand of greenery. Modest clinker-brick pedestals are all that mark the narrow entry drive. Once inside this brief break in the lush greenery of the street frontage, a vast gently rolling meadow comes into view, then at the far end of the lawn, the house. Its strong symmetry is greatly enhanced by the playful freedom with which Henry dealt asymmetrically with the recesses, cantilevers, and structural and textural considerations. Bands of casement windows, covered porches, and open balconies catch the breezes, overlook the gardens, and offer a multiplicity of views.

■ This is a house and garden composed of simple materials. It is not precious, yet it is one of the firm's most successful achievements in establishing a relationship between structure and surroundings. Within the Oak Knoll neighborhood the Spinks house has found its own privacy, its own quiet land, its personal vista, and has borrowed its own portion of the San Gabriel Valley for the enjoyment of its occupants.

Dr. S. S. Crow House, 1909
Edward S. Crocker House & Garden, 1911

*Dr. S. S. Crow house, 1909/Edward S.
Crocker house and garden, 1911.
Designed entirely by Henry Greene while
Charles was in England, this sensitive
and restrained design is one of the finest
houses carried out by the firm.*

Just two blocks from the Spinks house, the grid pattern of the
Pasadena street system obstructed views from the Crow house and
challenged Henry's abilities with a different set of determinants.
Despite the madness in the office brought on by the absence of
Charles and a tremendous amount of work, Henry managed to
create an elegant little house, his own particular masterwork. It was
a jewel. The roof lifted gently, overlapped, and adjusted to the
internal needs as quietly as the soft roll of the broad green lawn
upon which the house rested. Its street elevation was unsurpassed.
It was all the more elegant because of the restraint exercised at
every turn. Broad banks of clear-glass French doors opened to the
covered front terrace yet were secondary to the elevation of the
house. The entire character and charm comes from the carefully
studied relationships between the beauty of the roof forms, from
the straightforward expression of the series of dual column supports
of the broad front terrace, from the ever-changing shadows that
bring life and constant variety throughout the day, and from
Henry's exquisite mastery of scale and proportion.

■ To contrast with the articulation and rhythm of the expressed
timber and rafter detail, Henry sited the house to allow broad
raised lawns to surround the two street elevations, and thus
provided a serene environment within the normal grid pattern of
the residential neighborhood. This was a very modest, extremely
interesting and sophisticated bungalow. Henry's plan was another
variation of the Greenes' courtyard studies, only here the central
space was narrowed to serve only as a visual garden parallel to the
wide sunroom connecting the various spaces of the bedroom wing.
Overhead he composed the largest skylight of the Greenes' career, a
magnificent linear composition drawing directly from structural
needs and creating a carefully disciplined hierarchy of wood and
stained glass. The simple U shape of the plan placed the living and
dining rooms across the front, with one wing for pantry, kitchen,
porch, and maid's room, and the other large wing accommodating
the sunroom, two bedrooms, a large dressing room, and a sleeping
porch—an arrangement seemingly intended for two people with
a servant and a guest room.

■ One of the most intriguing features was the change in the floor
levels of the living and dining areas. Between two banks of
bookcases, three risers ascended to the dining level, maintaining
intimacy by a common ceiling height. Floating across this opening

Henry Greene allowed the structural integrity of the support elements for the sunroom skylight of the Crow/Crocker house to guide his careful linear composition.

1. Author's interviews with Leonard W. Collins, circa 1958.

was a cap, which cantilevered over the structure, from which to hang draperies. This closed off the lower dining area from sight yet allowed the upper portion of the room to continue through. It was unusual and typical of Henry's inventiveness.

■ The origins of the Crow house and the Crocker additions by Greene and Greene have long been in question. The project for Dr. S. S. Crow came into the office as Job. No. 245 in mid-1909, with construction drawings dated September 7, 1909. Building Permit No. 7867 was issued to Dr. S. S. Crow on October 5, 1909, with A. C. Brandt as contractor and Greene and Greene as architects. The sewer connection was made to the completed structure on October 9, 1909. The following year Robert R. Blacker briefly considered purchasing the Crow house for his siblings but they preferred another location. Whether Dr. Crow ever took occupancy has also been a matter of question. However, on January 21, 1911, slightly over a year after the house was completed,

the *Pasadena Star* published a story that discussed the sale of "the handsome Oak Knoll bungalow owned by Dr. S. S. Crow to E. S. Crocker, of Fitchburg, Mass. The consideration involved in this sale is $25,000. . . . This property is magnificently improved with shrubs and lawns. It also has a garage and servants' quarters. Mr. Crocker will make his home here."

■ What confused the issue of occupancy was a Grant Deed for the sale of the property by Dr. Crow to Edward S. Crocker, dated January 17, 1911, for the amount of $100, the same amount paid by Crocker to John and Margaret Wadsworth on January 30, 1911, for the two vacant lots to the rear of the Crow property. Regardless, the house as documented above was designed and built for Dr. Crow and later sold to Edward S. Crocker.

■ A close study of the plan reveals a very specific living arrangement indicative of a client with every intention of taking up permanent residence. That Dr. Crow placed the house on the market within months of completion suggests a dramatic change in his plans. Leonard W. Collins, chief draftsman in the Greene office, recalled in an interview that the plan was intended for a person confined to a wheelchair.[1] This has led to speculation that the sale of the house was possibly the result of a death in the family.

■ Following the purchase of the house in 1911, Edward Crocker immediately engaged Henry to make some changes, and over the years came back to him for the addition of a guest house, a teahouse, and extensive landscaping. In 1927 he requested brief sketches for a proposed second floor to the street facade of the house, but, fortunately, this project went no further than the drawing board. Henry's quick sketch likely convinced Crocker of the error of such a proposal.

Earle C. Anthony House, 1909

The Anthony commission had come into the office about the time Charles left for England in early 1909, and, again, the house was primarily the work of Henry, although on his return Charles did design the leaded-art-glass windows as well as some hanging lighting fixtures that, fortunately, were never carried out. These windows, however, represent some of the best art glass of the Greenes' career.

■ Anthony, whose interests were in automobile sales and radio broadcasting, had selected a site on Wilshire Boulevard at the corner of Berendo Street, on the outskirts of downtown Los Angeles. The Anthony house related more to the Greenes' larger

Poinsettia window detail from the Earle C. Anthony house, 1909. Built in Los Angeles, the house was moved to Beverly Hills in 1923. at which time Henry Greene handled the re-siting, alterations, and the landscape design.

bungalows, and was more complex in its exterior configuration and in its detail and rooflines than the Crow house. However, unlike the masterworks, its interior room arrangement was much more in line with Henry's interpretation of the relaxed Southern California lifestyle. But he had misjudged Mrs. Anthony's taste. Soon after the house was finished, she grew disenchanted with the bungalow character, and because of the friendship that had developed between her husband and Charles during the Packard showroom project, she engaged him, rather than Henry, to modify the upstairs sitting room in 1913 and to make other alterations, including painting portions of the wood detail to lighten the interiors.

■ Not long after the house was finished, commercial development created "the Miracle Mile" of Wilshire Boulevard, which replaced the single-family residential neighborhood. In 1923 the house was purchased by silent-film star Norman Kerry, who moved it to Beverly Hills and commissioned Henry to handle its redesign. The original site had been a tight corner parcel that prompted a linear composition of the floor plan, but the new lot was irregular in shape and covered considerably more land. Henry expanded the gardens, rearranged the garage facilities, and created a high degree of privacy with high sweeping walls of richly darkened clinker bricks.

Earle C. Anthony Automobile Showroom, 1911

Although architects Parkinson and Bergstrom had designed the basic structural shell of the automobile showroom, Anthony, whose house had just been completed, turned to Greene and Greene for the æsthetic features of the public rooms.

■ Although by the time he left for England Charles felt he had taken the wooden bungalow style to its peak, upon his return he was excited at the prospect of designing the detail, entrance, and interiors for the Packard showroom in downtown Los Angeles. His designs were unprecedented and unique, expressed in molded plaster, inlaid tiles, wrought and cast iron, wood and an array of dissimilar motifs that somehow hung together in spite of their great diversity. Charles made drawings depicting the design and of the three-dimensional relief of each tile. The relationships of the various patterns he devised were then elaborated in drawings and in watercolor renderings that illustrated for the craftsmen both the arrangements and the color combinations he desired. Pencil sketches went back and forth in the development of the tiles with notes such as "a little deeper," referring to the relief detail. The great octagonal columns in the center of the showroom, as well as portions of the balcony and ceiling pattern inlay, were carried out in these tiles, with the capitals of the columns in molded plaster, remnants of traditional staff work.

■ In the ceiling, executed in plaster relief and radiating out from the capitals, were fan-shaped sunbursts that, for Greene and Greene, was their only reference to the later Art Deco period. The teakwood screens and the wooden partitions for sales personnel were remarkably contemporary for their time. Large plaster lighting fixtures, octagonal in form and inset with more of the tiles, were suspended from the high ceilings on long wrought-iron rods and suffused the ceiling detail with a soft light. Charles was now exploring new materials and new techniques, and the Anthony showroom was an opportunity for just such a venture. Some of the most unusual features were the wrought- and cast-iron railings and screens, which evoked the imagery of the Greenes' earlier interpretations of oriental life and their interest in Japanese *tsuba* forms. Their execution in sand molds brought about a soft sculptural quality and texture unprecedented in their earlier work.

■ Charles had found the Pacific Ornamental Iron Company of Los Angeles to carry out much of the detail work on the entry canopy and its sweeping Art Nouveau character. This fortuitous

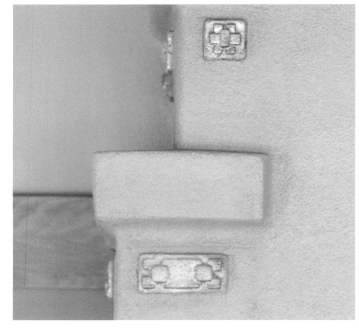

Above left, interiors for the Earle C. Anthony automobile showroom, 1911, Los Angeles. The building was designed by architects Parkinson and Bergstrom.

Above right, Charles's interior designs for the Anthony automobile showroom included custom tiles, most likely manufactured by the Pewabic Tile Company from Charles's detailed drawings and sketches. Charles used examples of the various designs of the tile in the remodeling of his own home the same year.

association inspired him to go forward with the designs for andirons, fire screens, and fire fenders for the Blacker and Thorsen houses in the years immediately following.

■ Several years later Anthony was upset by Charles's purchase of a Hudson automobile, and expressed his displeasure by turning to Bernard Maybeck for the remarkable addition to the Los Angeles showroom and the building and interiors for the large San Francisco Packard agency. But following the reorganization of the Greene firm in 1921, Anthony returned to Henry Greene for the design of his mother-in-law's house.

■ Mrs. Anthony's reaction to the craftsman qualities in the Anthony home was an early clue to changing tastes as the public turned from the earthy principles of the Arts and Crafts movement to the traditional designs that had previously been identified with affluence. The Greenes, however, were creative artists who had found an architectural vocabulary with which to express their own particular art form, and they were confident that this art form was the ultimate expression of the bungalow style. Moreover, they had been spoiled by wealthy clients who had made it easy for them to demand only the best in materials and workmanship, and had been equally spoiled by their freedom to be very selective in accepting commissions. And in 1909 there was still so much work remaining on both the masterworks and their furnishings, they were kept too busy to sit back and analyze or even notice the changing tastes of the public.

New Directions, 1910

As the new decade opened, Henry continued to produce wooden designs for a series of smaller commissions that came into the office, while Charles was very busy with the execution of furnishings for the five masterworks. But in spite of the intensity of his work, Charles's creative juices would not allow him to pass up several major commissions that he believed called for a differing palette of materials on which his imagination could draw. Several of these new commissions never progressed beyond the drawing board. Only the designs for Mortimer Fleishhacker and the Culbertson sisters were constructed and today exhibit the extraordinarily rich character of the new direction of the firm's work.

The John Lambert House Project, 1910

The first major departure from the wooden shingle-clad style was an elaborate project for John Lambert designed early in 1910 for a large and prominent corner site on Millionaires' Row along South Orange Grove Avenue. The house was to have a stucco dash-coat exterior finish similar to the early experiments on the Robinson house. Its forms responded to the plasticity of the material, and the overall character was softer, more sculptured and less linear than the Greenes' earlier work. The roof construction and the use of heavy timbers in the porch structure were, however, unmistakably part of their previous vocabulary. The very large scale of this house was accentuated by drawing the service wing out along Orange Grove Avenue, providing a handsome street elevation and sheltering the rear gardens from public view. Vast terraces flanked the dining and living rooms to the rear and along the side street elevation, and great retaining walls and planter areas reached out from the structure into the gardens. It was one of the firm's most expensive designs to date—and the principal factor in the decision not to build. Perhaps the Greenes had gone too far, had expected too much, had refined their art to such a high level that costs had become prohibitive. Although the Lambert design was never carried into construction, the mental vision of this magnificent structure was nevertheless exciting.

■ With fewer and fewer commissions coming in, Greene and Greene could no longer afford to be so selective, but there was still considerable activity in the office. The year 1911 was the most productive and diverse period of these transitional years. But Charles was discontented. He was appalled by the inferior quality of the reproductions of the firm's work by other architects and builders. And he had changed his own priorities since his return from England but still refused to sacrifice his principles. Fine materials were becoming increasingly hard to get. Also, with the coming of the income tax, he predicted the end of quality construction and doubted that clients would be willing to pay for his kind of work. His long-standing interest in the missions was rekindled, and he was rapidly moving toward the establishment of his own individual identity.

■ Henry was more willing than Charles to deal with the changing attitudes of the public. He found new challenges fascinating. Lesser budgets called for inventive ideas, and he approached each new opportunity with the same energy that had always been a part of the firm's dynamics. He was highly respected as a dedicated professional and in 1911 was appointed by Mayor William Thum, along with Myron Hunt, Elmer Grey, and Frederick L. Roehrig, to formulate the first city "code of building procedures," a document that later was adopted as the formal building law of the City of Pasadena. It was an interesting grouping of architects, inasmuch as Greene and Greene lost a number of earlier competitions and clients to Roehrig and within a very few years Hunt would replace the Greenes as the architect of choice with his popular Spanish Colonial Revival style.

John Lambert residence project, 1910. This was the first of three large house designs by Charles Greene following his return from England. Feeling he had carried his wooden style to the fullest, these new designs explored other materials; however, their scale and escalated costs allowed for the construction of only the Cordelia Culbertson house, 1911. This sculptural design for South Orange Grove Avenue in Pasadena would have been a magnificent addition to the Greene and Greene legacy.

RESIDENCE FOR JOHN LAMBERT, ESQ. AT PASADENA, CALIFORNIA.
GREENE & GREENE, ARCH'TS. 215-31 BOSTON BLDG. PASADENA, CALIFORNIA.
SHEET Nº 5.   MAR. 11ᵗʰ 1910.

FRONT OR WEST ELEVATION
Scale—one eighth inch equals one foot.

Previous page,
Cordelia A. Culbertson house, 1911.

Above, Charles Greene's marble urns for
the entrance of the Culbertson sisters'
house were designed for its second owner,
Mrs. Francis F. Prentiss, for whom he
and Henry carried out many additions
to the furnishings and grounds
throughout the 1920s.

The only one of the large commissions representing Charles's new directions to be built in Pasadena was the large home for the three maiden sisters of James A. Culbertson. Although from the street view the design was modest, this house was one of the largest and most extensive of the firm's designs and cost nearly $200,000—three times the cost of the Gamble house and twice the amount of the Blacker.

■ Cordelia, Kate, and Margaret Culbertson selected a site directly across from the Blacker grounds in the Oak Knoll development. It sloped away from the street and offered views of the canyon to the rear and beyond to the San Gabriel Mountains. They wanted a one-story house that would appear quite modest from the street, but they did not want bedrooms on the ground level. Charles responded with a courtyard plan form, taking every advantage of the sloping site. The north, or rear, wing contained the bedrooms, which were on the main level of the house yet were sixteen feet above ground level. The street, or south, wing encompassed the living, entry, dining, and kitchen functions, and belied the large scale of the estate. Connecting these two wings on the west were servant's and guest rooms. The east edge of the large central courtyard was defined by a long pergola of white wisteria. The frontal wings and the garden court stepped down to allow for the mountain vistas from the front of the property and from the garden court.

■ In response to the fall of the site, a large loggia was placed under the sleeping wing and opened to the panorama of the extensive formal gardens developed in the lower glen at the rear of the property. These gardens revealed the influence of the elaborate imagery that Charles had captured on film or in watercolors during his trip to southern Europe in 1909. The classical formality of the design was softened by the sculptural details, which seemed to flow from the walls of the lower fountain. This had been crafted while the gunite was still wet, the texture of the cement gun application providing an added textural fluidity. From the Pewabic tile details of the small octagonal fountain on the entry axis of the garden court, water reappears in the two-inch Grueby tile chases that cascade down the splayed stairways to the lower reflecting pool. Gunite was also chosen for the walls around the property, sprayed over a woven-wire reinforcing mesh with concrete carved out in Charles's desired pattern. Even the gates were crafted with the blown concrete. The green Ludivici roofing tiles were given variation by differing shades and colors of glaze, which were also

The courtyard of the Cordelia A.
Culbertson house featured a tile fountain
of iridescent Pewabic tiles.

used on the garden structures and the shelters over gateways. The roof tiles clearly reflect Charles's interests in the oriental arts and, with the exception of the Oaklawn portals and waiting station, further distanced this work from the firm's earlier roofing materials. Subtle overlapping gables and voids bring a careful sculptural quality to the roof forms, responding to the high portion of the bedroom ceilings, which seem to reach high into the attic to capture morning and early afternoon light and allow air to flow in above the two long galleries that separate the bedrooms from the inner garden court.

■ Nowhere did Charles leave a detail of this house, its furnishings, or its garden to chance. This was his opportunity to explore another style regardless of cost. The interiors were what he had wished for the John Lambert project on Millionaires' Row. There were no natural woods except in the furniture, and the forms emerging from the plaster were soft and fluid. Some walls were covered in fabric. Wood-trim detail was sculpted and painted as though it were the multi-lacquered finish of a Rolls Royce. Throughout there was a distinct hierarchy, a highly sophisticated unity, and yet each space had its own unmistakable character. The Culbertson sisters worked closely with Charles and in 1912 sent him to New York to select additional furnishings to be complementary to those of his design. While there he also purchased lighting fixtures, wall fabrics, and a variety of accessories.

■ In an article he wrote for the March 1914 issue of the *Pacific Coast Architect,* Charles revealed a far more tolerant attitude toward furnishings of the interiors than in earlier days:

The furniture of the hall consists of two tall backed chairs of very dark crotch mahogany, inlaid with Koa, lilac roots and Vermilion. This design is a delicate band with twining wild roses. There is a large case or wardrobe of the corresponding design and material. Also two smaller tables at each side of the opening to the living room. The floor covering is Bohemian hand tufted rugs in shades of blue, with a touch of soft dull gold after a Chinese pattern. The same is in the living room.

Above, the lower gardens of the Culbertson sisters' house provided Charles Greene the opportunity to express ideas he had carried in his mind since his honeymoon trip to southern Europe and England in 1901. Subdivision of the property in the 1950s preserved only the upper stair and railing.

Right, two-inch Grueby tile chases along each wrought-iron rail, allow water from the courtyard fountain to trickle down the stairways to the reflecting pond of the lower garden. European tiles and examples of ceramic copings that Charles had found were inserted in abstract composition into the soft, sculptural, undulating surfaces of the gunite garden rails and columns.

Right, entry hall of the Cordelia Culbertson house displays the five paintings Charles Greene carried out for the upper walls for the second owner, Mrs. Francis F. Prentiss, circa 1918.

The living room furniture is of the same material, but slightly different design from the hall. The chairs and two couches are covered with silk brocade, black and gold. . . . The walls of both rooms are covered with linen velour specially designed for hangings. The color of this and the woodwork is something near café au lait, but being changeable, it harmonizes well with the rugs and tones with the dull gold. There is a large desk table with a dull black marble top, delicately golden veined. There is a bookcase and a secretary, both with glass doors. A cut design of roses suggests the inlaid design of the hall pieces. . . . The curtains and bandeaux are of the same brocade as the covering of the furniture.

Discussing the furniture for the dining room, he continued:

This furniture is of mahogany, but lighter and warmer than that of the hall and living room. The center table is round and has simple ribbon inlay in the top. . . . The serving table and sideboard have tops of numidian marble, to match the panel in the mantel.

Further in the article Charles discusses the furniture purchased for portions of the house, some of which included Queen Anne carved-walnut chairs and settees, lacquered chairs, secretary, and other pieces of the same period. In his final paragraph he states very clearly that the furniture and the fittings of the Culbertson house were either selected or designed and executed by the architects.

■ Between 1912 and 1916, the sisters continued to call upon the Greenes for additions to the estate, including another pergola, garden storage structures, another fountain, lamps, vases, and other furnishings. Enthusiastic as the sisters were, the project began to overwhelm them, and in 1917 the property was sold. For a brief time the three ladies considered a new and smaller design by the Greenes, and Charles, who was now planning to move permanently to Carmel, offered them his house. Finally, however, they purchased the 1906 Bolton house, engaging Henry to make alterations for their occupancy.

Culbertson/Allen/Prentiss House

The purchase of this Culbertson house in 1917 by Mrs. Dudley P. Allen of Cleveland, Ohio, assured the involvement of both Charles and Henry for another two decades. Immediately after the purchase, Mrs. Allen met with Charles in Carmel to discuss alterations and additions. She was completely taken by the design and wished to contribute and enhance the original vision of both Charles and the Culbertson sisters. Charles probably brought up some of the items he had not yet been able to accomplish, for he began work immediately on the five murals to be hung on the high upper walls of the entry hall.

■ Mrs. Allen also purchased an additional one and one-half acres to the east of the house and more land across the canyon to the rear to prevent others from building and thus obstructing her view of the San Gabriel Mountains and engaged landscape architect Charles Gibbs Adams to develop these new gardens. Additional fencing was needed to surround the nearly five and one-half acres of her new estate, prompting several neighbors to commission the Greenes to continue these specially designed fences around their own properties.

■ Within weeks of purchasing the Culbertson sisters' house, Mrs. Allen wed Francis F. Prentiss, also of Cleveland, and under this name continued to commission furnishings for the Cordelia Culbertson house, which she had named Il Paradiso. Throughout the 1920s she called on both Henry and Charles for various designs. In either instance, the brothers communicated constantly during the Prentiss work and once again dealt with the issue of costs. Charles's letter of February 15, 1928, to Mrs. Prentiss provides another glimpse of the man and his perception of his art:

I am both sorry and pained to know that you are dissatisfied with the cost of this year's work. Speaking of estimates, it seems to me that you do not know, or you have forgotten that your house and all in it were completed without an estimate and exceeded all expectation. But your discriminating taste singled it out from many others; won't you believe that this was the reason? It seems plain to me.

There is nothing reckless or extravagant about the work, only more than ordinary care and the persistent will to make it beautiful. No artist can figure original work for only one set of objects, even the factory multiplies sets till the original cost is only a fraction of the cost of each set sold.

Colored-pencil cartoons by Charles Greene were designed for the nine murals (plaques) he had proposed for Mrs. Prentiss in 1927.

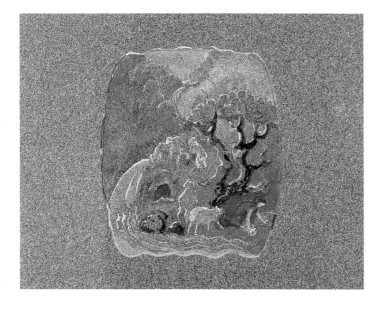

2. Letter from Charles Greene to Mrs. Francis F. Prentiss, February 15, 1928, Documents Collection, College of Environmental Design, University of California, Berkeley.

3. Letter from Charles Greene to Henry Greene, dated March 28, 1928, Documents Collection, College of Environmental Design, University of California, Berkeley.

If you had come to me to build the house, but had limited me to an estimate, 1188 Hillcrest could never have existed. Is not this a good argument for having added work done in the same way? Business, I admit, must be run upon business lines, but this is not business, this art of helping to make living pleasurable and beautiful beyond the merely useful. . . .

Please consider this matter a little more at your leisure, remembering that your relation has only been one of good fellowship and I trust a mutual pleasure. May you not give me your confidence now when you have accepted so much of mine in the past.[2]

Mrs. Prentiss had become as much involved with the house as had the Culbertson sisters themselves. She had engaged Henry to do several pieces of furniture for her during the 1920s and been most pleased. Equally, Charles was commissioned to do additional furniture, marble sculpture for the entry garden, screens for the bedrooms, nine carved-and-painted plaques for the dining room (only three of which were accepted and placed in the loggia), and sundry other items, all of which Henry tried to coordinate from the Pasadena office. However, the timing of the completion of some of the commissions, the surprisingly high costs, and Mrs. Prentiss's dissatisfaction with the carved panels for the dining room required considerable renegotiation and correspondence. Despite Henry's attempts to mediate, the final decisions were those of the client, prompting Charles to write to Henry: "I have settled with Mrs. Prentiss and she says the pieces are to go in the loggia. I am thoroughly disappointed, but it can't be helped. . . . I feel the plaques are as good as anything I have ever done and the dining room will always seem unfinished to me."[3]

Previous page, Mortimer Fleishhacker estate,
1911-27, Woodside, viewed from the formal
gardens in the rear of the house.

Rear terrace of the Fleishhacker house.

Mortimer Fleishhacker Estate, 1911 - 1927

The second of the two large commissions to which Charles turned his full attention in 1911 was that for Green Gables, the country residence for Mr. and Mrs. Mortimer Fleishhacker high in the hills of Woodside, California. The property was located in the midst of mountainous terrain just north of Palo Alto and within driving distance of the Fleishhacker home in San Francisco. Mortimer Fleishhacker was the president of the Great Western Paper Company, located in Woodside. His family had been a major force in the business and cultural affairs of San Francisco and the Bay Area over several generations, and Fleishhacker Park and Fleishhacker Zoo had been made possible by various family members. According to Charles's son, Nathaniel Patrickson Greene, Mortimer Fleishhacker offered the brothers a million dollars in commercial building in the Bay Area, an offer the Greenes refused because of their desire to work at a more personal and residential level.

■ For some time Mr. and Mrs. Fleishhacker had considered a number of architects for their new country home. Although aware of the work of Greene and Greene, they were not interested in what they perceived to be the Japanese influence on timbered structures they had seen in Pasadena. In spite of this, they met with Charles, who very likely charmed them with his new ideas inspired by his visit to England. Shortly thereafter, in the latter months of 1910, the commission was awarded to the firm.[4]

■ Charles was elated. The Fleishhackers wanted an English house with thatched roof similar to those they had seen in the East. This challenge rekindled his architectural interests and he took over this design completely, maintaining a close relationship with the Fleishhackers for several decades and carrying out one project after another on both the Woodside estate and the San Francisco house.

■ The timing was important to Charles. On his return from England, he felt that he had taken his new style in wood to its most sophisticated level and if he was to continue with architecture, he wanted to venture into other techniques. During his work on the Thorsen house, he had been attracted by the sea breezes of the Bay Area in contrast to what he considered the "bad

4. The author is grateful to Robert Judson Clark for access to his personal interview notes with members of the Fleishhacker family.

air" developing around the San Gabriel Valley. The opportunity to design in Northern California was a welcome and exciting change. The overall size of the Fleishhacker house and its extensive landscaping promised a new kind of freedom that Charles liked. The scale of the site made possible casual meandering forms on the one hand and a strict discipline in the axial geometry of formal gardens. He was eager to explore further the winged floor plan similar to what he had begun on the Pratt house, only here on a much grander scale. Moreover the vastness of the mountainous site allowed him to develop his ideas on the subtle relationships of the man-made environment and the natural chaparral of the surrounding hillsides and valleys.

■ The imagery of the "thatched roof" was carried out by steaming redwood shingles to respond to the soft curving edges of the multiple gabled roofs, which turned and overlapped in response to the irregularity of the angled plan of the large house. The most significant feature of the construction was the external skin of gunite, a thin layer of extremely fine-quality concrete blown under pressure through a hose while controlling the correct amount of moisture at the nozzle. This produced a fire-resistant surface material far more durable than stucco or plaster and an undulating variation in texture in the resulting surface.

■ Charles's attention to the exterior of the house and the elaborate gardens was more obvious than in the interiors, where the clients were less willing to give him the extraordinary latitude he was enjoying in the concurrent work for the Culbertson sisters. Here, for the Fleishhackers, the large rooms were dramatically simple by comparison with those of the masterworks of 1907 to 1909. Plaster was the predominant material, and, as in the Culbertson house, he explored the sculptural nature of the soft lines molded around the ceilings, at corners, and in details. The use of wood was minimal and now painted and rubbed to a glosslike finish. Beading in ebony along the transom trim offered extraordinary subtleties, including a crisp touch to the softness of the light natural earth tones of the plaster surface. Nowhere in the Fleishhacker house were there the special Greene and Greene fittings and lighting fixtures so familiar to their work, nor was there any furniture designed initially for the house. Charles was probably comfortable with this because at the time his attention and energies were again being taxed to the fullest with demands for the furniture for the major houses just completed, the Cordelia Culbertson house, gardens, and furnishings and several other designs that were never constructed, as well as the revival of his interest in writing.

■ In 1914 Charles began a series of alterations and additions to the Fleishhacker formal home on Pacific Avenue in San Francisco. These designs went on for many years, although some were never carried out. By this time Charles was functioning more as an interior decorator. He had become fascinated with patterns of folded ribbon and other historical motifs sculpted in the fresh plaster, in the imagery etched into clear glass windows, in the marble carvings for mantels, and in the various pieces of furniture projects. In December of 1916 there were as many as eleven men engaged in the San Francisco alteration.

■ The various Fleishhacker projects kept Charles working in his Carmel studio during the lean years. In 1923 they commissioned the enclosure of a side porch off the living room for the development of a game room. Charles jumped at the opportunity, which also gave him his first chance to design furniture for the house. The design and construction of the game room took him two years. He paid special attention to the variegated hand-glaze finish of the molded plaster wall surfaces, which included tiles that he placed himself, and to the scenic carvings for the panelings, frieze, cabinet doors, game table, its four chairs, and an armchair. This furniture was similar to that designed but never made for the James house of the same period, an example of Charles's persistence in carrying out his new ideas for wood carving and furniture concepts in the 1920s.

■ His details for the game-room furniture forced him to make the instruments with which he tooled the leather of the upholstery and the leather top of the game table. These surfaces were then accented with the application of color lacquers in the detail and then glazed. Charles's handcraftsmanship was superb, but he lacked the joinery equipment that he had been able to use in the Hall shops and therefore had to use simple hardware-store metal fasteners similar to those used in 1904 on the early Tichenor furniture.

■ Charles must have discussed with the Fleishhackers a vision he had kept at the back of his mind ever since his wedding trip to western Europe in 1901, for in 1928 they agreed to one of the most

tranquil yet breathtaking designs of the brothers' long career. With Henry's advice regarding certain aspects of the project, Charles designed an enormous reflecting pond that mirrored the distant mountain ranges. From the formal garden, great stone stairs wound down each side of the bluff to a lower landing on top of the arched stone retaining wall tucked into the base of the slope. At the opposite end the pond terminated with the image of a curving Roman aqueduct silhouetted against the far distant hills.

■ From the terrace of the house, only the stone arches at the far end of the water garden are visible, enticing the curious observer along the raked gravel paths to the brow of the hill. Here the view of the whole complex is arresting. At the level of the water, plantings in stone pots march along each side of the pond, and small edge bands of the gravel walks leading to the stone arches are made up of slivers of the stone structure set directly into the earth. Every detail was carefully planned to draw the visitor down to the water's edge, along the pond's entire length, around the arcaded end structure, and back along the opposite side. The transition from the upper formal gardens was handled with such finesse that the lower water gardens appeared to be an integral part of the original 1911 landscaping design.[5]

■ Mrs. Fleishhacker had long desired a setting in the natural environment of the site where she envisioned serving afternoon tea. In the year following the completion of the water gardens, she decided to have a stone dairy house built on the edge of a ravine across the main road that circled the site and led to the entry motor court. Charles, who was eager for another project, combined the dairy house with the facilities for afternoon tea in a charming two-story stone structure. But it was rarely, if ever, used. It was considered too far from the house, and the sensory combination of serving tea directly above the dairy house below was so intolerable that the generations of Fleishhacker family continue to refer to the dairy house as "Greene's Folly."

■ In spite of the failure of the dairy house, the Fleishhackers continued to be intrigued by Charles's impassioned imagination. When they considered a major addition to the San Francisco house, they were once again charmed by Charles's vision of a room drawing upon Gothic imagery, with a high vaulted ceiling and medieval stonework with wooden detail encasing the doors and windows to tie into the Greenes' articulated wooden vernacular.

■ Identified in time as the Gothic Room, this project, according to Charles, presented the greatest challenge and was the hardest work he ever attempted. Numerous sketches were done, many drawings

5. For further study of the Fleishhacker property see:

David C. Streatfield, "Echoes of England and Italy 'On the Edge of the World': Green Gables and Charles Greene," *Journal of Garden History*, vol. 2, no. 4, 377-98.

Ann Bloomfield, "The Evolution of a Landscape: Charles Sumner Greene's Designs for Green Gables," *Journal Society of Architectural Historians*, vol. XLVII, no. 3 (September 1988): 231-44.

Game room Charles Greene created in 1923
by enclosing the covered porch adjacent to
the Fleishhacker living room. In his Carmel
studio, Charles crafted the furniture and
carved the panels for the wall cabinets and
the frieze panels above the windows.

Left, vista overlooking the water gardens Charles designed for the Fleishhackers in 1928, viewed from the upper-level reflecting pool of the original formal rear gardens built in 1911.

Right, the stone arches of the closed end of the water garden recalled the imagery Charles had admired on the 1901 trip through southern Europe.

carried into refined stages, and estimates for construction were sought well into late 1931. Charles's letters to Henry continued to express his optimism, but the project was plagued with problems and in spite of the countless hours of planning never progressed beyond the drawing board. This was particularly unfortunate, as some of the later drawings revealed a sensitive weaving together of traditional Gothic forms and clearly recognizable characteristics of earlier Greene and Greene work, all of which were so carefully executed that the end product would certainly have been one of the most unusual spaces ever created by either of the brothers.

Fleishhacker water garden.

Left, the open, curved, arcaded terminus of the water garden recalls Charles's careful order and highly disciplined stratification of the stonework on the James house a decade earlier.

Right, Nathan Bentz house, 1911, Santa Barbara.

Nathan Bentz House, 1911

During 1911 Charles and Henry continued to separate the responsibilities of the firm between them. A few smaller bungalows moved through the office by one or another of the lead draftsmen. Henry, in the early part of the year, focused much of his attention on the Nathan Bentz house in Santa Barbara. This was principally his design of late 1910, with an angled plan developed on the slopes of the hills with a vast panorama of the Pacific Ocean. It featured a timber bridge to the entry, plaster interiors with wood detail, and trim was kept to a minimum.

■ Nathan Benz, like his brother, John Bentz of Pasadena, was passionately interested in the oriental arts, and his shop and home in Santa Barbara reflected this devotion. The association with the Greenes dated many years earlier and may account for the design of his large home being more closely allied to the Greenes' earlier wooden-bungalow era than any of the other work of this period. The Bentz house was thus the last of the large wooden designs in the full Greene and Greene style, although the use of steel I-beams and the soft sculptured forms of the living-room ceiling were totally new to the brothers' vocabulary.

■ While few residential commissions were coming into the office, a number of challenges interested Henry more than Charles. These included the Earle apartments, a small house for Mr. Blacker's siblings, a two-story bungalow in Sacramento, two houses with an English derivation, and one that explored the use of the gunite exterior. These were the years when the Greenes were stretching, again trying new ideas, concepts, and materials.

Annie Blacker house, 1912.

Annie Blacker House, 1912

Robert R. Blacker continued to turn to his architects not only for additional work on his own estate but also for a number of other structures, including a beach cottage at Santa Monica for himself in 1910, two cottages at Long Beach in 1912, and a new house for two sisters and a brother, built two blocks from his own home and across the street from a house rented by their nephew, Edward J. Blacker. Robert Blacker had loaned considerable money to the owner of the Vista Del Arroyo Hotel on the bluffs of the arroyo. In 1909 he took personal possession of the hotel and brought his nephew, Edward, to Pasadena to work there.

■ The Annie Blacker house plan differed from earlier Greene and Greene plans. It was dominated by a long central hallway that formed the core of both the first and second floors. The interior was simplified, and Henry's hand is evident in the linearity of the exquisite compositions, particularly of the clear leaded glass of the dining-room and hall cabinets. In this house may be the first use by the Greenes of Batchelder tiles—for the fireplace, using both plain and patterned stock designs. In order to control costs, commercial lighting fixtures were selected and interior walls were primarily plaster, with the exception of the special woods selected for the cabinetwork in the dining room and living room and in the door panels.

■ A very practical house, this was a smaller cousin of the Greenes' articulated timber houses. It featured Henry's careful composition of the front elevation—an asymmetrical design dominated by the strong central gable and given extraordinary grace by the line of the opposing roofs to each side over the one- and two-story portions of the house.

Mrs. Parker A. Earle Apartments, 1912

Pasadena's surge of interest in apartment quarters was prompted by the overflow crowds from several hotels along Colorado Boulevard. Mrs. Parker A. Earle purchased an existing wood-frame apartment property one block parallel to the north, turning the major expansion over to the Greenes. Their first move was to relocate the existing structure to the rear of the site, allowing the further development to front upon the Herkimer Street thoroughfare. As in the Annie Blacker house, Henry used the central hallways as the spine of the design, connecting to the original building in such a manner that from the interior the new and the old were scarcely discernable. The symmetrical arrangement of the rectangular floor plan was emphasized by the cubistic composition of the exterior elevations. The outer walls projected above the roofline. The long dramatic overhanging eaves of their earlier work was gone. Now featured were the bold exterior gunite materials and bilateral symmetry as well as the careful proportions of the street facade. The uneven, pneumatically applied stucco softened the rigid formality of the elevation and contrasted with the soft natural color tones of the sand-aggregate surface. This was accented only by the delicate green of the oriental tiles at vents and the warm brown of the transparent, penetrating oil stain of the wooden timber pergolas to each side of the structure. The overall effect of the exterior design was totally new, another one of their explorations into materials and style so prevalent in the Greene and Greene office in the years following the construction of the masterworks.

■ On the interiors, the general detail was consistent with the Greenes' earlier work. In the wood trim, detail, and cabinetwork were the familiar soft natural stains enhancing the natural grain of materials. The degree of articulated joinery was kept to a minimum to reduce costs; and in an effort to conserve space, Henry slid beds out from under closets, and breadboards out of bookshelves to provide writing surfaces. Although these apartments were intended as small, temporary quarters, Henry was concerned to provide the occupant with as much graceful living as he could. With this in mind, he designed a modest complement of furniture for each apartment. Although these pieces were much less complex in form and detail than the Greenes' previous furniture, they were more closely allied to the designs of Gustav Stickley. As the same furniture was supplied to all the apartments, producing it was as close as the brothers ever came to multiple production.

William M. Ladd House, 1913

For William Mead Ladd of Portland, Oregon, Henry designed a winter home in Nordhoff, California (now the Ojai Valley), just down the road from the earlier Pratt house. This clean linear design, essentially a return to the Greenes' earlier wooden bungalows, was composed of modest materials, and its planning and construction were most appropriate to the ruggedness of the site and the client's wishes. Ladd's personal reserve, his love of hunting, fishing, and the out-of-doors, drew him to the quiet rural atmosphere of the Ojai Valley. Here, in contrast to his demanding professional activities in Portland, his winter home was to be an extension of his camping interests and a part of the dry rocky barrancas and foothills.

■ Henry's elongated plan was a string of rooms along the high ridge of the site with a view to the road below. On the inner side, the long connecting gallery opened to the broad terrace overlooking the lower slopes of the rolling terrain to the canyon beyond. The living room, somewhat off the major axis, was anchored at one end of the plan with the dining, kitchen, and service rooms at the other end. In between were the bedrooms separated by a bath and a staircase that led to the master bedroom on the second level, thus providing another dimension to the overlapping gable forms of the interrelated roofs. These were punctuated by the three natural stone chimneys. The massive stonework of the living-room fireplace, designed for the interior as well as the exterior, was a powerful sculptural statement appropriate to the natural environment. With the undulation of the high retaining wall supporting the terrace, it tied the modest shingle-clad ranch-house bungalow to the earth. Most of the large grounds of the Ladd property were left in their natural state and contrasted well with the crisp lines of the house.

■ The differences between the Ladd and Pratt houses reveals not only the Greenes' ability to adapt themselves and their talents to the different lifestyles of their clients, but also Henry's and Charles's own personal expressions of their art. Each of these houses was a remarkable creation for its respective owner. Each contributed to and enriched the Ojai Valley, and each represented the varied and comfortable elements of earlier designs that had helped to change and give dignity to the broader cross section of American domestic architecture.

■ While both Charles and Henry were now beginning to recognize by this time that the public response to the bungalow style was waning, Gustav Stickley seemed unaware, or at least unwilling, to admit it. In the August 1912 issue of *The Craftsman* he devoted thirteen pages of text, as well as many plans and photographs, to the significance of the work of Greene and Greene as leaders of "California's Contribution to a National Architecture," stating that:

The value of Western architecture, locally and to the nation at large, and its widening influence upon home building all over the country are facts not to be estimated lightly. Every day it is becoming evident that America is writing her own architectural history, and writing it with no uncertain hand. The East, on the whole, has still a good

deal to learn—and perhaps even more to unlearn. . . but the West has for some time been recording on the fair page of the Pacific Slope what promises to be an important chapter in the life of the people.

The significance, moreover, of this Western accomplishment arises chiefly from the sincerity of spirit in which it is being undertaken. . . . And among those who have helped to make the homes of California proverbial for wise planning and structural beauty, perhaps none has contributed more effectively than the well-known Pasadena firm of Greene and Greene.

One of the first impressions gained. . . is the unusually wide variety of the designs. True, there is throughout a resemblance in spirit and purpose, due to the old Mission source and the similarity of the general surroundings. Each building has the typical features of the California home—the low, wide spreading roof lines, the solid yet picturesque walls, the frank use of structural beams, the luxurious spaces of porch and balcony and the quiet loveliness of the interior. And yet, so ample has been the range of the architects' imagination, and so diverse the treatment in each particular case, that one feels each house possesses a definite personality of its own, a certain uniqueness both of ideas and expression. . . .

. . . in every instance, the dominant note of their work is sincerity— and that, after all, is the thing that is going to make California's architecture a vital record in the chronicle of the nation, and help push forward the art of home building toward our great democratic ideal.

Stickley's timing suggests his own anxiety lest his Craftsman ideals become simply a part of history.

■ About this time, Charles, who had often been dissatisfied with his own buildings, turned to writing as a way of expressing his own very personal feelings about architecture. In both fiction and nonfiction he attempted to set down on paper his various thoughts at this point in his own career. Within his unpublished novel, "Thais Thayer," a melodramatic plot about an architecture student, Charles reveals his inner thoughts on art and architecture, and at times in this rambling text lapses into a form of bitterness:

The large terrace off the living room of this ranch house was embraced by a serpentine wall carried out in local soft stone and laid up consistent with the ruggedness of the nearby barranca.

Henry A. Ware house, 1913.

Architects don't have a chance. The educated public wants skill not soul. It can't judge because it can't feel. It only knows what it had learned. There isn't any culture. The other public is too ignorant to know what it really does want, and too busy money-making to try to find out. It takes to fads, discards the old for the new. . . .[6]

6. Charles Sumner Greene, "Thais Thayer," Greene & Greene Library, The Gamble House, USC.

The first of Charles's serious articles to be published was written for *The Architect* magazine, appearing in December 1915, in which he states that "the haste of speculation and sordidness of commercialism" was responsible for the worst of California architecture. He criticized the use of preliminary renderings by architects because:

nothing should be put on paper for them to see at the time. . . once the design. . . is fixed by means of a picture, it is very hard to change it. Properly no perspective for the owner of a bungalow should be made till after the plans are ready for bids; otherwise many a valuable opportunity may be lost to the betterment of the work.

In discussing the rights of the owner related to the design of his or her own home, he continued:

Not long since I heard an owner say, in regard to decoration and furnishing a room about which I happened to know the facts, "I would not think of asking my architect about that. It wouldn't be my room." However, this same owner had no hesitation in visiting a department store decorator, who showed her the latest consignment and made a very good bill. The owner herself honestly believed she had made her own selection, but it was entirely the cleverness of the salesman that did the trick, and he had never seen the room which, needless to say, became extraneous to the whole scheme of the house.

Drawing of the Charles S. Witbeck house, 1917, Santa Monica.

Both the Stickley article and that by Charles spoke clearly of their discomfort and indicate that neither of them would be able in the coming years to adjust to the changes in the social and the architectural scene, though each would attempt for a while to believe that the written word would hopefully bring believers back into a scene that was by now a part of the past.

■ Hardly more than half a dozen commissions for new work came into the firm's offices between 1913 and 1917 and none of these captured Charles's interest. There were frequent small requests from former clients for continued furnishings or additions to the great houses, but even these did not mitigate Charles's growing discontent with the architectural scene in Southern California as he observed it. Henry, on the other hand, maintained a steady hand on the work that came into the office and actually enjoyed the challenges from some clients that led him to explore building languages he had not dealt with before. In each of the commissions for Ware and Witbeck, in 1913 and 1917 respectively, the clients' strong preferences for the English tradition were carried out by Henry with considerable skill and much to the owners' satisfaction.

Henry A. Ware House, 1913

In the early part of 1913, when the firm had nearly completed the Kew house in San Diego, somewhat reminiscent of the English Tudor style and quite similar in plan and form to the James Culbertson house of 1902, Henry Arthur Ware offered Greene and Greene the commission for his own new house in Pasadena. Ware had recently come from Duluth, Minnesota, where he had been vice president of the Commercial National Bank of Chicago, and he definitely wanted the new design to resemble his former home. Like the Culbertson and Kew houses, the upper portion of his house was clad in shingle, with the ground floor of stucco. The plan was compact, revolving around the strong central hall and stairwell that formed the core of the circulation pattern. In the railings and structural detail there was less of the recognizable Greene and Greene language than in the living room. The dining room drew more on the English tradition. A personal request for an indirect lighting system due to Mrs. Ware's poor eyesight proved

a challenge to Henry, who developed the living room with its detail in redwood with a sculptured indirect light trough that encircled the entire space. The soft roll of the wire-brushed redwood light shield was repeated in the soft graceful lines of the transition trim to the beamed ceiling and in the equally fluid forms of the fireplace surround and mantel design. The balance of the living room was a light sand-colored plaster with ample natural light from the banks of windows to the south and west. The overall character of the living room was thus quiet, and expressed a strong sense of unity emphasized by the natural raw finish of the redwood.

Charles S. Witbeck House, 1917

Henry again drew upon an English Tudor expression for the second home for Harriet and Charles Strong Witbeck in Santa Monica. Although they maintained their principal residence in Pasadena, the Witbecks and Henry went through a series of variations to the two-story shingle-clad design. In each instance Henry penciled perspective renderings for the clients, a privilege which time had seldom permitted him to carry out during the more active years. The final design was quiet, straightforward and slightly less complex than earlier versions, though a study of the specifications reveal that the attention to detail and craftsmanship was held to this design as tightly as on any of the Greenes' earlier or larger commissions.

Dr. Nathan H. Williams house, 1915.

Right, detail of the gunite technique placed over wire mesh and carved out while the concrete remained wet. The soft gunite brows over the windows' concealed rolled canvas awnings.

Dr. Nathan H. Williams House, 1915

One of the more experimental concepts the office carried out during these lean years was the two-story, two-bedroom house for Dr. Nathan H. Williams on the slopes of Altadena just north of Pasadena. Williams had been living in the Herkimer Arms apartments and with two other people had purchased properties around Mar Vista Avenue and Albany Street. As he liked the gunite exterior of the Herkimer Arms apartments, he chose this pneumatically placed concrete material for the exterior of his own home. Considerable character was achieved by lightening the mass of the columns and railings by carving out certain portions of the concrete in patterns relating to the forms of the webbing of the wire-mesh reinforcment, in much the same manner as Charles had done for the Cordelia Culbertson walls. While this was again primarily the work of Henry Greene, there were elements of the design on which Charles participated, specifically on the stair detailing of the interior and the living-room marble fireplace mantel. Henry's interest in the development of the grounds and his careful shaping of berms and platforms upon which the house was placed was shown by his entitling the drawings "Residence and Gardens for . . ."

John T. Greene House, 1915

The John T. Greene house, 1915.

In 1915 some clients were still enamored with the Greenes' contribution to the bungalow style, and John Greene (no relation to the architects) was one of these. In Sacramento, he and other members of his family had acquired a number of acres of land on H Street at a time when East Sacramento was annexed to Sacramento. John Greene anticipated that the city would grow in that direction and decided he would set the standard for the area with the design and construction of his own house. In his extensive travels to the Bay Area and to Southern California, he had been very attracted by the rustic Japanese character of many of the bungalows. In time he met with Henry Greene, who carried out on both the interior and the exterior a simple design of bilateral symmetry, respectful of John Greene's interest in the Orient and yet honoring the integrity of the earlier Pasadena bungalows. The client intended to create a Japanese garden in front of the house facing the neighboring park, but this project never progressed beyond the installation of a stone lantern on top of a cobblestone pier at the entry terrace.

■ It was in the interiors that Henry's careful sense of scale and proportion coupled with his sensitive restraint produced, on a modest budget, a graceful, spacious, and harmonious California Arts and Crafts living environment.

The Westmoreland Gates, 1916

Ever since Charles had visited Berkeley and Woodside for the work on the Thorsen and Fleishhacker commissions, he had grown increasingly interested in the Carmel artists' colony just south of Monterey. He was attracted by the intellectual stimulation he found there and was disenchanted with architecture in Southern California. Consequently it was not long before he began to consider moving north.

■ His last executed work in the Pasadena office was the design for portals and gates for the control of Westmoreland Place for David Gamble and his five neighbors along the private street. The increasing amount of motor vehicle traffic shortcutting through the private roadway of Westmoreland Place was a real irritant to the residents, who had purchased their particular sites to escape the public curiosity and the hustle of sightseeing buses on Millionaires' Row along South Orange Grove Avenue. Now they, too, were subjected to tourist trams moving slowly by their homes and megaphones spewing out personal information. Consequently, Mr. Gamble, in consort with his neighbors, commissioned the Greenes to design the means by which their private drive could be limited to their personal use.

■ The Greenes' designs restricted access from the north end of Westmoreland by constructing handsome boulder piers between which wrought-iron gates were installed. At the entrance to the south, the design developed an island, splitting entry from exit by narrowing each in an effort to identify the privacy of the roadway. Located at the entry to the Park Place tract, the new Westmoreland Place entrance was labeled "private" and was carefully landscaped with sculptural boulder markers and carved wood signs.

■ In June of 1916, Charles and his family left Pasadena to explore a new life among the writers and artists around Carmel. Charles rented his Pasadena home in the event that he should decide to return, but he never did. Clay Lancaster, in his account of his interview with Charles in Carmel in the early 1950s, stated that the move was "partially motivated by a desire to delve into the profundities of Buddhist philosophy."[7] Also on Charles's mind was his desire to become a serious writer, anticipating further articles in *The Architect*. His earlier article for the periodical had been his frankest statements on the course of current architecture, and in his mind, writing was his best means of communicating his beliefs. As it turned out, it was an appropriate parting comment to his career in Southern California.

■ Henry continued to operate the Greene and Greene office, communicating with Charles at his rented residences in Carmel until the reorganization of the firm in 1922. A series of letters between Carmel and Pasadena in the subsequent months tells much of both the disenchantment and the dreams of Charles. To his father he wrote, "I am beginning to get my articles together for The Architect but so far I have done no other writing. I have been reading lately some books on Art and am beginning to feel as if I must start soon at my serious work."[8]

■ A short time later his father's response stated: "I do hope the pleasant intercourse with people who appreciate you will be beneficial to both of you and end in good friendships which will endure. . . . In Pasadena you saw a class of suddenly rich and another of regular creeky fanatics that you did not like and neither do I."

■ Charles replied: "Alice is giving another dinner tonight. The people here are much more simple and direct and nearly all are interested in something in contrast to people there."

■ Charles, in his second article for *The Architect,* entitled "Architecture as a Fine Art," rambled on about the current state of architecture, predicted a pessimistic future for the architect, and revealed much of his own frustrations. It may have been far too blunt for the editors of the magazine, who remained courteous but on the grounds of a restricted budget firmly rejected the plans for future articles that Charles was looking forward to writing. The second article for *The Architect* would be his last published writing.[9] At the same time, he had worked considerably on a proposal for a major book to be entitled "Truth in Building: A Plea for an American Democratic Style." Once again, Charles's optimism was not regarded and the book never progressed beyond the initial outline.

■ In the years that followed, Charles and Henry each entered into a new and important period in their lives, a period in which they would each bring to the architectural perspective a few more masterworks that will forever attest to their extraordinary collective and individual creative genius.

In retrospect the Westmoreland gates were prophetic. Charles's last design before moving to Carmel, they represent the end of the firm as it had long been known.

7. Clay Lancaster, "My Interviews with Greene and Greene," *Journal of the American Institute of Architects,* XXVIII (July 1957).

8. Letters, Document Collection, College of Environmental Design, University of California, Berkeley; and Greene & Greene Library, The Gamble House, USC.

9. Charles Sumner Greene, "Architecture As A Fine Art," *The Architect,* April 1917.

6

INDEPENDENT WORKS
1917-1928

D. L. James house rises naturally from the craggy cliffs of the Northern California coastline.

In 1914 when Charles sold his five-passenger Chalmers and bought a seven-passenger Hudson, he was not yet anticipating a move north. He was more interested in planning excursions to the California missions, where the family would camp for a few days while he painted. But with the San Francisco Exposition coming up the following year and Mortimer Fleishhacker encouraging him to come and work on some commercial building in Berkeley, Charles crowded the whole family into the Hudson and drove them up to the Bay Area for a visit. On the way back from San Francisco, they stopped in Carmel for a day and were all captivated by the sparsely populated artists' colony. For the next several months they talked enthusiastically of moving to Carmel for two years and then continuing on to Berkeley, where Charles, presumably encouraged by Fleishhacker, would set up his practice.

■ In the late summer of 1916 Charles moved his family north to the City of Carmel-by-the-Sea, which had recently been incorporated. Here he rented the boarded-up house of a Colonel Frye not far from the water. This was not a particularly convenient arrangement as he disapproved of the way the house had been wired, and therefore never had the electricity hooked up during the two years the family lived there. The great advantage of the place, however, was the ample room for his five children and enough space for a garden.

■ On the ground floor he set up a room similar to his personal office in Pasadena, complete with oriental rugs, his large bookcase, and his works of art. This was his domain and the children knew he was not to be disturbed.[1] Despite the move, he still had ties to the office in Pasadena and almost immediately went to work on a design for a large house along Pasadena's Linda Vista Avenue for Colonel John Poole, a rambling angular plan that, like many designs during this period, was never built. In April of 1917 when Mrs. Dudley P. Allen (later Mrs. Francis F. Prentiss) purchased the Culbertson sisters' house in Pasadena, she turned to Charles for the alterations and additions she desired. He was thrilled and immediately rented a simple studio space a few blocks away from the Frye house. Other responsibilities connected with the Greene and Greene practice necessitated frequent trips by train between

Salinas and Pasadena. Sometimes these trips lasted for two weeks or so at a time, particularly after Henry contracted a prolonged illness that kept him away from the office for months. By midyear, while still continuing the work for Mrs. Allen, Charles received the commission for a swimming pool on the Fleishhacker estate. By this time the family was so well settled in Carmel that he rented his Pasadena house and continued shuttling between the two cities until early 1918. By that time Henry had recuperated enough to take over the responsibility for the office as well as for the alterations to the Bolton house for the Culbertson sisters and a large garden design for Theodore Kramer in South Pasadena, along with numerous other projects.

■ Despite his frequent absences, Charles was becoming more and more involved with community activities in Carmel, and he and Alice made new friends among the neighboring artists, writers, and freethinkers. Foremost among these was Theodore Criley, who had given up the business world to settle down in the Carmel Highlands and paint. It was in his home where Charles met D. L. James, a meeting that changed his life. With the prospect of designing a house for Mr. James, it was finally easy for him to turn down Fleishhacker's offer for commercial housing. Thus ended forever any thought of his leaving Carmel.

■ The drawings for the James house were done on the drawing boards in Charles's office in the Frye house until, in 1919, the house was sold. By necessity he rented another house nearby and shortly thereafter purchased seven lots along Lincoln Street from his friend Andrew Stewart, whose nearby dairy ranch backed up to the rear of the Carmel Mission a few blocks away.

1. Information regarding Charles's move to Carmel and the building of the Carmel house and studio is from the author's interview notes with Thomas Gordon Greene, September 1997.

D. L. James house, Carmel Highlands.

2. Document Collection, College of Environmental Design, University of California, Berkeley.

3. Elmer Grey, "Some Country House Architecture in the Far West," *The Architectural Record*, vol. LII, no. 289 (October 1922).

4. D. L. James had no given name, only initials.

5. Excerpt from a draft of an unpublished manuscript sent to the author by Daniel James, May 25, 1964.

6. Elmer Grey, "Some Country House Architecture in the Far West," *The Architectural Record*, vol. LII, no. 289 (October 1922).

A simple masonry arch separates the pace of the present day from the quiet stone structure that appears to be a part of this small rugged site along the California coast north of Big Sur and high above the turbulent waters of the Pacific Ocean. This is no ordinary house. It rises from the craggy cliffs and stands firm against the wind blowing through the hardy pines and bringing in the sounds and scents of the sea. This is Seaward, an American architectural treasure of extraordinary subtlety and artistic genius, a majestic house created by Charles Greene for D. L. James.

■ This house at Carmel Highlands is the most creative and ambitious design outside of the Greenes' wooden-bungalow style and is essentially the independent work of Charles Greene. It hints of the California missions and of the stone ruins of Tintagel Castle in England, yet it is neither of these. Here the various stones selected and the creatively handled roofing tiles blend so harmoniously with the natural rock that only upon close examination can one discern where the site ends and man's masonry begins. As Bernard Ralph Maybeck wrote: "Beyond Carmel, Greene and Greene have built on the rocks by the sea one of the most beautiful pictures of our time."[2] In 1922 Elmer Grey, writing in the *Architectural Record*, devoted considerable space to the house, concluding that: "This kind of work is not architecture as now commonly known—it savors of a more plastic art, of the building of a home in thorough keeping with its rugged site."[3]

■ D. L. James[4] shared Charles Greene's vision of this house, a vision that sustained him throughout the delays and escalating costs of construction. James's background is described by his son, Daniel, in an unpublished manuscript as follows:

D. L. James and Lillie Snider James were born and spent most of their lives in Kansas City, Missouri, though romantically enough they first met in Athens on the Acropolis during the course of Mr. James' post-graduate studies at Oxford. After marriage Mr. James entered the family business founded by his grandfather. As manager of its retail operations, he dealt in fine imported china, silver and glass, but nearly all his free time he devoted to writing. Some of his plays were professionally produced both in the United States and abroad but none achieved the commercial success he hoped for.

Both the James and Snider families had been pioneers. Thomas M. James founded his mercantile business when Kansas City was still a small western outpost. A sternly devout pillar of the Baptist Church, it was his scourge to have as nephews the outlaws Frank and Jesse James. . . .

The James first visited Carmel in 1914 at the urging of Theodore Criley, an old classmate of Mr. James, who retired from the business world to paint. . . . It was at Criley's studio that they first met Charles Greene and invited him to see their building site. Two days later he returned with sketches and an elevation drawing which more than met the challenge of the spectacular site. On the spot Mr. James gave Charles the commission and authorized him to start on the house. It would be for the time a summer home but there was also the hope that Mr. James' writing would soon permit him to retire and live there permanently.[5]

From the early sketches and watercolor drawings by Charles Greene, it was clear from the outset that he had chosen quarried stone as the building material. However, the disciplined irregularity of the stone construction was an important part of his artistic vision and a concept that did not lend itself easily to communication through architectural drawings, which in this instance served only as a rudimentary suggestion. Consequently, Charles's presence was required throughout the masonry work, and he felt so strongly on this point that he later set out his thoughts on paper:

Ordinarily when plans are made for a house after careful study, they are practically final, and the specifications minutely exact. These are turned over to a contractor who by contract, produces the completed product. . . . Now the James house was not built that way. The architect hired the men and directed the work personally; except for the plumbing, electric wiring and tiling, there were no contracts.

Here is the difference: prevailing custom is a system of administration by recorded instruction; mine is not any system, but personal direction on the job. The first is fixed, the second is elastic, yielding to contingencies, open to inspiration.[6]

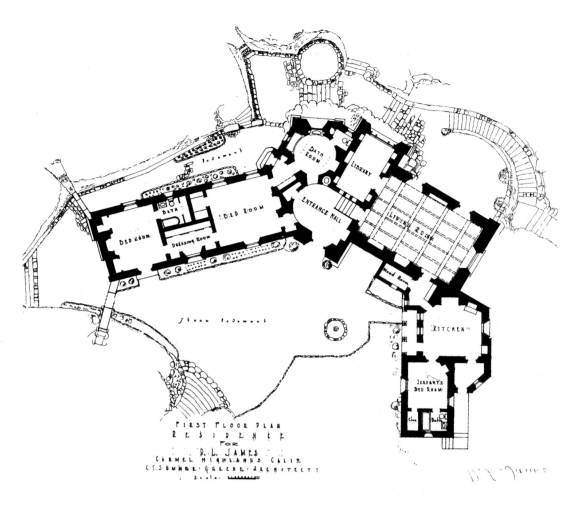

*Charles Greene pen-and-ink
drawing of the house and site plan
for D. L. James.*

7. Ibid.

8. Notes from the series
of personal interviews
between the author and
Daniel and Lilith James
between 1954 and 1985.

This would certainly prove to be true. In the composition of the stonework itself, Charles directed that the courses begin and end at random, creating varying horizontal levels. So intent was his concern for the exact effect he desired that he virtually stood over the masons as they worked. On occasion he traveled to San Francisco to direct the marble carving, but on his return he would often order sections of the wall dismantled and done over. Though Charles had known the stonemason, Fred Coleman, from earlier work in Pasadena and had requested that he come north for the James house, they battled continually over the four years of masonry work.

■ Throughout the construction Charles would redesign details responding directly to the existing conditions as they surfaced. This was particularly relevant to the foundation construction of the house. Once having determined that all footings rise from bedrock, he refused to bridge across a chase or break in the rock at some major point where support was needed, but instead chose to go forty-five feet down the cliff and build up from solid bedrock. This resulted in what appeared quite dramatically as great masonry arms reaching down to grasp onto the rugged site.

■ The stone selected for the basic construction of the James house was quarried from nearby Yankee Point. This rock, when quarried, was sharp and more golden in color than the weathered grey of the natural site although essentially of the same material composition. Soft sandstone used for detail came from the beaches of Point Lobos, and for the interior treatment Charles chose a limestone from the Carmel Valley. The terrace overlooking the sea was paved with carefully selected lichen-encrusted rock.

■ The roof tiles, furnished and laid by Gladding McBean and Company, added a rich light terra-cotta color to the stonework. Again traditional practices were discarded in order to achieve Charles's sculptural configurations of the varying roof forms. Breaking from the normal geometric lines both horizontally and vertically, he not only bent all traditional rules but seemed to have gone out of his way to violate them. In Elmer Grey's words, "The ridge rolls up and down with delightful waywardness, and the vertical lines of the tile appear and disappear as their usual course has been intentionally broken."[7]

■ James's son, Daniel, was a teenager during the construction of the house and a close friend of Charles's eldest son, Nathaniel, and he remembered Charles Greene as a tiny man with a sharp nose, little glasses, and a carefully curled pageboy haircut. He spoke very little and only in short sentences, his voice so soft that the listener had to lean forward to hear him. However, his small stature and nervous laugh belied a will of iron that enabled him to battle successfully with the various craftsmen on the job.[8]

■ The interiors of the James house were dramatically different from the exterior. The soft and gentle treatments of the curved plaster surfaces offer a sophisticated contrast to the rugged coastal cliff and the harsh weather. For the walls Charles and his son, Nathaniel, had scouted the area for special beach sands selected according to their color, and the plaster with which they were mixed was left natural and unpainted. Because of the plasticity of the material, Charles was able to give subtle sculptural form to the transitions between roof and wall and to the fireplaces and window and door openings. He took great pains to avoid straight lines by achieving this irregularity in the plaster walls, a characteristic most noticeable when the rooms were illuminated by candlelight. Chiseled stone blocks were inserted into the walls to receive Charles's hand-carved solid redwood timbers of the all-redwood ceiling detail. Elements of the sea were the source of form and details, particularly effective in the marble relief carvings of the fireplace surrounds. Because

Viewed through the natural landscape of the coastline, the James house appears as though it had always been a part of the rocky coastline.

Right, Careful observation is
required to detect just where nature
ends and where man's masonry genius
begins in Charles's subtle, discontinuous
stratification of stonework.

Left, Charles Greene watercolor drawing
of the ruins at Tintagel, England, 1909.

Right, the images from the Tintagel
watercolor served as the source for the
James arch and its window to the
crashing sea below.

Charles provided wood carvings as patterns for the San Francisco marble artisans, the marble relief work was more evocative of woodcarving forms and techniques than of normal marble work.

■ During the progress of the construction, a letter from Charles to the Jameses dated September 22, 1921, discusses an adjustment of architectural fees and made reference to furniture and fixtures on the same 6-percent fee basis. This was not surprising, for existing drawings reveal that Charles undoubtedly had plans for the complete furnishing of the house. But the Jameses felt these designs much too light for their taste. They preferred more massive antiques and selected instead seventeenth-century Italian and English pieces.

■ In spite of Mr. James's enduring faith in Charles's artistry, he did on occasion express his frustration over the delays and added costs with which he felt himself unable to cope. While Mrs. James's involvement was initially very supportive, these exchanges were complicated by her greater impatience with the pace of construction. Clearly the project was a vision shared by Mr. James and Charles.

■ As construction ran into the fifth year and costs exceeded the estimated $30,000, the Jameses began to feel that Charles wanted to work on the house forever. Consequently, in 1922 Mr. James insisted that Charles modify his concepts and bring construction to a point where they could move in. As a result, certain interior details and the lighting were hastily fitted for temporary use and thoughts of furniture were forgotten.

9. For further study on the James house, see:

Charles Miller, "The James House, Charles Greene's Masterpiece in Stone," *Fine Homebuilding*, no. 24 (December 1984/January 1985).

Elizabeth Gordon, "The Undiscovered Beauty of Our Recent Past," *House Beautiful*, vol. 99, no. 1 (January 1957).

■ The house, however, was everything that Mr. James had desired. He continued to regard Charles as its true creator.[9] Although they saw very little of each other for a decade and a half, both men continued to share a mutual respect and high regard for each other, even though Charles, as usual, felt the house was unfinished and kept hoping James would return with further work. But as the years passed, James's lack of success as a playwright never allowed him to retire early to his stone house on the bluffs of the Carmel Highlands. It was not until late in life when he took up permanent residence that he returned to Charles for the addition of a library for his collection of rare books. Charles was elated and began a series of concept drawings in 1939. He developed several schemes, locating the library on a second level over the kitchen, over the living room, and in the ground-floor circular bathroom area, but none of these designs pleased either Charles or the Jameses. Finally it was James's son, Daniel, who suggested that the narrow space under the house behind the stone arches be dug deeper into the bank for the library. This prevented any internal access from the house, but James was satisfied and Charles worked on the design for most of 1940. When he ran into problems constructing the new fireplace or with elements of structure and bearing, he again, as always, relied upon his brother, Henry, to come to Carmel and work with him.

■ Construction on the library addition was begun in 1941 and moved slowly along until finally nearing completion in March 1944, when the sudden death of Mr. James halted the project. Charles had already completed the magnificent bookcases—the final elements ready for installation—but it was not until the early 1950s when Mrs. James, encouraged and subsidized by *House Beautiful* magazine editor Elizabeth Gordon, decided to complete the library.[10] The project was a complete success. Charles's bookcases fit so exactly that not a detail needed to be altered and his total vision for the space was complete.

10. Elizabeth Gordon, "New—But Well Rooted in the Past," *House Beautiful*, vol. 99, no. 12 (December 1957).

■ Unfortunately, a design commissioned by *House Beautiful* for an additional bathroom off the end of the library showed little attempt to understand the integrity of the overall house. To the great credit of a more recent owner, the unfortunate bathroom was removed in 1996 and replaced with great sensitivity. Appropriately making no attempt to be Charles Greene, the architect provided a thoughtful addition to the house that remains one of the most romantic of architectural expressions.

The massing of the rooms and the window and doorway voids were casually but carefully placed so that each interior space had its own unique vista of the turbulent waters below.

Right, the original main-floor library of the James house rests directly off the main hall and maintains visual connection to the entry hall beyond.

The rugged, undulating surfaces of the natural sand-plaster walls of the James house main hall support the high ceiling of redwood beams and panels hand-carved and shaped by Charles Greene prior to the installation.

Charles Greene's last commission was in 1940 for the design and crafting of Mr. James's new and expanded library, built into the extended recess under the living room and accessed from the exterior only. Carried out in softer, more sculptural forms than the balance of the house, its capital shapings and the careful detail of the bookshelves remain the extremely important singular example of Charles Greene's extraordinary aesthetic at the end of his long and honored career.

Charles S. Greene house, Carmel, 1920,
C. Sumner Greene, architect.

11. Specifications for The
    Carmel Country Club,
    Greene & Greene
    Library, The Gamble
    House, USC.

Charles S. Greene House, 1921

Over the years Charles claimed that his Carmel house was the least costly he had ever built and was as close as he ever came to repeating the design form and construction techniques of the 1903 Arturo Bandini house in Pasadena. In his own house, however, there was more symmetry to the U-shaped plan than was usual for his compositions. The courtyard was much smaller and its few plantings were indigenous to the surrounding wooded site. Across the base of the plan were the master bedroom, living and dining rooms, kitchen, and service porch. The two wings were developed as dormitories, separating the boys from the girls. In the boys wing, the largest of three closets soon began to serve as a guest room for friends of Charles's two sons, among them Robert and Hubbard Hunt, sons of Myron Hunt; various children of John Galen Howard, dean of the Architecture School at Berkeley and also neighbors in Carmel; and Jack Mullgardt, son of Louis Christian Mullgardt.

■ The house was framed of redwood board-and-batten construction, assembled on the ground, and lifted into place. Charles was adamant that the house be built on a concrete foundation, contrary to the other Carmel cottages built with redwood sills directly to the ground. The interiors were left with no wall covering—a detail, so it was said, that Charles intended to complete at a later date. However well-intentioned he may have been, this idea was never carried out in the more than thirty-five years of his occupancy.

■ The family recalls it as an unusual house, heated by a Franklin stove, with no room for any kind of help, and considerably less sophisticated than the house in Pasadena with its velour upholstered walls and Port Orford cedar paneling and timber detail. But it was comfortable. The Greenes moved in during the fall of 1921, and in the following year Charles had a smaller three-room cottage constructed on a corner of the site for his parents, who began to spend more and more time in Carmel and less in Pasadena.

■ Following the completion of these two houses, Charles became involved with the design and specifications for a one-story frame clubhouse for the Carmel Country Club to be located near Junipero Serra and Ocean Avenues. This structure, housing a kitchen, billiard room, dance hall, and chatterbox room as well as showers and toilet facilities, followed much the same system of redwood board-and-batten construction as Charles's own house. Bids were opened on October 17, 1921, by Argyll Campbell, secretary of the club, a subsidiary of the Carmel Development Company.[11] According to various stories in the *Carmel Pine Cone* between October 8, 1921, and March 16, 1922, the contract was let to M. J. Murphy, but due to site changes and doubtful financing the project was never carried out.

Memorial Fountain, 1921
C. Sumner Greene, Architect

Charles donated his architectural services for the Memorial Fountain, which was dedicated "To those who served in the late war" and presented to the City of Carmel-by-the-Sea by the Community Club and Others. The drawings were identified as those by C. Sumner Greene, Architect, Carmel, apparently the first use of his individual name, suggesting that the imminent changes in the firm would distinguish the separate, independent work of each of the two brothers. The emphasis on Charles's second name, Sumner, acknowledged respect for his great-great-grandfather Thomas Waldron Sumner (1758-1849).

*Memorial Fountain, City of
Carmel-by-the-Sea, 1921, C. Sumner
Greene, architect.*

■ The Memorial Fountain was constructed on the site of the town's
former sheltered watering trough. The cornerstone was laid
during ceremonies on November 11, 1921, in the median strip on
the main thoroughfare of Ocean Avenue at San Carlos Avenue.
Charles's design was a simple stone arch, very different from any
of his former work. For some unknown reason he had the stone
cut to such precise form that it lost its distinctive quality. Equally
uncharacteristic were the stones at the top of the arch that were
forced into shapes to accommodate the unnatural line of the
curve. His familiar touch was evident, however, in the shaping of
the wood timber within the arch from which hung a bronze bell.
In its support of several fund-raising campaigns, the *Carmel Pine
Cone* wrote: "If you can't be a capitalist, come on with the rest of
us and be a dollar guy."[12]

12. "Work Resumed on
Soldier Fount,"
Carmel Pine Cone,
September 1922.

■ The memorial was completed for the Armistice Day ceremonies
in November 1922. A year after completing the Memorial
Fountain, Charles carved an elaborate plaque listing the names
of Carmel residents who were veterans of foreign wars, to be hung
in the Veterans Hall. So important has the memorial been to the
permanent citizenry of Carmel that after it was demolished by
a runaway car careening down Ocean Avenue in 1977, it was
rebuilt and once again dedicated during ceremonies on
November 10 of that year.

■ Charles continued to donate his time to various community
projects, including the design for alterations and additions to the
Little Forest Theater, where the Greene children performed in
various programs and which was run by the Carmel Club of Arts
and Crafts. At this time he also did a sketch for the Carmel City
Hall as well as proposals for the public library. The principal donor
to the library had already commissioned Charles to begin
the design, but her sudden death halted his work, and her heirs
awarded the commission to Bernard Maybeck.

■ Meanwhile in Pasadena Henry was very busy. He had handled
the conversion of the Bolton house for the Culbertson sisters and
had designed a number of projects including another scheme for
Colonel John Poole, a large craftsman house project in Ventura for
Thomas Gould Jr., and residences for Edward H. Angle and Kate
A. Kelly, as well as carrying out the large garden development for
Theodore Kramer in South Pasadena and the J. H. Jones
alterations and gardens in Altadena. In addition, Mrs. Allen (now
Mrs. Prentiss) was calling for additions and alterations on the
house Charles had originally built for the Culbertson sisters, and
Charles was calling on him for help on the structural designs for
the James house. In 1921 his time was also being taken up by
administering the major move of the Anthony house from Wilshire
Boulevard to Beverly Hills and its new garden development, as
well as a new design for Anthony's mother-in-law, Mrs. Kate A.
Kelly. After Charles moved to Carmel, Anthony had broken
off his association with Bernard Maybeck, whom he had chosen
as his architect during his quarrel with Charles over his purchase
of the Hudson, and in 1922 returned to Henry Greene with
the commission for the Kelly house in the Los Feliz hills
above Hollywood.

■ By this time Charles had given up all thought of moving on
to Berkeley, and Southern California was definitely out of the
picture. Moreover, the interests of the two brothers were further
diverging. Henry was becoming more and more social and Charles
more and more withdrawn, concentrating on his studies of art
and delving into the profundities of Buddhism.

Reorganization of the Firm, 1922

After Charles's return from England in 1909, both he and Henry recognized the growing differences in their interests, differences that had prompted more and more individual work. By the time Henry had recovered from his illness and was again assuming the responsibilities for the office in Pasadena, Charles had settled down in Carmel and was busily involved in the construction of the James house and the building of his own home. The geographical distance between Carmel and Pasadena, coupled with fewer and fewer commissions coming into the office, forced the brothers to realize the necessity of reorganizing the firm. The following statement was published in the April 1922 issue of *Architect and Engineer:*

Henry M. Greene, formerly of the architectural firm of Greene and Greene, 216 Boston Building, Pasadena, through office reorganization, has assumed entire charge of the business which will be continued at the same address under his name alone.

Charles had already indicated his independence from the firm by identifying himself as C. Sumner Greene, Architect, Carmel, on the drawings for the Memorial Fountain the previous year.
■ In spite of the dissolution of the partnership, the brothers remained close, and while their developing interests were worlds apart, they would continue thereafter to call upon each other for assistance on their independent commissions. Neither Henry nor Charles had any intention of retiring. Each continued to work independently as well as together on commissions for former clients, and over the years they did not hesitate to call upon each other's expertise as needed.

C. Sumner Greene Studio, Carmel, 1923, C. Sumner Greene, architect. Along the rural road and in front of his unfinished board-and-batten house, Charles built his personal studio of bricks from a demolished hotel in Pacific Grove and tiles left over from the James job.

C. Sumner Greene Studio, Carmel, 1923
C. Sumner Greene, Architect

Beyond 13th Street, Lincoln Street today remains almost as quiet as it was before the tourists discovered Carmel. The street is now paved, though it has escaped the harshness of concrete curbs. Indigenous plants and lush green ferns are a part of the rugged landscape of the parkway between the road and the brick-walled, tile-roofed studio that once served as a sanctuary for Charles Greene. Just a few feet to the rear and to the side stood the simple wooden board-and-batten courtyard house that was never really finished after ground had been broken for the studio. The studio is a modest structure but one of enormous historic importance to both residential architecture in California and the Arts and Crafts movement.

■ The idea of a studio first occurred to Charles when he was given the opportunity to purchase 60,000 used bricks after the demolition of a nearby hotel in Pacific Grove. He had always been a scavenger of available building materials. He had built his small shop at the rear of his property in Pasadena of cut stone from a demolished building in Los Angeles, and when that shop was torn down to make room for the new kitchen wing to his house, he used the stone again in the construction of the garden shelter to the side of the living room. Following the construction of his modest house in Carmel in 1921, the completion of the James house in 1922, and the sale of some property he owned in Long Beach, he was now in a position to build his studio and took out a building permit in 1923.

■ Because of all the hardwood he had purchased over the years for his various clients, he was given all the oak for the flooring and teakwood for the doors by the White Lumber Company of San Francisco. The Gladding McBean roof tiles, left over from the James house construction, covered half of the roof, and the balance was protected temporarily with building paper that remained during the next thirty-five years of Charles's life. With the help of his son, Nathaniel, Charles did much of the work on the studio himself, which kept the costs down to approximately $2,500.[13]

13. Information related to Charles's move to Carmel, the family activities, and the house and studio are from notes taken by the author through a series of interviews with various members of the Greene family between 1955 and 1997.

Charles playfully made use of the sculptural opportunities in the masonry construction of the fence connecting to the corner of the C. Sumner Greene studio and particularly in the curled brick detail.

■ Inspired by the California missions and by the flexibility he had discovered in both masonry construction and plastic materials, he planned his studio as a microcosm of his life and activities. It was to be his own space for painting, carving, writing, and drawing. It was to house the vast collection of books and portfolios, the paintings, furniture, and collected objects of oriental arts from which he drew so much inspiration. The main studio was also to be a place for musical events featuring his daughter Anne, who was well known in Carmel for her talented playing of the Steinway provided by the Fleishhackers. In time the studio would also be a haven for discussion groups studying Buddhism, *Goddard's Buddhist Bible*, and the teachings of Gurdjieff and Ouspensky.

■ The main hall was large, with a tall gabled ceiling supported by two massive redwood beams specially selected and cut at a local mill in Palo Colorado Canyon and then carved by Charles before being lifted into position. On the north a large twelve-panel skylight dominated the ceiling, which was finished throughout in natural sand-aggregate plaster and formed to provide excellent acoustics. The sand for the plaster, selected for its color, was taken right from the ground in front of the studio. The result was a subtle variation in soft earth tones that contributed to the artistry

of the undulating finish of the hand-troweled surfaces. Charles pressed into the soft plaster patterns of varying combinations from wood-block carvings he had made for this purpose, molds that the children called his "cookie cutters."

■ The entry hall in the front of the main studio was entered directly from Lincoln Street. To the left was a small bathroom and at the end of the studio a study where Charles would do most of his writing. At every turn was evidence of Charles's craftsmanship. Carvings on door panels or cabinets were virtual storyboards recording his interests; the central marble grid in the floor of the entry was framed by a mosaic of colored-marble scraps from other jobs; most of the fine furniture from the Pasadena house was moved into the studio, as well as the mahogany and teakwood bookcase that he had designed for his Pasadena office. As his collection of books increased, he made another large bookcase, compensating for its lesser quality of wood by adding his carvings and then finishing it with a painted surface distressed to simulate age, a practice he had strongly opposed in his earlier work. Oriental rugs were scattered around the floors, sometimes creating an altar effect for his collection of oriental arts. The studio was not only to be the workplace of its artist-architect-writer but also a showcase in Carmel for musical recitals and philosophical discussions.

■ Now that Charles was a part of the artists' colony, it was not surprising that several commissions for studios would come his way. In 1920 Professor and Mrs. Rudolph Schevill, friends of Frank Lloyd Wright, were so taken by the James house construction and its on-site architect that they asked Charles to do the alterations to their entry hall. So pleased were they that, although David and Jessie Holms had originally designed their bungalow in the Berkeley Hills adjacent to the university, they returned to Charles two years later to add a spacious music studio to the house. Acoustics were the primary concern, and Charles took advantage of the sloping site to accommodate the two-story height of the space and the split-level connections to the original house. On the exterior, long natural redwood shakes were used to coordinate the new wing with the original house, and Charles utilized tall windows and doors and a box balcony to join the soft roll of the plaster interior surfaces with the natural landscape of an adjacent garden. The Schevills were very happy with the acoustics and even more pleased when Wright, on a visit in later years, commented that this was one of the finest rooms he had experienced. Wright's earlier respect for the Greenes' work had been evident during his visits to Pasadena a decade earlier when he had visited with Charles at his Park Place home and studio.

The main hall in the Carmel studio served not only as the gallery for Charles's objets d'art, but also as a studio for his woodworking, painting, and writing as well as a recital hall for his daughter Anne. In addition, he held meetings there for studying the writings of Gurdjieff and Ouspensky.

A chiseled-stone capital set into the undulating natural-sand finish of the walls of the studio supported Charles's elaborately carved redwood timbers. The patterns about the borders of the room were pressed into the soft plaster with the series of wood-block carvings that Charles's children called his "cookie cutters."

While Charles had been kept busy following the reorganization of the firm, Henry's lengthy illness had forced him to curtail new commissions for several years and concentrate on various remodelings, the moving of the Anthony house, and various schemes for the Kelly house. Several projects had been designed but had not yet taken form. Robert Blacker partially funded a student center on the campus of the California Institute of Technology in response to student laments over the loss of a modest sandwich shop where they had been able to relax and talk. The 40-by-50-foot wooden craftsman hall, built in 1923 and named "The Dugout," was essentially a large low bungalow with three enormous exposed trusses supporting the large span of the open roof structure inside. On the exterior, the hall was surrounded on three sides by a covered pergola carried out in the Greenes' traditional detail. Upon completion the trustees assisted in the furnishing, with Henry M. Robinson providing a billiard table and piano.

Above, entrance hall of the studio as viewed from the main hall. The teakwood doors flanking the arch between the spaces are incomplete, and Charles's notes to himself in pencil and chalk remain, denoting works yet to be carved.

Left, designed for use in his studio, Charles never quite finished this cabinet, leaving to speculation the materials to be used in the upper door panels.

Thomas Gould Jr. House, 1924
Henry M. Greene, Architect

14. Author's interview with
Thomas Gould Jr. (age
87) at the Gould home
in Ventura, California,
January 12, 1973.
Subsequent interviews
with Richard and
Virginia Gould,
1973-90.

As early as 1911, Mrs. Thomas Gould Jr., a subscriber to *The Craftsman,* had decided that she would one day live in a Greene and Greene bungalow similar to those published in the magazine. So confident was she that she began immediately to purchase Arts and Crafts furnishings. But the Goulds could not seriously consider building until 1920, at which time they journeyed to Pasadena to meet with Henry and show him the sketchy floor plan Mrs. Gould had been doodling with for some time. They found Henry very understanding but wondered at first if he was too gentle to handle the builders.[14]

■ At first Henry urged them to consider the Mediterranean style, which he believed would insure a better resale value should the house be sold. But that would not do. Mrs. Gould had set her heart on a Greene and Greene wooden bungalow, and so Henry developed a large, two-story craftsman house through floor plans, elevations, and a pencil rendering, only to be interrupted by the Goulds' purchase of a large farm on the foothills of South Ventura. In 1924 Henry, at his own request, spent the night with his clients in order to get an idea of their lifestyle. As a result, he discarded the large scale of the initial project of 1920 and designed a more modest bungalow but one that took advantage of the magnificent panoramic views across the waters of the Pacific Ocean to the Channel Islands. The new plan was a narrow symmetrical rectangle with a partial second story over the center portion. Henry's engineering planned for an addition to the second floor to the rear, if desired, at some future date. For budget reasons, the post-and-beam timber joinery work of their earlier residences in Pasadena was limited to the entry and to the window boxes and the projecting outriggers supporting the open-gable roof structure. The exterior remained wood, but Henry accented the horizontality of the design by using clapboard siding detailed with two narrow bands between each wide band. The interiors were primarily carried out in plaster. Wherever wood was used in the trim or cabinetry, Henry demanded the same care as in the Greenes' most sophisticated work. Despite Mrs. Gould's initial fear that Henry would be too gentle in supervising the workmen, she soon learned that he exercised absolute control. So insistent was he on excellence that the sanders working on the finish of the interior woods frequently had to take time off to allow their fingers to heal.

■ As straightforward as the design of the Gould house was, Henry's designs for the leaded glass of the dining room revealed talents that had hitherto been overshadowed by Charles's more dramatic work.

Here his designs wove together a highly linear composition with the lyrical flow of line in the handling of floral elements and birds in flight. In the mirror cabinet at the landing of the stairway and in the cabinetwork of the dining room, the carved detail, color inlay and custom knobs were carefully balanced with the elegant simplicity of this quiet bungalow.

■ The following year Henry sketched out a project along Mediterranean lines for Mrs. Gould's sister, Mrs. C. P. Daly, also in Ventura. Though this project was never built, it illustrated again Henry's strong belief in this style as appropriate to the Southern California environment.

William Thum House, 1924
Henry M. Greene, Architect

The Thum house did not reflect the earlier Greene and Greene style. It did not embrace the prevailing Spanish Colonial Revival. It did not acknowledge the imagery of the modern movement. Instead, the overall statement is a gentle expression of Henry's beliefs and, regardless of popular trends, his ability to adapt to what he felt were the appropriate decisions to answer the needs of his client.

■ William Thum, a long-time friend of Henry's and former mayor of Pasadena, was most concerned about the security, fire protection, and acoustics of his library. His extensive collection of documents and books attested to his long service in government. His belief in the efficiency of public ownership of utilities manifested itself in his success in bringing about the municipal ownership of the water systems and the city power facilities. The progressive Colorado Street Bridge across the arroyo, the flood-control systems, the beautification of the arroyo, the development of Brookside Park, and the Municipal Golf Course were all implemented under his administration.

■ Henry's general two-story design of the Thum house was a perfect square, developed around the important library—a reinforced concrete fireproof and soundproof room with the rough character of the concrete ceiling structure expressed internally. The interiors were carried out very simply, finished in plaster with a minimum of natural wood trim and sculptural detail.

■ It is in the treatment of the exterior that Henry showed his respect for certain aspects of the popular Spanish Colonial Revival of the day, yet at the same time he remained free enough to proceed confidently on his own. The result was a handsome, straightforward house of quiet dignity yet possessed with the careful sculptural forms drawn from the plaster materials and details drawn from the expanded-wire and gunite construction used in the earlier Williams house. With its tiled roof, subtle arches at the entry, and the lyrical handling of the side terrace and its railing, Henry demonstrated that he was his own man, with the strength and conviction to meet one professional challenge after another.

■ In the latter part of the 1920s, both Henry and Charles deplored the impact of the machine on craftsmanship, but while Henry wrestled with new ideas, Charles continued to work with his handcrafts, spending most of his energy on projects for former clients. There was, however, one new client, Martin Flavin, who became mesmerized with Charles's gifts, calling on him first for the design of a modest table and later for extensive alterations and additions to his house in the Carmel Highlands. Had they met earlier, Charles would undoubtedly have been chosen as architect for the entire house.

*Stone walls and gates of the entrance
court for the Martin Flavin estate,
Carmel Highlands, 1925-39, C. Sumner
Greene, architect.*

Library addition for Martin Flavin, designed, carved, and constructed by Charles Greene circa 1930.

15. Letter to the author from Martin Flavin, dated March 16, 1966.

16. Interview with Flavia Louise (Flavin) Edgren, Carmel, September 10, 1978.

"Spindrift" is the name of the road, the house, and the estate of Martin Flavin on the spectacular thirteen-acre peninsula of Yankee Point, just a short distance south of the James house. Designed for Flavin by Charles E. Gottschalk of San Francisco, and built by M. J. Murphy in 1922, the large stone house with steep-gabled shingle roof rested openly among the cypress trees on the windswept promontory. Flavin, a screenwriter for Metro-Goldwyn-Mayer, believed his northern retreat to be a perfect setting in which to write. With his interest in drama, he had also directed that his dining room be raised from the living room to serve as a stage for the various performances he and his children frequently presented.
■ Around 1928 Charles began the designs for stone walls defining the property and the motor court, wrought-iron gates, and several schemes for a handsome gate lodge project that was also to have been used as a guest house. Many years later Martin Flavin wrote:

Charles Greene was not the architect [for Spindrift], but over a long period of years he contributed to it almost everything of value and distinction, both inside and out, that it possessed. . . . Charles Greene was my friend and my consultant. . . . I regard Charles Greene as its creator.[15]

By 1929 construction was proceeding on the walls and gates, and sketches began for a breakfast porch off the dining room with a view down the peninsula to the sea. The original builder, Murphy, was involved in much of the new work between the years 1930 to 1934, which necessitated alterations throughout the house and grounds, balcony railings, lighting brackets, carved panels for the living room, and the continued work on more massive masonry garden walls.[16]
■ The distinguishing feature of the house was the new library, in both design and execution. Flavin soon found that he needed a more private space for his writing. With the encouragement of Charles, he relinquished one of the bedrooms for his private library. The fact that the library became the access to the entire master bedroom suite seemed to be of little concern to Flavin or Charles, although when Flavin locked the door to the living room, which he frequently did, there was no entry to the remaining master bedroom. Be that as it may, the Flavin library, and a decade later, the James library, represent two of Charles Greene's most sensuous interior spaces and a fitting end to his extraordinary career.
■ The intimate Flavin library was developed in natural unfinished redwood and was crafted and carved in its entirety by Charles in his Carmel Studio. Alternating triangular panels made up the

ceiling of the library, with varying patterns given to each of the carved medallions. The effect was both dramatic and unique. Carvings were equally dominant in the panels of the closed cabinets to each side of the walls of bookshelves. At one end of the library was a built-in seat suitable for sleeping, and over this were stained-glass windows with handblown rondels making up the three panels of the windows. To compensate for the relative lack of natural light and the muted quality of the all-wooden interior, Charles designed and crafted hand-beaten copper hanging light shades suspended from scrolled wrought-iron brackets that swiveled from the wall, one at each side of the window seat and a larger version at the opposite end of the room. On each side of the two doors on the central axis of the library were similar copper hand-lights with wooden handles and long cords, allowing them to be lifted from their wall mounts and carried along the shelving in search of some particular book. Major double doors opened directly to the living room, one with a hanging carved-wood and copper bar to be swung across the doors, locking the library from the living room. Each of the panels carved in Charles's studio were so accurately measured and crafted, little more than a day was required for their hand installation.
■ The small library for Martin Flavin evoked more of the spiritual energy of Charles Greene in his later years than any other interior space. The imagery in his carvings reflects his deep interest in symbolism, his philosophical excursions into the teachings

of Gurdjieff and Ouspensky, his search for the "oneness of all that exists,"[17] and his passion for the crafting of soft wire-brushed redwood with tools that he had made for himself in his own studio. This was architecture as he knew it to be. He was not willing to give up the principles of the soul and pride of craftsmanship that had been at the heart of all his beliefs throughout his long career. Like Henry, he believed that the machine was only another tool to be used by the creative hand rather than being the genesis of design itself. In a letter to his friend, Professor Vladimir Ulehla in Brno, Czechoslovakia, dated June 29, 1929, Charles attempted to put these feelings into words.

Building today is engineering, not architecture. The ideal of engineering is precision and economy, the slogan of manufacturers. Both of them have a fever of facts and figures, but the public is immune from this malady. It is the merchant who molds the nation with his publicity stuff. . . . Careless of the quality of material and work he sets a premium on clever design that discreetly covers the engineering it can never be a part of. The real modernist architect turns with disgust from this unmeaning display to aesthetic denial and beauty.[18]

Charles was clearly expressing his own passionate beliefs here. Had he been able to exercise the same vigor and dynamic energy that had driven him to rebel against the eclectic historicism at the turn of the century, could he have discovered that his ideals of beauty and inspiration were also a part of the new technological world? No, not in his mind. Instead he retreated into his studies of oriental philosophy, which not only appealed to his inner feelings but also reinforced his refusal to accept the crass realities of commercialism. So out of touch was he with what was going on in his own profession during the 1930s that he spent his creative energy in crafting furnishings, some of which were not accepted by his clients. Instead, these pieces remained in his studio until his death.

■ Yet Charles rebounded again in 1939 with his brilliantly sculpted design for the library for Mr. James at Seaward. Once again he broke all the rules and produced one final testament to his creative genius.

■ While Charles was clinging stubbornly to his beliefs, Henry welcomed the challenges of new materials and changing conditions of construction with renewed vigor.

Walter L. Richardson, who had been a developer in Pasadena, was well acquainted with the Greenes' work, although he had never had any direct contact with them. As a young man he had been an avid outdoorsman and had accompanied Theodore Parker Lukens, California's "Father of Forestry," on a High Sierra horseback trip from Visalia north into Yosemite, a very rugged excursion.[19] He was always ready for new challenges, and after a very successful business career in Pasadena, he sold his "Richardson" building block, which housed his offices, and bought a large citrus ranch in Porterville in the San Joaquin Valley. There he built a small house along the road on the lower slopes of the ranch. By 1929 the ranch had prospered enough for him to suggest to his family that they build a swimming pool or a new and larger house. To his surprise they chose a house![20] With a quick sketch in hand, Richardson returned to Pasadena to meet with Henry Greene and lay out the special circumstances of his needs. He had thought of a simple U-shaped courtyard plan with an internal garden in dramatic contrast to the rugged hillside terrain. He wanted the house built of adobe blocks formed on-site by his ranch hands from the natural materials found on the ranch, and with the framing, hardware, and entire construction carried out by his own crews. Henry was intrigued. He accepted the commission, and the two men agreed that Richardson would act as his own contractor and Henry would handle the supervision through the mails with occasional trips north when deemed necessary.

■ As soon as Henry visited the ranch, he persuaded Richardson to change the roadside site to one higher up on the brow of the hill that had a commanding view over the valley and the citrus groves. The house was thus named "Tanalu," the name given to the hill by the Koyote Indians who had used it as a lookout station from which they could send smoke signals.

■ In order to start the construction before the winter rains, Richardson had to break ground as soon as Henry had completed the basic concepts of the design. From that time on, Henry kept forwarding through the mails page after page of detailed drawings along with lengthy instructions that seemed to arrive almost daily. While much of the detail and some of the materials were new to him, Henry maintained firm control and insisted that the workmen adhere strictly to his word. On one occasion when Richardson wrote proposing that a wall be moved a few inches, Henry rejected the idea in a nine-page letter in which he wrote:

17. C. Sumner Greene, "Symbolism" (1933), Greene & Greene Library, The Gamble House, USC.

18. Greene & Greene Library, The Gamble House, USC.

19. Shirley Sargent, *Theodore Parker Lukens, Father of Forestry* (Los Angeles: Dawson Book Shop, 1969).

20. Interviews with Marge and William S. Richardson, John and Beverly Richardson, and Julie Richardson, 1974 - 1997.

Walter L. Richardson residence,
Porterville, 1929, Henry M. Greene,
architect. The Richardson design repre-
sented the last complete structure carried
out by either of the brothers.

The ranch house at the Richardson ranch, "Tanalu," in Porterville was Henry Greene's first and only work in adobe. Henry selected native lichen-covered stone from the surrounding site for the basement level and foundations, concrete beams for lintels and headers, adobe blocks made by the workmen on the ranch, and redwood and Douglas fir for the roof structure. This was one of his most timeless and site-appropriate designs. It is still comfortably at home in the operation of the ranch today.

*In doing work this way there is always a tendency of both workmen
and Owner to start changing the plans. But remember that the
Architect works out the things "on paper" in advance, and often when
a change is made without consulting him, things don't work out and
discrepancies occur which would not have happened if the plans had
been followed, or his instructions asked for. This may make some delay
or trouble, but it is the only way.*[21]

Capitalizing on the gentle slope of the site, Henry developed
the main-floor opening directly to the rear garden upon an
eighteen-inch-thick rugged stone foundation, nearly eight feet in
height, creating a full series of basement spaces and lifting the
entry sitting-porch high to take advantage of the magnificent
panorama over the valley. Lichen-covered natural stone from
the site was used for the foundation, and a massive concrete
bond-beam tied the entire structure together and provided a
precise base for the orderly nature of the adobe construction of
the house proper. Henry's deliberate decision to allow these
concrete bond-beams to be expressed boldly on both the exterior
and the interior of the structure gave a remarkable integrity to
the overall design. Simple lines of the strong gabled timbered
roof forms provided an equally powerful silhouette against
the sky, and long overhangs supplied welcome shade from the
hot rays of the sun.

■ The adobe blocks—the fundamental building material—were
principally the work of one family on the ranch whose experience
in such work made their use possible. With the assistance of other
ranch hands they drew materials at hand and produced, in short
time, the multiple numbers required for the project. In the laying
out of the plan, Henry had used the modular nature of the blocks
to calculate very carefully the position of doors and windows
and made every attempt possible to draw upon their natural
aesthetic to provide integrity to the design. The heavy timber
work of headers, posts, and roof structure were enhanced by the
retention of adze marks in his attempt to relate the various
elements of the structure to the nature of the rocky site.

■ While the adobe blocks were expressed at various openings, the
interiors were principally plastered with a muted earth-color
aggregate left natural, and wood trim and timbers were waxed with
soft color. Detail and door woods were sandblasted or brushed
with a stiff brush. The on-site blacksmith crafted Henry's designs
for hardware, hinges, lighting fixtures, and door plates in forms
reminiscent of the Greenes' earlier works, though appropriately
adjusted to the on-site craft.

■ During construction, Henry was emphatic about the aesthetic
aspects of his design. On one of his rare visits to the site, he found
that the test sample of the stain on the exterior beams was too dark
and insisted it be sanded off and lightened. He also noticed that
there were too many carpenters at work at one time and was firm

in his request that their numbers be reduced because he felt that Richardson's attempt to hurry the work would result in mistakes.

■ Henry's hopes for designing furniture for the house was never realized, except for the walnut dining-room table. Its structure, while direct and light in scale, is softened by certain characteristics that identify it with earlier works of the firm, yet with a simplicity that reaches to the future. Henry composed a system of drop leaves at each end of the table that, when not in use, folded under and were kept in place by the notch in the end of the stretchers used to support the leaves when lifted into place. Except for the simple, straightforward fastenings of the top, there is no applied decoration. The purity of its line and his sensitivity to its proportion demonstrated a remarkable talent that had too often been overshadowed by the sheer number and drama of Charles's creations.

■ One of Henry's letters written after the completion of the house reveals his personal thoughts regarding handcraftsmanship versus the machines of the modern age:

I was glad to hear that the walnut table came out so well. . . also that the cost was so reasonable. Those "old fellows," some of them, turn out fine cabinet work. There are left a few of these older men, Swedes, Germans and English, who really learned their trade and love their work. . . . In my opinion, they give the work a quality which cannot be secured in any other way; modern machinery to the contrary, notwithstanding. Machines can never supply that personal human factor.[22]

22. Ibid., February 17, 1931.

During the Great Depression years, there were few opportunities for Henry to practice his profession. In 1944 there were sketches for a house project for his son and daughter-in-law, William Sumner and Harriott Greene, in Pittsburg, California; and in 1951, he designed and detailed a concrete-block house for his daughter and son-in-law, Isabelle and Alan McElwain, in Woodland Hills, California. By then Henry was over eighty years of age, but he got out his drawing board, a copy of the Los Angeles Building Code for regulations on a material he had never before addressed, and simply stated, "Bring me a block," with the same confidence with which he had first handled the adobe for the ranch house for Walter L. Richardson.

■ There was a brazen honesty about that rugged adobe ranch house, which stands today as a landmark of American architecture. At a time when the ideological discourse of historical revivals was battling the voice of the modernist, Henry, in the last building to be built by the brothers, held steadfast to his own principles and composed one of the most logical buildings of a long and honored career.

Seascape carvings by Charles Greene
for Mrs. Willis Walker.

Three-panel teakwood and
leather-hinged screen
carved by Charles Greene for
Mrs. Willis Walker
of Pebble Beach, 1934.

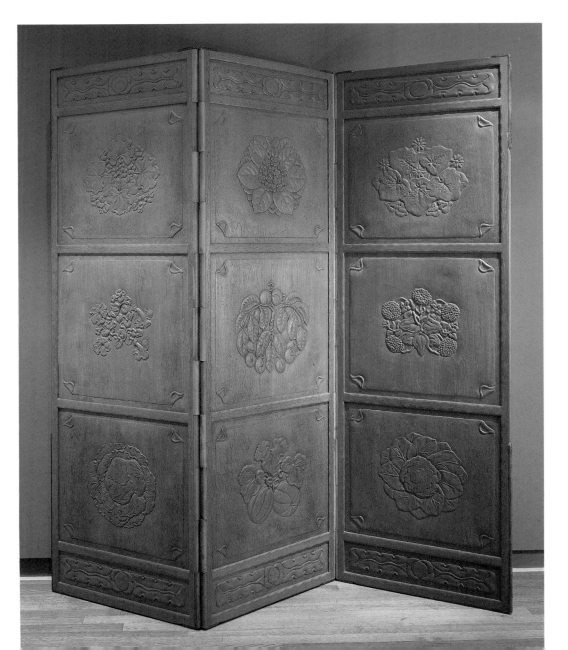

Charles Sumner Greene and
Henry Mather Greene at
the D. L. James house in 1947.

EPILOGUE

It was an overcast afternoon in November when I arrived at the brick studio on Lincoln Street thirteen blocks from the business center of Carmel-by-the-Sea. This far out of town there were no sidewalks, no curbs, no commercial buildings, but the road was paved, and on each side small wooden cabins nestled among tall pine trees, conveying a sense of affinity between artisan and environment.

■ I had no difficulty identifying the studio of Charles Greene, for it was set close to the road and dominated by the most extraordinary carved door I had ever seen. It was made of solid teakwood with expressed round pegging. The carvings depicted tomato vines rising from two urns twisting up the vertical elements of the structural frame of the door and joining the imagery of fruit, vine, and leaf patterns in the arc at the top where the door was arched in response to the masonry construction. After decades of the wind and rain, the oiled exterior had weathered to a grey patina that, as the clouds lifted momentarily, gleamed almost like silver.

■ I paused for a moment in nervous anticipation. It had been just one year since O'Neill Ford had introduced me to the wonderful symphonies in wood created by the American architects Greene and Greene, those two legendary brothers who had given genuine substance to the Arts and Crafts movement and new directions to domestic architecture in the western United States and as far away as Kilara, Australia. And here I was, a student of architecture, about to enter Charles Greene's own sanctuary.

■ I knocked hesitantly on the door. There was no response. I knocked a second time. Still no answer. Uncertainly I turned to a split-rail redwood gate in a brick wall extending along the edge of the street, and entered a naturally wooded clearing in the middle of which stood an unpretentious board-and-batten cottage with several pairs of glazed French doors opening out to this simple courtyard.

■ As a light rain began to fall, I knocked again, this time on the doors to the right of a brick chimney. They were slowly opened by a tiny man who stood there silently, shoulders bent, long white hair curling around the collar of a white shirt, small round glasses pinching his nose, and lips curved in a welcoming smile. Mrs. Alice Greene stepped up behind him, invited me inside, and commented that she had been telling Charles throughout the day

that I was coming to visit him, and that I was a student interested in his work. "I think he understands," she said, placing a coat over his shoulders and asking if I would help him up the path to the rear entrance to his studio. He smiled again, and gripped my arm so tightly that I can still imagine the feel of his long thin fingers above my elbow.

■ Once inside I was overwhelmed by the knowledge that I was standing here in his workplace, in this most intimate space where Charles Greene had created his designs, had drawn, painted, written, meditated, and spoken out his thoughts to his closest friends. Earlier in the day Alice had lit a fire to warm up the studio, and now the crackle of the logs mingled with the sound of raindrops on the skylight. A simple hanging light with a small five-inch cylindrical white shade was suspended over the couch opposite the fireplace and revealed the natural sand finish of the plaster walls and the cookie-cutter patterns Charles had pressed into the wet material during construction. With the lighting of table and floor lamps, the full studio came into view with its wonderful clutter of mementos signifying Charles's many different interests. All around us were examples of his own furniture designs, a chair for his wife crafted after a design for Mrs. Belle Barlow Bush, two dining chairs designed for the Freeman Ford house, a small table created as a wedding present for one of his children, a three-panel teakwood screen for Mrs. Willis Walker, and the boudoir bench for Mrs. Thomas Vernor Moore, both items refused on completion, primarily because of costs. From pictures I had studied, I recognized the large mahogany bookcase he had designed for his Pasadena office and which was now filled with books, portfolios, and plates of drawings. Against another wall was an open bookcase with a distressed finish, with which I was not familiar but that clearly represented imagery identified with his work in the 1920s. There were his collections of Japanese sword guards, his old Imari china, and paintings by himself as well as photographs and prints by his friends Louis Christian Mullgardt and Eugene and Cole Weston. There were also examples of Chinese household furniture, a few pieces of Chippendale, a remarkable oriental screen sitting on the floor, and Chinese urns placed about on high tables as though on altars, and in his writing room a desk piled high with correspondence. Such diversity in such a small space and yet, somehow, the diversity of objects seemed to illustrate "the oneness of all that exists," to borrow a line from his 1932 essay on symbolism.

■ As Alice began to point out the various items about the studio, she remarked sadly that in his forgetfulness of recent months, Charles had recently tossed a manuscript for his book on furniture into the fire. While she spoke, Charles rose from a wicker couch partly covered with oriental rugs smaller in size than those scattered around the floor, and moved slowly but gracefully across the room, taking an object from his wife's hands and trying to tell me about it. However, it was not his attempt to connect words to objects that communicated the most to me, but his facial expressions that clearly attested to the affection he still felt for the beauty of these objects. Once, when I was examining a richly carved teakwood screen in a corner of the studio, he came over to me, took my hand, and ran my fingertips over the soft patina of the wood. Moments such as these are rare, but on that rainy evening in his own studio, Charles Greene's efforts to impart his feelings to me were so gentle, so caring that his lack of words was never missed.

■ I was concerned that my visit not tire Charles, but Alice remarked on how stimulated he seemed to be by my interest in all the items around the studio that had been so much a part of his life. Yet it was time to end my visit, and standing in front of his mahogany bookcase, I presented him with the first photograph I had taken of the Gamble House. Charles held the photograph for a long while and then looked up at me with a hint of mischief in his twinkling eyes and smiled the broadest smile of the evening. As he did so, Alice picked up my camera and captured that moment on film, providing me with the most precious of gifts, an image that will remain with me as a continuing reminder of that first meeting with one of the two mentors who, through their artistic gifts and personal vision, had unknowingly changed the balance of my personal and professional life.

This photograph was taken in the Carmel studio by Charles's wife, Alice, in November 1955 as Charles Sumner Greene and the author review an image of the Gamble house.

The D. L. James house atop the bluffs at Carmel Highlands.

ILLUSTRATION CREDITS

The following individuals and institutions have made illustrative materials available for this book:

Photographers

■ Thomas A. Heinz, AIA, photographer, © 1998 RLM Associates, iv, viii, 11 L, 17 BR, 18T & BR, 19, 23, 25 TL, 26, 28 T, 30, 31, 32, 36, 41, 44 B, 46 R, 50, 54, 55, 56, 58, 62, 63 B, 65, 67 TR, 72 R, 73 L, 74, 82 T, 83 TL, 84 L, 85, 86, 87, 109 B, 110, 124, 125, 126, 128, 131, 132, 133, 134, 136, 138, 146, 148, 149, 150, 154 R, 156, 164, 166, 169, 170, 171, 172, 173, 174, 175, 176, 177, 178, 180, 183, 184, 189, 190 R, 191, 192, 194, 195, 197, 198, 200, 202, 203 T, 204, 205, 206, 207, 211, 212, 214, 220.

■ Randell L. Makinson, HON. AIA, © 1998, xiv, 1, 11 R, 19, 47 R, 67 BL & BR, 77 L, 88 R, 112, 130, 137, 153, 154 L, 181 R, 208, 209.

■ Erika Marrin, © 1998, ii, x, 15 TL, MR & BR, 16, 17 T, 22, 37, 52, 53, 64 TR & BR, 77 R, 78, 82 B, 83 R, T & B, 84 R, 90, 92, 93, 95, 99, 100 L, 101 B, 102, 103 L, 140, 141, 142, 143, 145, 152, 158, 159, 160 B, 161.

■ Julius Shulman, © 1953, 35 B.

■ Cole Weston, © 1947, 216.

■ Toshi Yoshimi, © 1998, 73 M & R, 76 L, 80, 103 R, 116, 118, 120, 121, 122, 215.

■ Lloyd Yost, © 1998 and courtesy Winogene Yost, 38.

Archival Sources

■ Author's files, 6, 27 TL, 28 BL & R, 34, 35 T & M, 43, 60 L, 88 L, 109 TR, 188, 196, 201, 218.

■ *The Architect*, December 1915, 104.

■ *The Architectural Record,* October 1906, 67 TL.

■ *The Boston Museum of Fine Arts*, Julia de Wolf Addison, 1910, 3R.

■ *The Western Architect*, July 1908, 40, 45.

■ *The Western Architect*, September 1920, 109 TL.

■ Avery Architectural and Fine Arts Library, Columbia University in the City of New York, 12 B, 14 B, 21, 71, 155, 179.

■ Greene and Greene Library, 2 TLL & BL, 3 M, L & R, 10 R, 18 BL & M, 20, 44 T, L & R, 46 L, 66, 69, 94, 96, 100 R, 101 T, 114, 163, 181.

■ Missouri Historical Society, 68.

■ Pasadena Historical Museum, *Pasadena Illustrated Souvenir Book*, Board of Trade Publication, 1903, 10 L, 12 T, 15 TR.

■ University of California, Berkeley, Documents Collection, College of Environmental Design, 72 L.

Other Sources

■ Margaret Bandini, 60 R, 61 R.

■ Christie's, New York, 203 B.

■ Betty and Thomas Gordon Greene, 190 L.

■ Nanine Hillard Greene, 25 BR.

■ Virginia Dart Greene Hales, 4.

■ Hall family, 79 T & ML.

■ William H. Jordy, *The Manual Training High School*, Calvin M. Woodward, 1887, 2 R.

■ Joan Kaas, 79 R & BL.

■ Marrin Collection, 106.

■ Martin Studios, 14 T, 160 TL.

■ Charles Miller, The Taunton Press, 186.

■ Kirk Myers, 8, 13, 47 R, 63 T, 98.

■ Ann E. Nourse and Kon Ammossow, 64 TL & MR.

■ Kathryn Novak, 48.

■ William B. and Marjoree Richardson family, 213 T.

■ Bruce Smith, 89.

■ Walter Johannes "Jack" van Rossem, 42 T & B, 46 L.

Drawings

■ D. Eric Bowyer, 51.

■ Daniel Nelson Bube, 24, 76 R, 94, 105.

■ Daniel Nelson Bube and Luther Paul Weber, 27 TR & B, 29 T & B.

■ Charles Sumner Greene, 188.

■ Dennis McGuire, 127.

Key:

T = top

M = middle

B = bottom

L = left

R = right

INDEX

COLOPHON

This book and jacket
were designed
by James Marrin
and the production was
done by Erika Marrin

This book was
typeset in
Adobe Garamond
with old style figures
and small caps

Printing and binding
executed in Korea
by Codra Enterprises,
Carson, California

I DISCOVERED THES CREATIVE ARCHITECTS WHEN I LIVED
IN FERNDALE MI, IN '46. THIS IS THE FIRST GOOD BOOK
OF THEIR WORK I HAVE FOUND.

Edan Knapp. AIA
EAGAN. MN.

PURCHASED OT THE WALKER ART CENTER
MINNEAPOLIS MN
OCT. 2000.